Praise for *Strength for Their Journey*:

"*Strength for Their Journey* is a great resource for African American parents."
—AJ Calloway, co-host of BET's signature series, "106th and Park."

"Reading this book is a 'must do' for parents invested in maximizing their childrens' chances for thriving in today's world. It's hard to imagine that a parent can get through the first chapter without realizing that this book is truly an invaluable gift!"
—Paulette Hines, Director of the Office of Prevention Services and Research, New Jersey Medical School-Behavioral Research and Training Institute

HARLEM MOON

BROADWAY

STRENGTH
for Their
JOURNEY

Five Essential Disciplines
African American Parents Must
Teach Their Children and Teens

ROBERT L. JOHNSON, M.D.

PAULETTE STANFORD, M.D.

HARLEM MOON

BROADWAY BOOKS

NEW YORK

Harlem Moon titles may be purchased for business or promotional use or for special sales. For information, please write to: Special Markets Department, Random House, Inc., 280 Park Avenue, New York, NY 10017.

PRINTED IN THE UNITED STATES OF AMERICA

The figure in the Harlem Moon logo is inspired by a graphic design by Aaron Douglas (1899–1979). Harlem Moon and its logo, depicting a moon and woman, are trademarks of Broadway Books, a division of Random House, Inc.

Visit our website at www.harlemmoon.com

First edition published 2002.

Designed by Cassandra J. Pappas

Library of Congress Cataloging-in-Publication Data

Johnson, Robert L., 1946–
    Strength for their journey : five essential disciplines African American parents must teach their children and teens / Robert L. Johnson, Paulette Stanford.—1st ed.
        p. cm.
    Includes bibliographical references and index.
    1. Parenting—United States. 2. Parent and child—United States. 3. African American children—Life skills guides. 4. African American families—Psychology. 5. Self-esteem in children—United States. I. Stanford, Paulette. II. Title.
HQ755.85 J645 2002
649'.1'0973—dc21

2002023224

ISBN 0-7679-0875-9

10   9   8   7   6   5   4   3   2   1

To our parents,
Robert Johnson, Clalice Johnson,
Edward Stanford, and Gwenilda Stanford.
They gave us the strength for our journey.

Contents

Acknowledgments

THE FOLLOWING PERSONS were instrumental in the creation of this work: Linda Konner, Janet Hill, Toisan Craigg, Jamie M. Forbes, Keith Bratcher, Marie Ellis, and Wadene Howard. Special thanks to our coauthor Gene Busnar—and to the thousands of African American families who have contributed to our collective expertise.

Foreword

I HAVE SPENT four decades as a pediatrician and a trainer of pediatricians. During that time, it has become clear to me that the most important task I can perform as a physician and a teacher is to help mothers and fathers become more competent parents. There is no question that, regardless of an infant's biological inheritance, his or her chances of growing up healthy and fulfilled increase in direct proportion to the quality of the parenting provided. Drs. Johnson and Stanford have written a book that shows mothers and fathers how to dramatically improve that quality by fostering the essential disciplines young African Americans need to thrive and succeed.

Strength for Their Journey is written in a clear, anecdotal style. Here readers will find a wealth of practical information and valuable advice. The chapters cover such universal parenting themes as talking to children about drugs, motivating young people to avoid high-risk sex, and recognizing how a parent's own problems can undermine discipline. The authors tailor these topics to the needs of African American parents, and never lose sight of the extraordinary challenges black children face in this society.

Given my professional background, not to speak of my personal experience as a father and grandfather, I would like to think of myself as someone well versed in the challenges faced by African American parents. But I must confess that reading this book gave me new insight and a new depth of understanding. I have every confidence that parents who apply the authors' Five-Discipline Program will be giving their children a powerful vaccine against racism and bigotry, which continue to be major health hazards for our kids.

I am so glad that Dr. Johnson and Dr. Stanford decided to write *Strength for Their Journey*. I truly believe that it can change lives—and save lives.

Louis Z. Cooper, MD
President, American Academy of Pediatrics

Introduction

WHEN WE GRADUATED from medical school in the early 1970s, we were the only African Americans in our respective classes. Even today, less than 4 percent of doctors in the United States are African Americans. Still, there's reason to be hopeful about the future.

As we teach and do our hospital rounds, we feel proud to see the growing number of black medical students in our midst. We especially enjoy hearing them greet us as "brother" or "sister," a greeting that our white colleagues sometimes misinterpret as a lack of respect. But we understand that these aspiring African American doctors are really saying, "Thanks for opening the door, and making the journey easier for me." They are also saying, "I'm proud of my own accomplishments, and I understand my responsibility to those who wish to follow my lead."

We credit our parents for teaching us that it's important to achieve—not just for ourselves, but also for the positive impact that individual successes can have on other African Americans. This sense of connection and obligation has always been a source of strength in the black community, but it is an ethic that parents must nurture in their children.

As black doctors and educators, we feel a responsibility to those who follow us professionally, and to our community as a whole. That's why we both find time to mentor inner-city youth, and why we decided that it was important to write a book that shows African American parents how to give their sons and daughters the tools to succeed on the often rocky journey of life.

The Evolution of an Idea

In many respects, black children's needs are the same as those of their white counterparts—especially during the first few years of life. However, once the black child enters school, he or she begins to face a number of race-specific challenges. The most effective way for parents to give children the strength to meet those challenges is by instilling discipline. However, discipline is not just about punishing kids when they get out of line; it's about giving young people the inner strength they need to achieve success and fulfillment. Setting firm limits is important, but it's just one of five critical, interconnected disciplines parents must teach.

The Five Essential Disciplines

- **Traditional Discipline:** The strength to accept and embrace parental limits
- **Racial Discipline:** The strength to negotiate the realities of being a racial minority
- **Emotional Discipline:** The strength to resist negative peer pressure and temptation
- **Practical Discipline:** The strength to excel in academic, career, and financial pursuits
- **Mind-Body Discipline:** The strength to maintain positive physical, mental, and spiritual health

For over three decades, we've developed and shared these disciplines with parents and families in our professional practice. We also give over one hundred talks and seminars each year that are attended by thousands of African American parents. Each week, our staff fields dozens of phone calls and in-person requests from mothers and fathers asking if we know of a book that will show them how to help their sons and daughters become more disciplined.

There are very few books for African American parents that even mention discipline, beyond a brief discussion of whether or not spanking and other forms of punishment are appropriate. We came across several books that talked about infants and school-aged children, but none of these offered a prescriptive parenting program that showed mothers and fathers how to inspire discipline. We finally realized that writing our own book was the only way to reach all the parents who could benefit from our program.

The Five-Discipline Program

Ours is a developmental program, consisting of the following five key interconnected disciplines:

- **Traditional Discipline:** Along with self-love and resilience, setting behavioral limits is something all parents must instill as part of a child's basic emotional grounding. In Chapter One, we show you how to help your child develop the inner strength and self-esteem he or she needs to meet the challenges of growing up. In Chapter Two, we show you how to help your child accept and embrace limits, so that he or she will have the foundation to acquire the other disciplines.

- **Racial Discipline:** Growing up black guarantees that a child will encounter a set of experiences that most white kids will never understand—much less face. In Chapter Three, we show you how to instill the special kind of discipline and strength your child needs to negotiate the formidable color-based obstacles that lie ahead.

- **Emotional Discipline:** Many black children are especially vulnerable to a variety of dangerous behaviors, including high-risk sex and certain kinds of substance abuse. In Chapter Four, we show you how to increase your child's emotional resilience and develop the discipline to say no to negative peer pressure. We help you to face the daunting challenge of adolescence—a time when a young person's impulse to rebel against parental restraints reaches its peak.

♦ **Practical Discipline:** In this three-chapter section we give you the tools to help your child succeed in school and in the handling of money and career choices.

Black children face a variety of obstacles in school. They are far more likely than whites or Asians to be singled out as discipline problems, diagnosed with Attention Deficit Hyperactivity Disorder (ADHD), or dumped into remedial and special education courses. In Chapter Five, we show you how to deal with teachers and school administrators, so that your child can avoid these early setbacks that often have a devastating effect on a young person's career and financial prospects. We also talk about the important role mentors play in the lives and scholastic success of black youth.

In Chapter Six, we show you how to prepare your child to deal with the academic and social challenges of college. We share tips for choosing the best college or university and for handling the challenge of paying for a higher education.

The discussion in Chapter Seven focuses on giving children the discipline to handle money and preparing them for the world of work. We show you how to help your child appreciate the value of a dollar and to develop the skills he or she will need to have a successful and fulfilling career.

♦ **Mind-Body Discipline:** African Americans are at elevated risk for a variety of chronic diseases—including hypertension and diabetes, conditions that often take root in childhood. To make matters worse, African American patients are less likely to receive quality treatment from a racially biased health-care system.

In Chapter Eight, we show you how to foster the kind of discipline your child needs to achieve optimal physical, mental, and spiritual health. We talk about the special health concerns African Americans face, and offer tips on how to receive better services from doctors and other health-care providers. We demonstrate that the discipline to maintain good health habits requires a positive self-image and the kind of faith in the future that helps a child choose long-term rewards over instant gratification.

As you go through the chapters, you may notice that there is a certain amount of overlap among the five disciplines. For example, you can look at avoiding drugs as emotional discipline or mind-body discipline. Or you can argue that overcoming racial bias is part of racial or practical discipline. We discuss these issues separately to make it easier for you to sort them out, and to come up with strategies to address various problems or questions as they arise. In Chapter Nine, we answer some of the most pressing questions parents frequently ask—many of which cut across the five disciplines.

No book can provide all the information parents need or anticipate problems that may arise. In Chapter Ten, we provide a comprehensive listing of resources you can turn to for help or specific information on a particular topic.

WE BELIEVE THAT you will profit most from this book if you start out by reading the chapters in the order they are written. At the same time, we know that some people don't like to read books from cover to cover. That's why we made the book user-friendly for readers who want to skip around, troubleshoot, or review certain sections at a later date.

We recognize that there is no one best way to parent. Some mothers and fathers tend to be more laid back, while others have a more intense approach. The Five-Discipline Program is both flexible and powerful. We encourage you to mold the techniques in the chapters to fit your particular style and needs. Above all, we fervently hope you will use the power of the Five-Discipline Program to make a positive difference in your child's journey through life.

DR. ROBERT L. JOHNSON
DR. PAULETTE STANFORD
(www.strengthfortheirjourney.com)

1

Teaching Black Children
to Love Themselves

Every child should sense that gleam in the parent's eye. That's
where self-esteem starts—the sense of being loved and admired.
As parents, that means putting in the time.

—DR. MARILYN BENOIT

President, American Academy of Child/Adolescent Psychiatry.[1]

What's in This Chapter

♦ Helping your child meet the challenges of growing up

♦ Understanding what's unique about parenting black children

♦ Constructing the towers of self-love

♦ Building your child's self-esteem

♦ Helping your child become resilient

♦ Setting the right example

♦ Laying the groundwork for success

♦ Helping your child make positive decisions

1

I N THIS OPENING CHAPTER, we talk about the importance of fostering self-love in children. We explore the special challenges parents who raise black boys and girls face, and show you how to construct the towers of self-love: resilience and self-esteem. We explore ways to build on children's strengths and to maximize their opportunities to grow up healthy and strong.

Making the Transition from Child to Adult

Childhood is often portrayed as a happy, carefree time—and parents do need to ensure that their sons and daughters experience their full share of joy. But childhood is also a training ground for adulthood. The more effective the training, the better prepared a child will be to face the real-world challenges that lie ahead. Throughout history, societies have used different approaches to moving children into adulthood.

In some cultures, children are trained to be adults through specific rites of passage and tests. Alex Haley, in his book *Roots,* describes how youngsters made this transition in traditional African societies:

> At twelve years of age, the boys of the village were separated from their families and taken to a camp in the jungle by the men of the community. Over a period of six weeks, the boys were taught all the lessons of adulthood. At the end of the encampment they were tested to determine whether they had learned these lessons. . . . Those who successfully passed the test were granted adult status. They had left their village as boys and they returned . . . as men.[2]

In contemporary American culture there are no uniform tests that prove that boys and girls have become men and women. In our society, youngsters learn the disciplines of adulthood, not from lessons that are carefully designed and taught by designated elders, but from watching and listening to the significant grownups in their lives.

In the African American community, extended families of grandparents, aunts, and uncles—as well as friends, neighbors, and clergy—have long participated in the parenting process. Many of these resources are still available, and we will talk about the best ways to access and utilize them throughout the chapters. Still, as more African Americans climb the economic ladder and move out of traditional black neighborhoods, families tend to live farther apart and neighbors don't always share the same concerns. That means parents must assume a greater responsibility.

No parent can provide all of the training and support a child needs. Which is why part of a parent's responsibility involves finding mentors and other role models to help children become stronger and more well rounded. If parents and other significant adults fail to provide the support and positive example children need, they are likely to seek the lessons of manhood or womanhood on the streets. And that spells trouble—especially for black children.

The Five-Discipline Program is an effective way to help young people flourish and succeed. Keep in mind that the word *discipline* comes from the word *disciple,* which involves achieving mastery by observing and imitating someone older and more accomplished.

Our goal is to help you apply the five disciplines in ways that provide children with lessons that make them stronger. These disciplines are especially important for black children, who need to feel good about themselves and confident in their abilities to negotiate a world that is often less than fair. It must also be said that all children face a world in which fairness is often little more than a pretty-sounding word. And this raises a question that white folks sometimes ask:

How is parenting an African American child different from parenting any other child? This question may sound naïve, but it's one that's at the heart of this book. All children need parents who provide love, strength, and discipline. That said, it's important to never underestimate the extraordinary challenges black youngsters face.

There are certain realities that come with being black in America, and there's no way to avoid them completely, no matter how wealthy or accomplished you become. There's no question that things are gradually changing for the better. Still, race is an issue that is likely to have an economic, social, cultural, and political impact on today's black children throughout their lives. One of our goals in this book is to help parents

make race a positive force in children's lives, despite the ongoing struggle to shed the following tired racial stereotypes.

Ten Racial Stereotypes That Won't Go Away

1. Blacks blame all their problems on racial prejudice.
2. Blacks expect special consideration and treatment.
3. Blacks don't take full advantage of educational and economic opportunities.
4. Blacks don't acknowledge that white people have problems too.
5. Blacks continue to use past oppression as an excuse for current social problems.
6. Blacks don't respect the police.
7. Blacks play the "race card" at every opportunity.
8. Blacks are lazier than other ethnic and racial groups.
9. Blacks are more likely to shoplift and to commit other crimes.
10. Blacks hate all whites.

Despite these entrenched negative stereotypes, African Americans
continue to move up as a people. Large numbers continue to move out
of urban areas and into upscale communities. Future generations will
have the opportunity to follow a growing number of role models up the
corporate ladder and into the professional ranks. The progress has been
dramatic, but it hasn't happened overnight.

African Americans have often been compared unfavorably to various
immigrant groups for not making the most of educational opportunities.
Those who serve up such comparisons conveniently ignore the many
hardships and obstacles black people have faced in this country. In any
case, this stereotype has been exploded in the past few years.

A recent study commissioned by the National Center for Public
Policy and Higher Education found that black parents are now 50 percent more likely than white parents to rank a college education as the
most important ingredient in a youngster's ultimate success.[3] Previous
studies have shown that the educational ambitions of black parents are

less dependent on socioeconomic class than those of their white counterparts. However, black parents' placing so much more value on a
college-level education is a relatively recent development. "Jews, Asians,
and other groups have used higher education as a means of social and
economic transformation," one researcher told *The New York Times*. "The
African American community now appears to be following a similar
path."[4]

Despite all this positive movement, no person of color is immune to
the ravages of overt and covert racial prejudice. So, it's not surprising to
hear parents express the following concern:

*How do we raise our children to have the strength to wrestle with and
make sense of all the adversity—and still have enough strength left to love
themselves—and their people?* You do so by taking the lead in embracing
life's challenges, by demonstrating a sense of pride in your heritage—and
by shaping the Five-Discipline Program in this book to the needs of your
children. All the while, you keep on fortifying the process by loving your
children and doing everything in your power to make sure that they grow
up loving themselves.

Building the Towers of Self-Love in Black Children

When parents ask: What is the most important thing we can do for our
children? Our answer is: Help them to feel good about themselves and
give them strength for their journey. We call these towers in a child's development *self-esteem* and *resilience*. They are the two keys to any child's
emotional health, and they go hand in hand.

Self-esteem simply means that when children look in the mirror, they
see someone valuable, deserving of love and respect, happiness, and success. Children who don't feel good about themselves are less likely to
thrive and achieve. They are at higher risk for drug abuse, depression—
even suicide.

Resilience means being able to rebound from setbacks and handle different types of adversity. Every person encounters predictable and unpredictable obstacles on the journey through life. Resilient people find
effective ways to deal with these challenges—while always maintaining a
vision of their long-term goals. Children who are resilient share the following traits:

- They are able to meet challenges head-on.
- They learn well from both successes and mistakes.
- They are optimistic, but also realistic, in their dealings.
- They are able to delay gratification.

Perhaps some of you are looking at the above characteristics and thinking that your child falls short in one or more areas. Don't worry. It's not too late to make positive changes.

Much of traditional psychology has operated under the belief that personalities are set by the time children reach age five or six. We know from our clinical practice that this is often not the case. We've seen adolescents rebound from early problems and emotional scars to lead fulfilling and successful lives. There's no question that the sooner you start building these towers of self-love the better. However, it's never too late to begin moving a child or adolescent in a positive direction. Here are some tips to help you get started now.

SET A POSITIVE EXAMPLE

Parents often ask us why their children don't heed their warnings and advice, even after countless repetition. The short answer is that boys and girls are far more focused on what parents *do* than what they *say*. It follows, then, that the mother who tells her daughter that it's important to read shouldn't be surprised if these words fall on deaf ears if she herself is constantly glued to the TV set. Likewise, the hard-drinking father who chides his son about the dangers of alcohol can reasonably expect those warnings to be ignored.

Your children are observing you all the time—looking for messages about how they should act and view things. The notion of "do what I say—not what I do" is a poor substitute for taking the lead in showing children the right way to act. Still, if you're going to engage in negative or unhealthy behavior, the worst thing you can do is to try to justify that what you're doing is right.

We all know people who will go to great lengths to defend their actions, however self-destructive they may be. "If I'm doing it," the flawed reasoning goes, "how bad can it be?" What makes this wrongheaded approach worse is telling your child that it's okay—or even desirable—to follow your lead.

We understand how difficult it can be for adults to change certain deeply ingrained habits and attitudes. Still, can you think of a better reason for making such positive changes than protecting your child's future?

Let's look at some examples of how parental behavior affects children. Take health habits. When it comes to habits such as eating right or avoiding tobacco and alcohol, your child is watching you carefully and comparing what he sees to the messages he gets in school, on TV, and from his peers. If the child has observed you eating moderately, and abstaining from tobacco and alcohol throughout his life, chances are good that he will follow your lead. If he sees you break an unhealthy habit and make positive lifestyle changes, that can have an especially positive long-term effect.

When parents make positive behavioral changes, children take notice and often ask questions. Here is an opportunity to discuss the matter in detail, and to explain the reasons for the change. You might talk about how hard it is to break long-time bad habits, and point out that it's easier not to start them in the first place.

We are well aware that some parents have difficulty with healthy eating, just as others find it next to impossible to stop smoking. In these cases, we suggest that parents explain their behavior as an unfortunate but human weakness, one that they will hopefully correct sometime in the future. At least then the parent can honestly say to a child: "Smoking cigarettes is wrong, but someday I plan to stop. I want you to understand that, once you start smoking, it's very hard to quit. Look at how much trouble I'm having. So, please, don't *you* ever smoke."

This approach is not an easy sell to skeptical teens, but it's far better than justifying your actions. For example, we know one mother named Mary who continued to chain-smoke while she breast-fed her infant son.

"Don't you realize that you are putting your baby's health at risk?" friends and relatives would ask.

"That's a bunch of propaganda by the baby formula companies that want women to stop breast-feeding and use their products," Mary would answer. "My smoking isn't going to hurt my child in the least."

There was a time when many more people smoked cigarettes around their children. But that was before the dangers of secondhand smoke to children became widely known. As always, there are some hard cases who refuse to change their behavior, or even admit that there's a good reason for making such a change. This destructive approach extends to many other key areas of life.

Caution: Passing on your own limitations to your children can stifle their potential.

Try to take a clear-eyed look at which of your behaviors and attitudes you want your child to emulate, and which ones cry out for change. If you are truly committed to your children's future, you don't want to burden them with your own destructive habits, outmoded ideas, and personal limitations.

The ability to help children go beyond parental limits is unique to human beings. In fact, humans are the only species in which each generation must teach its young different skills from the ones it possesses. These unique generational shifts among humans make parenting in the twenty-first century an exciting but complex challenge.

Coping with change is never easy. Still, in this fast-moving age, it's important to recognize the skills and social codes that may have been totally foreign to our parents—and even to us—have become critical to the future of today's children.

Take the Internet, for example. Many of today's parents grew up in an era where computers were not widely used and the Internet hadn't even been invented. Today, grade-school children know how to log on to Web sites to search for information and exchange e-mails with their friends.

People tend to be comfortable with the things they know and believe, even if they no longer make much sense. Too often, they pass these attitudes and behaviors on to their children without thinking about the possible consequences. It's as though they're saying: "This is the way I've always done it. Therefore, it must be the right way. I want my child to follow my lead." This approach to parenting is not in a child's best interest.

If, for example, you aren't computer literate, would you tell your child that computers are useless? Or, if you didn't attend college, would you tell your child that higher education is a waste of time?

Parents of black children need to be particularly careful about the way racial attitudes are conveyed. The beliefs and attitudes you grew up with may not be the ones that are most helpful to your child. In Chapter Three, we show you a disciplined and practical approach to race relations, one that fosters effective dealings across racial lines. We call this approach racial discipline, and it is a skill set of tremendous value to any person of color.

Racial discipline is not something they teach in school—although children can pick up a good deal by observing racially smart teachers and other adults. But, for the most part, racially disciplined children pick up this skill by observing their parents.

If you are disciplined and effective in your racial dealings, your child is likely to imitate your behavior. If not, your child may first have to reject your values, then go about learning how to deal with different kinds of people through a painful process of trial and error. In the worst-case scenario, children mirror their parents' unproductive ways of dealing across racial lines, and open themselves up to all kinds of trouble.

HELP CHILDREN BUILD ON THEIR SUCCESSES

Every person has strengths and weaknesses, and children are no different. Some girls and boys are good students; others excel in athletics; still others have outstanding social skills. Throughout childhood and adolescence, young people evaluate themselves in terms of what they do well and what they don't. These perceptions have a profound effect on how they feel about themselves.

Can you recall how proud your child felt when, as a toddler, she took her first independent steps? As time goes on, there are many other steps for a child to take. The first time she balances herself on a bicycle. The first time he receives an A on a test. Her first hit in a softball game. The first dollar he earns helping a neighbor clean out his attic. Each of these seemingly small steps is a building block that gives children a sense of mastery and the confidence to deal with future challenges.

When parents show their support and excitement over a child's accomplishments, the youngster gradually develops a catalogue of successful experiences on which to build. We call these building blocks *competencies.*

Children who are able to succeed in one area can, with proper parental encouragement, use that as a foundation for success in other areas. Children who feel successful or competent also have an easier time coping with stress and facing life's daily and long-term challenges.

Parents need to provide children with a wide variety of experiences so that they can find out which areas they are good in and what they enjoy doing most. When children succeed, it's essential that parents credit them for those successes.

For example, when Jamal comes home with an A on a reading test, the parent needs to convey that this good result was a product of the child's effort and skill, even if it was an easy test on which most of the students did well. Likewise, when Charlene gets a hit in softball, you want to congratulate her and say "great job," even if the pitch wasn't particularly difficult to hit.

This is not to say that you should unrealistically inflate a child's efforts or accomplishments. It's not helpful to tell a child that he's a top athlete or student if that's not really the case. Such an approach creates unrealistic expectations and sets the stage for disappointment. At the same time, you never want to downgrade a child's accomplishments, however modest they may be. The following are common mistakes parents make that can undermine a child's sense of competence. We urge you to avoid them:

- **Don't push children toward your preferences or strengths.** Children develop a sense of competence by finding their own niche. Whether or not it's something you've envisioned for them is beside the point. We have counseled many children who become discouraged or depressed because their parents don't value their successes. For example, twelve-year-old Keisha is an outstanding athlete but a mediocre student. Her parents are both attorneys who could care less about sports.

"My mom and dad are always on me about my grades," Keisha told us. "Just once, I'd like to hear them compliment me when I do something good on the field."

To make matters worse, Keisha's younger sister is an A student who has no interest in athletics. As a result, she receives a great deal more praise and approval than Keisha.

It's not unusual for parents to favor a sibling who more closely meets their expectations over one whose talents lie elsewhere. This kind of preferential treatment can weaken the less-favored child's motivation to do well.

Reminder: Every child has unique talents and a unique personality.

One of your primary responsibilities as a parent is to help a child achieve that unique potential. That means accepting the child for who he or she is—even if what you see doesn't always coincide with your desires and expectations.

◆ **Don't pay more attention to what's wrong than what's right.** Too often, parents concentrate on shoring up a child's weaknesses instead of building on strengths. You're likely to get a lot further if you identify your child's strong points and use them as building blocks that help the child feel competent about confronting tasks and situations that may be more difficult to navigate.

Many schools also seem more concerned with students' weaknesses and problems, and often neglect shoring up children's strengths. This is not a productive approach—or one that is grounded in the realities children will face.

When today's children eventually enter the workplace, the questions prospective employers are likely to ask will be focused on what the young person does well and can contribute. For both practical and emotional reasons, parents and teachers need to spend at least as much time and energy encouraging and cultivating a child's strengths as they do correcting problems and weaknesses.

◆ **Don't expect children to succeed without your help.** While it's sometimes easy to spot a child's talents or preferences, parents need to take an active role in helping their sons and daughters develop and pursue interests that foster a sense of competence. If you see a child sitting around and doing nothing, don't allow that to continue. It's your job to get the child actively involved doing something productive—be it in sports, the arts, or some other area. That means demonstrating an interest in the activity yourself—even if it's not something that you particularly favor. The key is letting a child know that you want to be a part of whatever he or she is doing.

◆ **Don't discourage children who aren't the greatest at their chosen activities.** A child doesn't have to be the most gifted athlete to benefit by participating in team sports, or the best singer to experience joy and success from participating in a religious choir or school chorus. Children get multiple benefits from taking part in a group effort even if they're not the star.

There's a flip side to this scenario: pushing children to pursue activities to which they're ill suited just because you favor them. If your child has a tin ear, it's simply not a good use of resources to encourage her to spend a lot of time practicing the violin or piano. Likewise, a child who is uncoordinated may not get much satisfaction playing competitive team sports.

We are not saying that children with limited athletic skills shouldn't be actively involved in physical pursuits. All children should try their hand at a wide variety of activities. However, given the limited amount of time in their (and your) schedules, there's something to be said for concentrating on activities that are both fun and well suited to a child's interests and skills.

Clearly, no child can possibly have equal exposure to the entire array of worthy time- and energy-consuming endeavors. Parents need to prioritize carefully, and to make certain that a child isn't being driven too hard or pushed in directions that are unproductive and uncomfortable.

GIVE CHILDREN RESPONSIBILITIES

One of the most important things parents can do to help children develop a sense of competence and mastery is to begin placing responsibilities on their shoulders. There are any number of ways to help children become responsible. These range from helping with chores around the house to participating in family decision making.

Children develop a sense of pride and accomplishment when they have an opportunity to contribute to their families, neighborhoods, and schools. The nature of these responsibilities depends on a child's age and temperament. Still, even very young children come to appreciate the opportunity to contribute their energies and ideas—even if some seem reluctant at first. The key is letting children know that their efforts and ideas can make a positive difference in their lives and the lives of others.

Assigning chores. "Moms and dads are often reluctant to give their youngsters jobs to do," author/educator Muriel Karlin Trachman observes. "They're too little," some mothers and fathers will rationalize. "It takes my [six]-year-old forever to clear her dishes," one mother complained. "I can get that work done in less than a minute."

"There's no denying that it can take a child much longer to complete a task than it does an adult. Still, the potential benefits of allowing a child to contribute to family life are well worth the extra time. Children who are given a continuous opportunity to participate in a family's household chores grow up to be responsible teenagers, and then adults."[5]

Try encouraging children to accomplish tasks that are slightly difficult for them. Be sure to allow for mistakes, and always offer praise for a job well done. By giving girls and boys an opportunity to make meaningful contributions to the household, you convey a trust and confidence that can do wonders for a young person's self image.

TEN CONTRIBUTIONS CHILDREN CAN MAKE TO HOME AND FAMILY

Helping prepare meals
Setting the table
Washing dishes
Sorting and folding laundry
Sweeping and washing floors
Taking out the garbage
Making the beds
Helping younger siblings with homework
Babysitting younger sisters and brothers
Caring for pets

It's a good idea to start assigning chores no later than age five. As children get older, gradually increase the number and difficulty of tasks without overwhelming the youngster. Make it a point not to use outdated gender stereotypes. Boys and girls are both capable of carrying out virtually all of the same basic chores, and you'd be wise to encourage them to do so.

If you haven't yet started an older child on a graduated course of responsibility, there's no time like the present. Begin by explaining why these contributions are important—to both the family and the young person. Then suggest a few chores for which the child will be responsible.

If the youngster complains or resists, don't show anger or threaten punishment. Instead, try to calmly talk things out. It's important to always respect the child's point of view, but this is one debate you should be able to win. All youngsters want their parents' approval. It's your job to let them know how much you value their taking responsibility and pitching in.

HELP CHILDREN BECOME EFFECTIVE DECISION MAKERS

Parents make all decisions for infants. But as children continue to grow, it becomes increasingly important to allow them to start deciding and choosing for themselves.

There are many decisions children can make—from the color of clothes they prefer, to which toys they want to share, to which books they want to read for school reports, to more serious decisions that affect family life. There are also more complex decisions that confront children, such as how much effort to put into schoolwork, how well to treat others, and whether or not to cheat on tests.

The moral and ethical values parents impart are a big part of any child's decision-making process. But, as with most skills, a child's ability to make value-based judgments is one that grows through opportunity and practice.

The following tips can help you strengthen your child's decision-making process:

◆ **Talk to the child about the thinking involved in making a particular decision.** If, for example, your fourteen-year-old has saved up some money and wants to spend it on something frivolous, like an expensive pair of sneakers, point out several other ways he might use that money, and discuss the pros and cons of each choice.

◆ **Talk about the possible consequences of each choice.** If you let your fourteen-year-old spend all his savings on sneakers, make it clear that she will not have enough to buy the new bike she's been talking about. As children mature and learn from their mistakes, they become more capable of seeing the long-term effects of their choices. Emphasize the benefits of thinking ahead instead of giving into their first impulse.

Remember, as with everything else, your child will be watching to see how willing you are to take the long view in how you reach decisions.

◆ **Encourage children to trust themselves.** Many decisions we make in life are based on a kind of inner sense we develop through experience. Children need to have an opportunity to develop and trust what their heart and gut tell them. When children make mistakes, parents need to help frame such missteps as valuable learning experiences, rather than defeats and causes for shame.

Thirteen-year-old Carl was offered a full scholarship to a private high school for academically gifted students. Carl's parents were very excited by this development. They did not have a great deal of money, and realized that this opportunity could greatly enhance their son's chances of receiving a scholarship to a top college. But Carl took a different view of things. He wanted to attend the neighborhood public high school, because that's where all his friends would be going.

Carl and his parents spent time talking about the pros and cons of each option. The young man knew full well the choice his parents favored—even though he was leaning the other way. After several long discussions, Carl's parents said: "We want you to make the decision. No matter which choice you take, you can count on our full support."

The young man wound up accepting the scholarship. "Being separated from my crowd was a drag at first," Carl recalled. "But I really wanted to please my parents—especially since they showed so much faith in my judgment."

Today, Carl is a successful attorney with children of his own. "I'm so grateful to my parents," he explained. "They trusted me to make my own choices, and that made me feel strong and confident. I think that show of trust had a lot to do with why I had the self-control to say no when many of my friends were messing with drugs. I'm working hard to show the same kind of trust in my young son and daughter."

Reminder: Don't blame every problem on low self-esteem.

While self-love is key to a child's successful development, it's easy to overlook other important issues if you attribute every concern you have about a child's performance or behavior to a lack of self-love or low self-esteem. The following examples are typical of the kinds of mistakes parents make in this regard:

◆ When sixteen-year-old Malik's folks learned that their son was dealing drugs, they blamed it on low self-esteem. After we spent time with Malik, it became clear that this was a young man who felt quite confident and good about himself. His problem had to do with faulty values—not a lack of self-love.

♦   Eleven-year-old Gloria's parents believed that her substandard grades were caused by low self-esteem. We suspected that this was not Gloria's problem—though all of her folks' talking and worrying about low self-esteem had taken its toll on the girl's once-sunny disposition. We ordered some tests which revealed that Gloria had a learning disability that her teachers had been unable to diagnose. Once Gloria got the help she needed, her grades improved, and so did her state of mind. But the scenario could have been very different if we hadn't found the real cause of Gloria's problem.

Self-love is a critically important issue. But, as we discuss in the upcoming chapters, it's hardly the only issue in fostering discipline and self-esteem in a child.

Summary

Ten Ways to Help Black Children Feel Good About Themselves

1. Help children understand the challenges African American's face.

2. Instill a sense of pride in their heritage.

3. Make it easy for children to build on the love you show for them.

4. Help children develop the strength to deal with adversity and recover from setbacks.

5. Always set a positive example.

6. Work to expand, not limit, your child's horizons.

7. Take a vital interest in what your child is doing.

8. Help children develop a sense of competence by building on their successes.

9. Give children as much responsibility as they can handle.

10. Help children recognize the consequences of their decisions.

2

∽

Traditional Discipline:
Setting Behavioral Limits

Train up a child in the way he should go: and he when he is old, he will not depart from it.

—PROVERBS 22:6

What's in This Chapter:

- Understanding why it's especially important for black children to embrace limits

- Understanding your parenting style

- Deciding when to be firm and when to be flexible

- Guidelines for moms and dads with different parenting styles

- Guidelines for married couples, single parents, and stepfamilies

RESEARCH SHOWS THAT setting behavioral limits is key to determining the course of how children fare. Traditional discipline is even more essential for black children, who will have to hurdle the additional roadblocks set up by a society that discriminates against people of color in both obvious and subtle ways. In this chapter, we share guidelines to help you figure out how strict or lenient you need to be in various situations. We help you understand the pros and cons of different parenting styles, and suggest effective strategies for setting behavioral limits.

By the time they enter kindergarten, all children are expected to respect authority figures and the rules of behavior they set. Black children who break those rules can find themselves in serious trouble with teachers, police, and other authority figures. To avoid these problems, skillful parents set behavioral limits and make it clear that certain rules are nonnegotiable.

Reminder: The mere appearance of breaking rules can lead to trouble for black youth.

Fifteen-year-old Michael was standing in front of his racially mixed high school with a group of five male classmates, all of whom were white. Three of the boys were passing around a marijuana cigarette when the school principal happened by. The marijuana was discarded, but the principal recognized the herb's pungent smell. He let the other boys go but proceeded to escort Michael into his office. He then accused the young man of smoking marijuana on school grounds. Michael was a B-plus student who'd never been in any kind of trouble. Suddenly he found himself suspended from school and accused of doing drugs.

Michael's parents were upset that their son was hanging out with boys who were smoking pot, but they believed his version of the story. The parents saw this as a blatant case of racial profiling on the part of the principal. They understood, however, that proving such suspicions is never easy. Michael was not about to squeal on the boys who'd actually been smoking; nor did he expect them to come forward in his defense.

We suggested that Michael give a urine sample to prove he was drug-free. The results established the boy's innocence. Nevertheless, the principal continued to insist that he was guilty. When Michael returned to school after a weeklong suspension, he felt that there was a cloud over his head.

"My teachers used to think of me as a good student who stayed out of trouble," he told us. "Now, they look at me differently. It's like I'm some kind of druggie who's a bad influence on other kids."

In Chapter Five, we detail the various steps parents can take to deflect the systemic racism African Americans too often encounter in school systems. There's no question, however, that any teenager would be well advised to walk away from a situation where drugs were present. And, as Michael found out, the consequences of ignoring such behavioral guidelines can be especially severe if you're black.

Michael's parents elected not to punish their son. They felt he'd suffered enough for his obvious lack of judgment. After talking to the boy about the various aspects of what had happened, his parents were satisfied that he'd learned from his mistake. They also understood that the situation could have been worse. "At least the police weren't called," Michael's mother remarked. "Thank God for that."

Michael transferred to another high school the following term, and made a fresh start. Still, it's frightening to think what this one faulty choice might have cost him.

When children fail to exercise discipline at school or on the street, they invite trouble. That's why it's important to establish behavioral limits in the home, where you can exert your influence early in a child's life. At home, lapses of discipline are easier to contain. When a child does misbehave, you have an opportunity to correct the substandard behavior and talk about the importance of respecting limits at all times.

All parents want their children to behave and to follow the rules, both in and out of the home. However, the question of how to best accomplish this goal is a much-debated parenting issue. Whether it's better for a parent to be strict or lenient has been argued for decades, and it continues to be a source of heated discussion and controversy. Some related hot-button issues include the following:

Should I punish my child for every infraction?

Is it better to give children lots of freedom or to keep a tight rein on what they do?

Is it ever appropriate to use corporal punishment?

Does it help to use bribery to motivate a child?

What happens when parents disagree on how to discipline a child?

There is no one-size-fits-all answer to any of these questions—no surefire way to guarantee that a child won't falter every now and then. One parenting expert will say that it's always better to be lenient. A second authority will offer proof that strict discipline is always the way to go. One study will show that spanking impedes a child's emotional development. Another will claim that spanking often has a positive effect.

We have found very few absolutes in our years working with children and parents. Nevertheless, all parents and caregivers need some guideposts to help keep children on the right track.

Whether you use a relatively strict or lenient approach, you need to understand your particular parenting style—which is very much a function of your own past experience and temperament. It's not easy to change your (or your child's) temperament. However, we urge you to use this book to enrich your experience and to expand the way you think about yourself, your child, and the style of discipline that works best for all concerned.

What Are Parenting Styles?

The term *parenting styles* describes the overall way mothers and fathers go about disciplining children. Parenting styles fit into three broad categories.

◆ **Authoritarian:** Parents who use this style demand strict obedience to the rules they set. Such parents are generally not responsive to a child's feelings and viewpoints. Authoritarian parents insist that things be done their way—essentially because they say so. This kind of parent tends to discourage discussion and negotiation, and takes a hard line on infractions.

◆ **Authoritative:** Mothers and fathers who use this style are more democratic in their childrearing. They set the basic rules, but are willing to listen to the viewpoints of children, and revise the rules in particular situations. Authoritative parents are willing to explain their rules, and are interested in helping children understand the reasons behind those rules.

♦ **Permissive:** Parents who use this style create a relatively loose environment, with few rules. Demands and punishments are often spotty and inconsistent. Outsiders who walk into the home of a family with overly permissive parents may be moved to ask: "Who's really in charge here?"

Keep in mind that these three approaches to discipline form a kind of sliding scale and there are lots of variations. For example, there are some authoritative parents who tend to be more lenient, while others favor a stricter approach. We also know parents who are quite strict in some areas and more lenient in others.

Even within the same family, it's not uncommon for parents to take varying approaches with different children. For example, a father might be lenient with his daughter and far stricter with his son. This can be driven by the parent's opinion about what a particular child needs, or some preconceived notion about the way boys and girls should be raised.

People don't always do what they say—and parents are no exception. We know moms and dads who spout the virtues of authoritative parenting, but run a very loose ship when it comes to disciplining their children. We also know extremely strict, unresponsive parents who talk a good game of flexibility—and who see themselves as authoritative, not authoritarian.

Parenting Styles in African American Families

Recent research suggests that many African American families favor an authoritative style of parenting. When it comes to setting limits, most of the parents surveyed prefer to discuss disciplinary matters with children—at least as a first step. This contradicts earlier studies that claimed African American parents had "very little give-and-take dialogue with their children."

When children challenge parental authority, African American parents often prefer to discipline by giving extra work or ordering the child not to persist in a particular behavior. This and other findings support the long-held belief that many black parents do not favor a particularly lenient approach.

A number of researchers have suggested that this is because "demanding obedience from African American children . . . is imperative, given the life circumstances imposed on [black] youth by the social, environmental, and institutional forces in American society." Nevertheless, there is a good deal of research to contradict the old stereotype that black parents are more likely to use corporal punishment than their white counterparts.

A study in the *Journal of Multicultural Counseling & Development* revealed that of the African American parents who use physical punishment, almost all do so in situation they perceive to be severe.[1]

HOW AFRICAN AMERICAN PARENTS DISCIPLINE THEIR CHILDREN

TECHNIQUE USED	POPULARITY OF USE
Discusses matter	Very popular: increases as children get older.
Orders child not to	Moderately popular: does not change much with age.
Gives extra work	Moderately popular: does not change much with age.
Promises reward	Moderately popular: decreases as children get older.
Gives warning look	Moderately popular: does not change much with age.
Yells at child	Moderately popular: does not change much with age.
Sends to another room	Moderately popular: does not change much with age.
Withdraws privileges	Moderately popular: increases slightly as children get older.
Ignores child	Unpopular: Decreases slightly as children get older.
Spanks with open hand	Moderately popular: decreases sharply as children get older.
Strikes with switch or belt	Unpopular: remains fairly stable as children get older.
Slaps child on face	Unpopular: remains fairly stable as children get older.

Tip: Look at your parenting style as if you were governing a nation.

How do you see yourself as a parent? Are you a dictator, a kind ruler, or the leader of a democracy? Although parents can raise strong children using any of the three styles, we find that an authoritative approach is a choice that works well for many parents. This style is comparable to a limited democracy—one that fosters open communication among family members. This is a far cry from saying that children should be allowed to do anything they want.

There are laws that must be obeyed in any system of government— even if some citizens don't think that all the laws are fair. In a democracy, people are free to speak out and question policy—and this same principle applies to parents who use an authoritative approach. Each family has to find a workable solution and no two situations are identical. In many families, the style of parenting is somewhat fluid.

There will be times, for instance, when an authoritative parent appears to be permissive or authoritarian, or when an authoritarian parent loosens the reins of power. Parents who are overly permissive, however, often find it hard to reverse course and suddenly start enforcing rules. Similarly, overly strict parents can instill such fear that children freeze when they're given an opportunity to bend the rules.

The key is to find a workable balance between demanding that children obey the rules and responding to their needs and feelings. The authoritative approach to parenting gives you the flexibility to maintain that critical balance. It rejects the need for taking either of the two extreme positions about how to discipline children. If you seek an approach that's neither overindulgent or too dictatorial, we recommend that you adapt the following guidelines.

Assert Your Authority But Respect the Child.

Make it clear to your child that you are responsible for setting the rules for what he or she can and cannot do. At the same time, encourage the child to ask questions and offer alternative views on how things might be run. This kind of approach helps children develop critical-thinking skills, and reinforces the sense that you value their feelings and opinions.

Use a Tone That's Both Friendly and Instructive.

What you're trying to do is create an atmosphere that is not built exclusively around the needs of the child or the parent. Instead, the goal is to blend the child's needs with those of other family members in ways that respect the rights and responsibilities of all concerned. This approach helps children understand that their rights and those of their parents are complementary, even if they're not identical.

SHOW PATIENCE IN THE FACE OF RESISTANCE.

When you lay down a rule to which a child objects, you may eventually have to assert your authority by saying: "You'll just have to do it my way." Don't be surprised if the child continues to protest or argue. Remember, most children expect their parents to set behavioral standards—even if they don't want those standards applied at the expense of getting their way at a particular moment.

Try to use discussion, explanation, and two-way communication to get your point across. Make it clear that you have sound reasons for your demands—even if the child is having trouble understanding or accepting them.

GIVE CHILDREN A FAIR HEARING.

It's important to always listen to what children have to say before deciding on a sanction or punishment. Too often, parents make these decisions without letting children express their views. Even when you sense that youngsters are lying, you still need to give them a chance to explain their actions. Children have a much easier time accepting punishment when they know that the parents have considered their point of view.

When you give children sufficient time to express themselves before deciding on a course of action, they are able to walk away feeling: "My folks listened to me; they considered what I had to say. I may not like what they decided, but at least I had some input."

PULL RANK WHEN NECESSARY.

Children become experts at pushing a parent's buttons at a very young age. They also have their own agendas, which include testing the limits of parental authority. When a disciplinary encounter can't be resolved through reason and discussion, it's time to exercise firm control, and let children know that there will be a price to pay if they don't meet the standards you set.

Reminder: *The impact of punishment depends on your parenting style*.

When authoritarian parents punish, they are simply asserting their unquestioned right to demand compliance under any circumstances. The threat of punishment by overly permissive parents is often a cry of sheer frustration—which the child feels he can safely ignore. However, in a balanced, authoritative home, punishment is applied judiciously and consistently, and is in sync with a child's developmental needs.

The rules of discipline are subject to change as children develop, but the need for discipline is ongoing. Clearly, the rules for a seven-year-old can't be the same as those for a seventeen-year-old. By ages fifteen or sixteen, many teens are largely independent of parental authority, and you're likely to find yourself negotiating hard for every inch of control. Nevertheless, if you've taken the kind of balanced approach we've described, adolescence doesn't have to be a horror show.

By the time children reach their teens, most parents are old hands at dealing with periods of compliance and rebellion. Infants accept parental authority without question. But even in the first weeks and months of life, parents are already making judgments about how well the child is complying with their needs. "She's such a good baby," a mother will say. "She sleeps through the night, and hardly ever cries when she's hungry."

As the child learns to walk, talk, and think, rebellion rears its head. The *terrible twos* is a term parents use to describe once-obedient children who are at a stage where they're no longer willing to listen. During this time, the word children and parents most often use is *no*. In the years that follow, children go through alternating periods of relative compliance and rebellion—and parents must know how to steer through both calm and turbulence.

As children move into adolescence, parents often find themselves facing a kind of 3-D version of the terrible twos. But now they have a lot less control over their children's lives and fewer punishment options.

Teenagers tend to be increasingly out of their parents' sight and subject to the influence of peers. Still, don't ever underestimate how much your child needs you to continue setting reasonable limits—even if he or she initially rebels or accuses you of being clueless or worse. During this time, your teen may flatly refuse to abide by your rules and force you to take a stand. Still, if you've laid a strong foundation, you can generally ride out these storms. The key is to hold your ground and continue setting a positive example. Here are some tips for dealing with teen discipline.

◆ **Take advantage of your supervisory powers.** Even though you no longer have much control over your adolescent's daily activities, you are still in charge of supervisory decisions and setting such parameters as curfew and family responsibilities. You also control where the family lives and which school your child attends. We know parents, including some of modest means, who've moved to different neighborhoods or transferred their children to other schools in order to get them out of a destructive environment.

◆ **Don't be too heavy-handed.** You have every right to make and enforce rules at this stage, but you are likely to find that it's a struggle. The more gracefully you can accept this battle of wills, the easier it will be to communicate with your teen. Remember that risk taking is a normal part of an adolescent's growth and development—even if it makes you uncomfortable. In Chapter Four, we fully explore the differences between healthy and dangerous risk taking.

Helping Black Children Appreciate the Value of Discipline

There are two major phases when it comes to disciplining children: setting the rules and applying the rules. Many parents have a far easier time deciding what they want the rules to be than they do implementing those rules. For instance, deciding that children are responsible for certain chores around the house is a lot easier than making sure they fulfill that responsibility. When children ignore rules, it's often because parents haven't spelled out their expectations and the consequences of not meeting those standards.

Reminder: Don't expect children to think like adults.

It's important to understand the way children think, so that you can adjust your expectations accordingly. Before a certain age, children simply don't understand the connection between actions and consequences.

As they develop, children are more able to use this kind of consequential thinking. Until then, they tend to use impulsive thinking. Rather than consider the impact of their actions, children focus on the immediate benefit or gratification they anticipate a certain action will produce. The younger the child, the less able he or she is able to connect actions to consequences.

The ability to delay gratification is key to achieving discipline. The sooner children grasp the value of trading something they want right now for something more valuable in the future, the stronger they will be. This is a gradual process, one that hinges on both emotional and neurological development. Still, the principle applies for all age groups and across the five disciplines, as the following examples demonstrate.

- Six-year-old Walter doesn't want to wash his dish, but he does so in order to please his mom.

- Ten-year-old Michael doesn't want to do his homework, but his folks have helped him understand that good grades are important to his future.

- Thirteen-year-old Destiny has a craving for junk food, but follows her parents' lead by opting for a snack that's better for her health.

- Sixteen-year-old Alexis is offered drugs by her best friend. She's tempted to experiment, but ultimately declines, because she under-stands the potential dangers.

- Eighteen-year-old Lamar wants to get in the face of the video store security guard who has profiled him as a probable shoplifter, but his dad has explained that this isn't the best time or way to vent his anger.

Each time children forgo their impulse in favor of a more long-range reward, they become stronger. A parent's love, approval, and example are the forces that put this process into motion. Even babies can tell when they are pleasing their parents—and this desire to please you is the foundation that gives children the strength to resist their impulses.

THE REAL MEANING OF QUALITY TIME

Nothing signals your love and approval more than spending time
with your child. There has been a good deal written about quality time, yet it's a term that's often misunderstood.

Quality time is not about planned activities or events. Children
are likely to get more value and enjoyment spending time doing
chores with you or just hanging out than going to a movie or a ball-
game. In fact, a father will take a child to a game, and think he's
spending quality time with the kid. In reality, parents sometimes use
such "special events" as a way to effectively be alone and not have
to communicate with children.

Real quality time is about activities that make it easy and natural for you and the child to communicate—the nature of the event
is unimportant. What is important is that your child spends time
with you, participating in your-day-to-day routines—whether it's
doing something around the house, running an errand, or reading a
book together.

As children develop, there are always new challenges and issues for
parents to deal with. Parents are not superhuman, so it's unrealistic to expect anyone to make the best choices all the time or always set the best
examples for their children. Which is not to say that there aren't more
and less effective ways to deal with the following real-life family situations.

When Two Parents Disagree About Discipline

One of the most common problems mothers and fathers encounter is a
basic difference in parenting styles. This is not something husbands and
wives tend to discuss beforehand. Once a baby comes into their lives,
people tend to play it by ear. This usually means either copying their own
parents or trying to do the opposite of what their folks did. Both of these
strategies are flawed—because neither is based on a thoughtful decision

about what makes the most sense. But the situation can get much worse when a mother and father are at opposite ends of the parenting-style spectrum.

Diane and Chris had been fighting over how to discipline their seven-year-old daughter, Ashley. Diane was angry that Chris was never able to say no to the child. Diane always felt like the bad guy—the one who always has to deliver the bad news.

Like many children with parents who fight about the rules, Ashley was confused. That's not surprising, since she was getting one message from her mom about how she should behave, and the opposite message from her dad. Ashley was a clever child who quickly figured out how to manipulate the situation. Whenever mom would put her foot down or refuse to give Ashley something she wanted, the child would go crying to dad, who would then say: "Let me try to talk your mother into it."

Diane told Chris she felt he was undermining her, but these complaints went in one ear and out the other. Diane was constantly after her husband to be stricter with their child. "Why do you always have to give in to her?" she'd say. "How will she learn to be responsible?"

Chris would nod his head, as if agreeing, but it appeared to Diane that his mind was somewhere else. It was left to young Ashley to figure out right and wrong for herself. After a while, the child picked up on the tension between her parents and started having temper tantrums. Something had to be done.

We suggested that Chris and Diane use the following three-step program to work out their problems—steps that can help you and your partner resolve conflicts about how to apply discipline.

1. Recognize that changes are needed.

Diane and Chris had been fighting the same battle since Ashley was in diapers. Clearly, they weren't getting anywhere. Many of their arguments were taking place in front of their daughter—who was becoming increasingly upset and confused. The first step for these parents was to admit that they were getting nowhere resolving their differences—and that that their disagreements were having a negative impact on both the quality of their relationship and their effectiveness as parents.

2. Talk out your differences using first-person statements.

When people argue, there's a tendency to focus on what the other guy is doing wrong. In order to resolve differences, it's much more productive to express how you're feeling, instead of talking about the other person's faults. It took a while, but here's how the dialogue between Diane and Chris sounded when they finally started to make some progress:

DIANE: I'm very uptight about this situation. No matter how much I talk, I can't seem to get across to you how strongly I feel about the kind of discipline I believe our daughter needs. I want to talk with you about our different ideas on bringing her up so that we can find some better solutions.

CHRIS: I want Ashley to enjoy her childhood without a whole bunch of restrictions. Look, she's not going to be a little kid forever.

DIANE: I also want Ashley to enjoy these years. But I feel strongly that she needs to have limits, which I think will make things easier for her in the long run.

3. Agree on a game plan.

Diane and Chris loved their daughter; both parents had their child's best interests at heart. We helped Diane and Chris understand that it's important for parents to be consistent when dealing with their young child, and that achieving this consistency takes planning. Diane and Chris realized they both had the same goal for their daughter—even if they had different ideas about the best way to achieve that goal. They were then able to agree on the following parenting strategy:

- Diane will take the lead concerning Ashley's responsibilities around the house.

- Chris will have more say in deciding about Ashley's weekend activities. Chris will also assume more of a role in deciding how much to spend on toys and other things Ashley wants.

- Diane and Chris both agree not to contradict each other in front of the child no matter how strongly one disagrees with the other's decision.

- The couple will set aside time to talk about how well this new approach is working and make adjustments when necessary.

If you are committed to keeping your marriage together and doing what's best for your child, try the following five communication tips:

- Stick to the issue you're discussing.

- Make an effort to listen to what your partner is saying.

- Don't keep blaming and finding fault with your partner.

- Don't use your children to get back at or send messages to your partner.

- If problems don't improve, consider seeking counseling.

Raising a Child on Your Own

According to recent census statistics, over two-thirds of African American families are headed by single mothers, compared to less than one quarter of white families. At the same time, more than half of all children in the United States are living in homes headed by a single parent, in a remarried family, or in a stepfamily.

Conventional wisdom has held that children are best off living in a traditional home, with the mother and father who conceived them. However, there has been enough research over the years to put to rest the outmoded assumption that a child who grows up in a single-family home is automatically at a disadvantage. Children can grow up strong and happy with either one or two good parents—or in any number of nontraditional family environments.

The traditional two-parent household is no longer the dominant family structure in America. As more single mothers are having children; more couples with children divorce and never remarry or enter into some type of stepfamily situation, there are many different types of family structures. A study of African American youth reported in *Family Journal* is one of many that supports our own view on whether this is a positive or negative development.

"It is the quality of family relationships, not the structure, that influence [childhood and] adolescent development. For both boys and girls, living in a supportive, positive, and controlled family environment is associated with fewer problem behaviors and positive psychological well-being."[2]

As with everything else, there are advantages and disadvantages to any and all circumstances. Single mothers don't hesitate to point out the many challenges of their situation. Parenting without a partner clearly has its downside. Many single parents are primarily responsible for making a living and supervising their children—and this can be stressful. On the other hand, single parents often consider it a plus to be able to raise children as they see fit, without having to fight over differences with a spouse.

There is a long tradition of successful single mothering in the African American community. Fueled by necessity and fierce determination, black single mothers have provided a special source of strength that continues to be passed down through the generations.

In part, this single-mother tradition evolved because black women's work history is different from that of their white counterparts. During slavery, work was assigned to male and female slaves without much regard for gender differences. After Emancipation, African American men faced formidable racial barriers, which meant that women had to work in order to provide basic necessities for their families. As a result, the traditional arrangement of men working outside the home while women functioned as homemakers was a lot less prevalent in African American families than in white families.

Historically, in African societies, there were strong communal networks, including extended families that existed for the purpose of caring for children. This tradition continued after the forced migration of Africans to the American colonies. During slavery, parents and children were routinely sold away from each other at their owner's whim. Consequently, the survival of slave children in this situation depended on other adults assuming parental roles.

During slavery, a phenomenon sometimes called *multiple mothering* became the norm. Related and unrelated women formed a kind of communal adoption society in which all pitched in to help rear and discipline whatever children were around. Beverly Greene, an African American scholar, provides an apt description of how this relationship between single mothers and extended families developed and why it continues to thrive to this day:

"This society of close friends, aunts, grandmothers, cousins, even neighbors who were part of a network that was considered *kin* to a child's mother continue[s] to provide emotional safety valves, sounding boards, and alternative role models to children. [They also provide] their real mothers with important tangible support in the form of child care. These arrangements also emphasize the important role for elder members of the family and the importance of their connection to members of the next generation."[3]

Single-parent families are a large and diverse group among black Americans and are not (as another cultural stereotype would have it) made up of mostly underage welfare mothers. We know many families headed by successful single mothers (and fathers) who are thriving, both emotionally and financially. The following tips can help you achieve the same kind of success.

Manage Your Time Realistically.

Full-time working parents have to decide on how to apportion their time. Many of the problems children have stem from parents who don't spend enough time with them. This is a problem in all types of families, but it can be an especially pressing issue for single parents, who often have trouble finding enough hours in a day.

There has been a lot written about quality time. However, as we detailed earlier in this chapter, much of that is a fallacy. Working parents who walk through the door at 8:00 p.m. and try to squeeze in forty-five minutes of so-called quality time with a youngster who is half asleep are short-changing their children—and themselves.

Reminder: There's no substitute for the hours parents spend with children.

Many of today's children are victims of too little parental attention, and it's leading to lots of problems—including a lack of discipline at home, classroom disruptions at school, drug abuse, and eating disorders. The following time-management tips can help you add more rewarding hours to your busy day:

Decide What's Most Important.

These choices are called *priorities*. If one of your priorities is spending more time with your children, figure out ways to reduce the time you devote to less important pursuits. For example, consider moving closer to work so that you spend less time commuting. By reducing your travel time from, say, an hour to a half hour going to and from work, you'll have five extra hours each week, twenty extra hours each month—and around 240 extra hours each year to spend with your children.

Don't Waste Your Time.

Everyone needs a certain amount of downtime, and hardworking parents are certainly no exception. Still, if you think about it, you are likely to find certain time wasters that you can eliminate—perhaps a little less TV watching in the evening. Another good idea is to eliminate people who are a drain on your time and emotional energy.

Set Aside Specific Time for Your Children.

Include both special times as well as times when you're just hanging out. If you have more than one child, spend a few minutes of individual time with each. Don't forget to make time to be together as a family. A short family meeting or conference each night is a good way for parents and children to share feelings and talk about the highs and lows of the day.

How to Turn Time Apart into Time Together

- *Prepare meals with children. Use that time to talk about your day.*

- *Plan to have at least one sit-down meal together with the entire family every day.*

- *Take children with you when you go shopping. Ask for their opinion about which items to purchase. Encourage them to select some of the items.*

- *Find a form of physical exercise you can do together on a regular basis—be it walking, bicycle riding, swimming, or some other activity.*

- *If feasible, take your child to work several times a year. If possible, find ways for him or her to help you with various job-related tasks.*

KEEP YOUR STRESS LEVEL OUT OF THE RED ZONE.

Parenting can be stressful, even when things are going well. For example, parents experience stress when children leave for college or go out on a first date. However, the type and level of stress are a lot different when you're called into school because a child is in trouble, or when he's having physical or emotional problems.

Studies show that stress-related illnesses are at least partially responsible for almost two-thirds of all visits to family doctors. Too much stress has been linked to headaches, digestive problems, back pain, insomnia, chronic fatigue, depression, and feelings of perpetual anger. People who are chronically stressed out are also at elevated risk for strokes and heart attacks.

Every person has a different way of dealing with stress. We know parents who are great at standing up in the face of a real crisis, but who lose their tempers when children commit a minor infraction. Parents who blow up this way don't get rid of their stress. Instead, they increase stress on themselves and on their children. The following techniques are especially useful for single parents who feel stressed out.

DEVELOP A STRONG SUPPORT SYSTEM.

As more African Americans move out of traditional black neighborhoods, there is less multiple mothering and communal parenting than there once was. However, there is plenty of help and support available if you know where to look for it. We list a number of helpful national and community organizations in Chapter Ten, and urge you to take advantage of them.

Reminder: The best neighborhood you can afford isn't always the best choice for your family.

When choosing a place to live, it's important to consider proximity to relatives and friends, for your sake as well as your child's. The local black church or mosque is often a good place to network and find support in the form of child care, mentoring programs, and counseling. Which is why you should consider living close to a religious or community center that addresses these needs.

Another proven stress buster is confiding in a friend—especially one who is a good listener. We believe that if more parents took advantage of this and other readily available networking opportunities, there would be a lot fewer cases of stress-related illness.

SLOW DOWN.

The life of a single parent tends to be particularly hectic. Nevertheless, there are a number of things you can do to relax. The following techniques can help cushion the stressful hits that can undermine your well-being and your effectiveness as a parent.

+ **Take a power nap.** Many single parents complain they don't get enough sleep at night. This makes them tired, irritable, and less able to handle stress. One effective way to deal with this problem is to take one or more short naps during the day. A power nap can last anywhere from ten to twenty minutes. Simply lie down on a couch (if available) or sit in a comfortable position. Then shut your eyes and let your mind relax. The cumulative effect of this additional sleep can make coping with stress a lot easier.

+ **Take a deep breath.** Deep breathing has long been used as a technique to relax the mind and body. Inhale slowly, drawing air deep into your lungs. Hold your breath for a few seconds. Then slowly exhale, as you visualize the stress being carried out of your body.

+ **Make time for yourself.** It's hard to be an effective, loving parent if you're always on edge. That's why it's important to make time in your day to do something relaxing and revitalizing. Some people enjoy playing or listening to music. Others like to jog, play tennis, or take walks. Whatever activity you choose, it's essential that you devote part of each day to doing something you enjoy—whether alone or with others.

Reminder: Don't expect you or your child to be perfect.
When parents are stressed out, they sometimes fly off the handle when a child makes an unimportant mistake or commits a small breach of discipline. Stress can also cause parents to beat themselves up for their own mistakes. When you demand perfection, you automatically create unnecessary stress. That's because there's no such thing as the perfect parent—or the perfect child.

Sometimes, the most important asset you can possess is a good sense of humor. It's often possible to find humor, even when you're faced with serious problems. Fortunately, most of the day-to-day struggles that come up between parents and children are not critical. When you can find humor in situations, you lighten everyone's tension and increase the chances of getting the result you want.

HELPING KIDS RELIEVE STRESS

*C*hildren pick up on their parents' stress. Children also have their own stress, something often ignored when parents are themselves stressed out. Doing one or more of the following simple stress-busting techniques with children will help keep everyone's stress levels out of the red zone:[4]

- *To relieve frustration, have the child count backward and slowly from 100 down to 1.*

- *Show a stressed-out child how to calm herself by controlling the breath. Demonstrate breath control by taking a long breath through your nose, and then exhaling through your mouth. Take twice as long exhaling than inhaling.*

- *Sit down on the floor with a stressed-out child and have him do a forward stretch. Demonstrate the move by closing your eyes and leaning forward as you move your fingertips toward your toes. Don't strain.*

- *Use progressive relaxation: Tense up your face for five seconds, then slowly relax those muscles. Next move down your body, starting with your shoulders, chest, arms, hands, legs, and toes.*

- *Have the child take a relaxing warm bath. Stress has a negative effect on circulation, whereas warm water tends to restore it.*

Creating a Functional Stepfamily

It is estimated that between one-third and one-half of all African American children live in a remarried or stepfamily. In some cases, one or both of a child's biological parents has remarried. These children may share their homes with stepsiblings. Such circumstances make it almost impossible to maintain the same degree of control or influence over children as in a first-time family.

There are other difficulties as well. Parents who become part of a newly re-formed family can find themselves torn apart by any number of conflicting forces. These can include the child's elevated need for attention, the new partner's need for time alone together, and the demands of an ex-spouse who may be hostile to the new relationship.

Children often have a tough time adjusting to these unfamiliar situations. They've already suffered the loss of their original family. Now they may be forced to move to a new neighborhood, attend a new school, and make new friends.

Part of your job as a parent is to recognize the difficulties that are part of stepfamily life, and do what you can to make the transition as painless as possible. Here are some steps you can take to make that happen.[5]

ENCOURAGE CHILDREN TO EXPRESS THEIR FEELINGS.

Do what you can to show you understand what family members are going through. If, for example, your son is having a tough time adjusting to his new home and accepting his new stepparent, you can avoid these common mistakes: Don't discourage him from complaining that he misses his dad and don't try to convince him how much nicer your new mate is than that nightmare of an ex-husband. Instead, tell the child you understand how he feels. Encourage him to talk about what he misses most, and assure him that you'll try to work things out so that he can spend more time with his dad.

ENCOURAGE OPEN LINES OF COMMUNICATION.

As much as possible, try to promote good relations among all concerned—ex-spouses, biological and adopted children, stepchildren and their biological parents, stepparents, grandparents, and other relatives, as well as concerned friends. The more cut off people are from their loved ones, the more conflict there will be among family members, and the harder it will be to have a successful stepfamily.

Caution: Don't badmouth your ex to your child.

No matter how bitter your breakup, it's important to remember that you and your ex have an obligation to leave the children out of your battles. Children can be permanently damaged when divorced parents are openly hostile to one another. They also have a much tougher time adjusting to a new family arrangement when their parents are in open conflict.

One of the most hurtful things estranged spouses do is use their children to deliver antagonistic messages to each other. An angry mother might ask her child: "Remind that deadbeat that he's two weeks late with this month's support payment." This strategy puts children in the middle of a conflict that's not of their making.

TAKE THE RESPONSIBILITY FOR DISCIPLINING YOUR OWN CHILDREN.

Remarried wives often expect their new husbands to become instant authority figures to their children, whereas remarried men often assume that their new wives will automatically assume the role of second mothers to their children. This is far from an automatic process.

Sometimes a child's stepparent has different ideas and a different parenting style than a child's biological parent. It's a mistake for a stepparent to be too forceful, no matter how strongly he feels about a particular way to discipline children. Newer stepparents are well advised to start off by being a child's friend or mentor—but not their boss.

It often takes years for a child to accept a stepparent's authority and affection. Meanwhile, the primary responsibility for providing discipline and love falls to the biological parent. As time passes, a concerned stepparent will have an opportunity to gradually earn the child's respect and affection. Still, it's a slow and sometimes tortuous process.

EXPECT THE UNEXPECTED.

When newly re-formed families contain children from different original families, any number of unanticipated complications may arise. For instance, the oldest child in your new husband's family may suddenly find that he has one or more older siblings. A reshuffled birth order can result in conflict. Still, it's far from the thorniest problem some stepfamilies encounter.

Teenagers are rarely easy for parents to control. But when adolescent stepsiblings live under the same roof, there can be constant and intense bickering. An even trickier situation is the possibility of a romantic or sexual relationship. There's no easy way to curb sexual attraction and inhibit sexual contact between stepsiblings. A wise course is to talk to your teens about the potential complications of such close-quarter affairs, and to spell out your expectations regarding boundaries and appropriate behavior. Talking may not do the trick, so keep your eyes open in order to spot problems before they get out of hand.

The most effective way to promote positive relations in stepfamilies is to give each member of the re-formed family space and time to adjust to the new environment. One technique that produces good results is to hold regular family conferences. Every family can benefit from a forum in which each member has as an opportunity to express feelings and air concerns. These conferences can be especially helpful for stepfamilies, because there are often more players with different backgrounds, viewpoints, and needs. The following guidelines will help you plan family conferences:

1. *Set a regular place and time.*

There's no need to set up strict or inflexible rules. However, regularly scheduled conferences give family members a shared sense of participation and structure. Try to get everyone to agree on a time and a schedule. Set a time limit for how long the meetings will run.

2. *Make sure each family member has the opportunity to speak.*

It's important not to let any one member dominate the conversation—especially if that person regularly does so. Change the order of who starts and who ends the session periodically. Give each family member an opportunity to contribute ideas and make suggestions about what is to be discussed. If feasible, give each member (including preadolescent children who demonstrate the necessary maturity) a chance to lead the conference. If there are too many ideas to discuss at any one session, take turns deciding which are most pressing and address those first. Agree to start the next session with those issues that were not included.

3. *Have members voice feelings and complaints in the first person.*

The main purpose of family conferences is to give everyone an op-portunity to express feelings openly. When a family member says, "I feel that you are shouting at me and that makes me feel bad," he is using an "I" (or first-person) statement. However, if he instead says, "You're always shouting at everyone," that's the kind of third-person or finger-pointing statement that is counterproductive. Remember, the goal of a family con-ference is to improve communication among family members in hopes of creating a more cooperative and supportive atmosphere.

4. *Put some effort into making other family members comfortable.*

The purpose of regular family conferences is not for each member to get everything he or she wants. Still, one or two accommodations on each person's part can make a big difference. For example, if another member says that he feels bad when you shout, agree to make an effort to change that behavior. If that person does something that bothers you, ask him to make an effort to curtail or modify that behavior. The more respect and consideration family members are willing to demonstrate the smoother things are likely to go.

Discipline and a Healthy Family Environment

A healthy family environment is key to determining whether a young per-son will have the strength and discipline to meet the challenges that lie ahead. As we've been discussing, there are different problems that come up in different family circumstances. However, no single type of family environment is inherently healthier than any other. We see healthy fam-ily environments in homes headed by mothers and fathers, single par-ents, grandparents, and other primary caretakers. In some of these families both parents work, whereas in others a parent is at home during the day.

We have identified fifteen common characteristics that go a long way in determining the health of a family environment. We have designed the following exercise to help you pinpoint the issues that need the most work.

Instructions: Read each statement, then put a check next to the letter-choice that most closely matches your assessment of your family environment.

Check [E] if you regard the statement as reflecting an area of exceptional strength in your family.

Check [S] if you regard the statement as reflecting an area that is just satisfactory.

Check [I] if you regard the statement as reflecting an area that needs improvement.

How do the Members of Your Family Interact?

1. Family members communicate and listen to one another. Members spend time together, conversing and sharing views, values, and experiences. [E] [S] [I]

2. Family members are affectionate to one another, and feel comfortable that their feelings and concerns are acknowledged and respected. [E] [S] [I]

3. Family members feel that each member is valued equally. [E] [S] [I]

4. Children are encouraged to think independently, as well as to comply with parental standards.   [E] [S] [I]

5. Family members resolve disputes and arguments without putdowns. Parents and children know how to forgive and make up. [E] [S] [I]

6. Family members work to recognize their collective and individual stress levels, and strive to create a less stressful environment. [E] [S] [I]

7. Family members support one another and try not to place undue pressure on each other.   [E] [S] [I]

8. Parents trust each other, and children are gradually given more opportunities to earn trust. Family members try hard not to break trust. Should trust be broken, the offending member is forgiven and allowed to reestablish credibility.   [E] [S] [I]

9. Parents do not allow work and other responsibilities to intrude routinely upon family time.   [E] [S] [I]

10. Family members have a sense of shared responsibility. Children are

encouraged to earn their rewards, and to value time and money. [E] [S] [I]

11. Parents teach tolerance toward those with different values and backgrounds. Children are taught the importance of treating others with kindness and consideration. [E] [S] [I]

12. Family members respect one another's need for privacy and space. [E] [S] [I]

13. Parents make it clear that what a child does is important, and try to participate actively in those experiences. [E] [S] [I]

14. Parents do not try to cover up mistakes or rationalize weaknesses. Nor do they expect perfection from their children. [E] [S] [I]

15. The family accepts problems as a normal part of life, and strives to develop problem-solving techniques. Problems are discussed without placing blame. [E] [S] [I]

Reminder: Small changes can make a big difference.

As you think about changes you'd like to make in the way your family functions, don't be too hard on yourself—or your children. Start by concentrating on those areas where a small shift is likely to be most effective.

If, for example, you feel you haven't been spending enough time together as a family, start off by setting aside a few extra minutes each night to exchange feelings and talk about the high and low points of the day. Then add a few hours on the weekend to just hang out or do something everyone enjoys. If family members disagree about what's enjoyable, give everyone a turn at selecting the activity. Small steps like this may not seem earth-shattering, but they can go a long way to help strengthen the bonds between parents and children.

Summary

Ten Rules for Setting Behavioral Limits

1. Help children understand the importance of obeying rules—both in and outside of the home.

2. Understand your parenting style, and the adjustments you may need to make to effectively discipline your child.

3. Find an effective balance between firmness and flexibility.

4. Respect the child's point of view—however much you might disagree.

5. Understand what you want the rules to be before you try to enforce them.

6. Choose your battles and punishment options carefully.

7. Set standards of behavior that are high, but within a child's capacity.

8. Find more *real* quality time to spend with your child.

9. Manage stress, and show the child how to do likewise.

10. Recognize the issues that can arise in your particular kind of family structure.

3
⁓

Racial Discipline:
Don't Leave Home Without It

My first memory of being called "nigger" was the same cruel rite
of passage it has been for black children the country over. I was
seven, playing football with a group of white kids. A boy, about
my age, saw me in a neighbor's yard. . . . He pointed at me ex-
citedly and chanted: "Nigger. Nigger. Nigger."[1]

—Don Terry, *New York Times* reporter

White parents worry about their kids getting into an accident.
I worry that my son will mouth off to an officer or make a wrong
move, and end up getting beaten—or killed.

—African American mother of an eighteen-year-old boy

What's in This Chapter:

- ◆ Explaining the challenge of being black in America
- ◆ Helping children become effective in their interracial dealings
- ◆ Teaching children to treasure their rich heritage
- ◆ Showing children how to operate in a multicultural world
- ◆ Preparing children to deal with prejudice and profiling

EVERY CHILD FACES tough challenges growing up, regardless of race, economic status, social skills, and talents. But black children have to carry the extra burden of racism—and that takes a special kind of resilience. In this chapter, we show you how to help your child recognize and negotiate the many challenges black people face in this country. We give you techniques to help you instill racial pride and positive human values—even in the face of adversity. We begin with a review of some of the unpleasant realities our young people can expect to encounter:

♦ Sooner or later, most black men (and some women) will be pulled over on the highway, and possibly get harassed by police for driving while black (commonly known as DWB). African American women who find themselves walking in the "wrong neighborhood" are apt to be stopped on suspicion of prostitution or carrying drugs.

♦ In stores, black shoppers are regularly followed by store security personnel and treated with less courtesy than their white counterparts by cashiers and sales clerks.

♦ In school, black students are more likely to be labeled as having discipline problems or Attention Deficit Disorder by teachers and administrators.

♦ In the world of work, black workers are often paid less for the same jobs than their white counterparts and kept out of the higher echelons of power.

♦ When seeking medical treatment, black patients are often given second-rate service by doctors and hospitals—sometimes with fatal results.

Without racial discipline, the cumulative effect of these and many other slights, indignities, and lost opportunities can be devastating. Unless parents help children develop the inner strength to surmount these assaults, boys and girls may find themselves emotionally and physically vulnerable and unprepared to negotiate the world as it really is.

It's not hard to understand why parents would want to shield children from the slings and arrows of racial prejudice. But sooner or later, every black child is going to find out that he or she is part of the minority that is the number-one target of racism in America. This is a tough thing for moms and dads to tell their kids. It's especially difficult for parents who've overcome discrimination in their own lives and achieved financial success to acknowledge that their children are likely to encounter trials and struggles similar to the ones they had to face.

Whatever your background or current economic status, it's unrealistic and potentially dangerous to let any child of color go out into the world without racial discipline. Our young people need to understand that, while they may not be able to control the racial bias of others, they do have a great deal of control and power over their lives. You can help your child unlock that power by emphasizing the following principles.[2]

How to Spark Racial Discipline

1. Teach your child to understand the impact of race.

2. Teach your child to know where "home" is.

3. Teach your child to cultivate positive human values.

4. Teach your child to recognize what's most important.

5. Teach your child how to win the race-relations game.

Teach Your Child to Understand the Impact of Race

It's been almost four decades since Dr. Martin Luther King, Jr., called for a world in which people are judged by the content of their character rather than by the color of their skin. Unfortunately, we are still a long way from realizing that dream. Race *shouldn't* matter; but in the real world, it's a factor that often comes into play.

One of the trickiest things to convey to a child is that black people often don't get a fair shake in our society. It's not easy to get this point across in a culture where children are bombarded with nice-sounding words about fair play and equality. Parents must help children understand the difference between outright lies, pie-in-the-sky thinking, and the truth about how things really are.

If there really was a level playing field, everyone would have an equal opportunity to succeed. That's not what's happening. There are certain circumstances most whites will never face that black people encounter on a regular basis, including the following ten examples.

1. If a white person happens to work for an affirmative action employer, her colleagues won't assume she got the job because of race.

2. If a white person moves into a neighborhood, it's unlikely that his neighbors will automatically dislike him based on skin color.

3. Accomplished white people are never called "a credit to" their race.

4. White folks are never asked to answer questions on behalf of their race.

5. If a white person is late for a meeting, she's not likely to be thought of as exhibiting irresponsible behavior that's typical of her race.

6. When white folks ask to speak to "the person in charge," they are likely to be correct in their assumption that they will be facing another white person.

7. White people can speak out against racism without being seen as self-serving.

8. A white person is not assumed to be financially unreliable strictly on the basis of skin color.

9. White folks can travel virtually anywhere without having to worry about being rejected or mistreated on the basis of race.

10. White parents can be reasonably certain that their children's race won't make it more difficult for them to succeed in school and in the workplace.

The upshot of all this is that white parents don't have to worry about showing their children how to recognize and overcome systemic racism for their own physical, emotional, and financial protection. It may be unfair, but no black parent can afford to ignore this responsibility.

Black children need to understand that their color is a factor in virtually everything they do. Still, you don't want them to feel like victims or to go through life with a chip on their shoulder. That's why it's important to help children of color understand that most prejudice they encounter has little or nothing to do with them. It's much more about the other person, and how he or she has been taught to react to members of a particular racial group.

Even though you can't eliminate prejudice, you can help your child develop a vision of what he or she wants to accomplish, and provide the discipline and support that make this vision a reality. The following guidelines will help you accomplish this:

- Help your child understand that people who have to overcome obstacles often wind up stronger and more successful than those who have it easy.

- Give your child opportunities to have contact with people of different racial groups. If those opportunities aren't readily available in your neighborhood, seek them out elsewhere. For example, you might consider enrolling your child in a sports or arts program in a nearby area that reflects the diversity he or she is likely to encounter in the years to come.

- Don't use the prejudice of others as an excuse for your own shortcomings. As with all five disciplines, it's essential that your child sees you as a positive role model.

- Let your child know that he or she can succeed, despite the inequities of an unfair world.

- Encourage an open discussion about race relations. Answer all questions frankly, in an age-appropriate manner. Use those discussions as opportunities to come to terms with your own feelings about race.

Caution: Pretending that race doesn't matter often creates more problems.

We know a number of successful African Americans who have moved into upscale, primarily white suburbs, hoping that their children would avoid the hardships and bias they experienced coming up. Once the family moves, it's not unusual for the children to be rejected or discriminated against in this "better" environment. This can be an especially devastating circumstance for young people who lack the training and social skills to handle racial adversity.

One African American family we counseled moved from a racially mixed lower-middle-class community to an upscale town some people sarcastically call "White-landia." The couple's thirteen-year-old daughter and fifteen-year-old son had been doing well, both socially and academically, in their previous school. Both teenagers continued to maintain good grades in the new school—which is rated as one of the best in the state. However, they were both having a tough time making friends, and weren't shy about expressing their unhappiness.

"What good is living in a bigger house on a nicer block if you're always miserable?" the daughter recently asked her mom. The mother, who was startled by the question, could only answer, "But, honey, we did this for you and your brother."

It's only natural for people to want to live better as they climb the economic ladder. At the same time, it's important to recognize that money often has a different meaning for children who've never lacked material comfort than for parents who came from more humble beginnings. Whatever your economic status, you can wind up doing your children a disservice if you don't help them understand the realities of being black in a white-dominated culture.

Teach Your Child to Know Where "Home" Is

The vast majority of black children who grow into successful, well-balanced adults find a way to take what they need from the dominant white culture—without buying into its stereotypes and biases toward African Americans. In order to accomplish this delicate balancing act, young people must learn to appreciate their heritage and find their place in the black community.

Boys and girls who take pride in their ancestry and identify with the accomplishments of their community are tapping into a deep source of psychic nourishment. This is a source of sustenance that draws from the accumulated strength of each succeeding generation of African Americans.

Despite lingering racism in every corner of society, there is no question that today's young people are enjoying unprecedented opportunities to forge a better life. It's important that you encourage them to appreciate these opportunities and understand that they are a direct result of the survival and success of previous generations—often against overwhelming odds.

You can inspire children to greater heights by helping them recognize the connection between their own success and that of the group. Young people who understand the value of being part of this intergenerational linkage benefit in the following ways.

- They are able to draw strength and courage from the accumulated history and collective memory of the group.
- They are able to strengthen their motivation and resolve by framing their individual accomplishments as a way of passing the torch to future generations.

Some people seek challenges and adverse situations in an attempt to stretch themselves, but growing up black in America presents its own special kind of obstacle course. African Americans have met these challenges with a deep sense of community, a burning desire to achieve, and a strong religious and spiritual orientation. The following are some things you can do to strengthen your child's (and your own) connection to this rich heritage.

BECOME ACTIVE IN A BLACK CHURCH

African American families reap many advantages by getting involved in a black church, and by helping children understand the vital role the church has played in our community.

The black church has long been the center of political, economic, and social activity—particularly in the south, where churches were segregated. This gave black people the opportunity to discuss problems and express their feelings openly, without interference from potentially hostile forces.

White folks approved of blacks attending church. To them, this interest in God seemed admirable—a sign that black people were accepting one of society's most sturdy institutions. It also followed that if blacks believed in God, they would accept the way He had planned a world that gave whites more freedom, wealth, and opportunity than blacks. However, astute African Americans had a much different agenda.

Black folks could see that the church offered a private meeting ground—a center for change and action—and a place where their children were taught to appreciate the history of their people. It's no accident that many prominent black leaders, from the Reverend Dr. Martin Luther King, to the Reverend Jesse Jackson, to the Reverend Dr. Calvin Butts, began their careers in the church. Today, such leaders continue to use the pulpit to reach out to and further the interests of the African American community.

As black families become upwardly mobile, they sometimes lose interest in going to church. In some cases, the parents work long hours during the week and feel they can't spare the time on weekends. Others think of the black church as a remnant of a life that's no longer important. We feel strongly that such a perspective hurts families as a whole, and children in particular. Black churches have a lot to offer, even if you are not attached to an organized religion.

The church provides one of the best settings for black children to learn about their culture and to become connected to their people. In previous generations, when families had less money and tended to live closer together, black children had a greater sense of community. Back then, a child often had grandparents, aunts, and uncles around to help instill racial pride and discipline. Neighbors also took a greater interest in one another's children—and this added to a child's sense of belonging. The church was the glue that held the community together. It provided both spiritual enrichment and a meeting place for its members.

Even if you live in a primarily white area, there is likely to be a black church or mosque in a nearby town or city. We suggest that you set the example by becoming active in that church, and encouraging your children to do the same. This experience can be especially valuable if the house of worship draws members from a variety of neighborhoods, because children have an opportunity to develop bonds that transcend money and social status.

CONNECT TO AFRICAN AMERICAN ORGANIZATIONS.

Many African American service organizations and clubs have cultural, academic, and mentoring programs for children and adolescents. These national service organizations include women's groups like The Links, Inc., and men's organizations like 100 Black Men, Inc., as well as black sororities and fraternities. (Please see Chapter Ten for a complete listing of organizations and other resources.) Many of these organizations have embraced the rapidly growing numbers of middle- and professional-class African Americans.

The oldest black social club is Jack and Jill, a national organization for black children. The group was started in Philadelphia in the late 1930s by twenty well-to-do black mothers who thought it was important that their children had contact with boys and girls who shared a similar background.

Today, Jack and Jill has over 200 chapters in 35 states—as well as a chapter in Germany. Now, as then, mothers gather monthly to plan activities for their children, who are grouped by age. According to the organization's charter, all activities must be educational, fun, and/or culturally uplifting.

There is also an unstated purpose that goes something like this: "You're going to have to make it in *their* world, but we want you to remember where home is too." So, in addition to picnics, movies, and parties, children are required to participate in group volunteer projects, attend concerts by respected black performers, and visit museums to admire works by black artists.

The need to give black children this sense of place and cultural pride becomes more pressing as a growing number of African Americans move to primarily white areas. These are the families who are most concerned that their children are losing any sense of who they really are.

One couple, both successful corporate executives, were talking about a case involving racial bias at the dinner table, when their twelve-year-old son started screaming, "You guys need to stop living in the past. Race doesn't mean all that much anymore."

The boy's parents realized that they had fostered this kind of denial by moving to a lily-white suburb, enrolling their son in a private school that had very few minority students, and not doing much to help the young man develop connections to the black community. This outburst helped them recognize that their son was growing up without the grounding and resilience he would need to deal with pressures and challenges he would face down the road. These parents also had some more immediate concerns:

- ◆ As boys and girls progress through their teens, those who are "different" may find themselves excluded from social activities—or included as cultural mascots by white kids who want to appear hip.

- ◆ White parents who may have approved of interracial friendships often take a much harder line when their teenagers start to date. Young people who are naïve about their racial identity and lack ties to their community often find themselves unable to handle this kind of rejection.

- ◆ A lack of racial identity hits some black adolescents in the face when they enter college. Those who get through high school believing that racial bias was a myth or an abstraction are suddenly confronted with the reality of being a minority in a white world. These boys and girls may also have problems with older African American students who see them as sellouts or in denial about being black.

By getting involved in one or more social organizations and taking advantage of the many programs available for children, you provide your son or daughter with a sense of self-affirmation and belonging that he or she may have a hard time finding elsewhere.

Teach Your Child to Cultivate Positive Human Values

As children develop an understanding of what it means to be African American, they must also learn to appreciate those common elements all human beings share.

Race is one of the first ways we identify people who are more or less like ourselves. Still, children need to understand that, once you look past those surface differences, all people are more the same than they are different. Black people undoubtedly have some troubling experiences that are unfamiliar to whites. Nevertheless, you don't want your child to think that all problems are based on race.

People of all races want peace, security, and good health for themselves and their families—and all of us suffer setbacks and losses in these areas. Members of different racial groups also share many of the same moral codes and core values—even if some events and incidents divide us along racial lines.

When an innocent black man named Amadou Diallo was shot forty-one times by New York City police as he was reaching for his wallet, many whites considered the incident unfortunate—but felt it was an understandable overreaction by the police officers. Many African Americans, on the other hand, saw the incident as outright murder by cops who automatically assume that black men are criminals.

All citizens rely on the police to protect them. But studies show that, while most whites trust the police to do their jobs, black people often see cops as enemies who regularly violate their civil rights.

On one level, these clashes in response to public incidents serve to highlight the disparity in what black and white people experience. When you remove race from the equation, everyone can agree that the murder of an innocent man is tragic. Once race enters the picture, though, people can lose sight of the shared values and struggles that bind us as human beings.

A racially disciplined person is able to embrace the common values and needs all human beings share. You can help your child achieve this perspective by helping him or her develop two key life skills: empathy and inner strength.

Empathy involves respecting and supporting others. This can be tough when the other person has experiences and viewpoints that conflict with your own. Help your child observe these differences without passing judgment about who's right or wrong. Encourage the boy or girl to walk a mile in the other guy's shoes.

When children encounter people who appear to be different, they may frame those differences in terms of good or bad, better or worse. It's important to teach children to build on their own feelings and experiences by pointing out similar feelings in others who appear to be different. When teaching your child to empathize, be sure to stress the following guidelines.

♦ Always show respect for where other people are coming from.

♦ Recognize other people's feelings and viewpoints, and how they differ from your own.

♦ Communicate your feelings, needs, and wishes without framing them as good versus bad.

♦ Never allow anyone to misinterpret your empathy as a sign of weakness.

Inner strength is a key component of racial discipline—as well as the four other disciplines we explore throughout the chapters. We live in a culture that values power—but power is a two-sided coin. Insecure people often wield power as a weapon—a way to control, dominate, and belittle others. Inner strength, on the other hand, is an absolute force that helps a person endure and move forward. Unlike power, inner strength has no negative side, because it is a tool—not a weapon.

Many acts of bias are based on the fear of losing power. Whether that power is economic, social, or political, insecure people often blame their own failure on others. What can be easier than to blame your problem on an entire racial group, or to use race as an excuse for your own shortcomings?

Reminder: All children are vulnerable, whatever posture they may assume.

Young people who lack inner strength often become bullies who pick on other kids. Those who become the victims of bullies also lack inner strength. Help your child understand that bullies and victims are generally unhappy and undisciplined people who don't achieve much success.

Teach your child to face his or her vulnerability, and explain that this is not a sign of weakness. Use the following explanations to demonstrate that possessing inner strength is always more advantageous than wielding power over others.

- ◆ Strength helps you to think and act independently.
- ◆ Strength helps you to stand your ground.
- ◆ Strength helps you to become a leader whom others respect.

Teach Your Child to Recognize What's Most Important

To succeed at anything, you first need to pinpoint your goal, and then pursue it without allowing yourself to get sidetracked. Young people, who tend to be more impulsive than their elders, often act without thinking. Even when they do take time to consider various options, youngsters may choose shortsighted solutions. You can help your child develop a disciplined, goal-oriented approach to decision making by encouraging him to take the following steps.

- ◆ Always ask yourself: What matters most to me in this situation?

- ◆ Visualize the consequences of pursuing different courses of action.

- ◆ Talk and act in ways that motivate people to give you what you want.

- ◆ Don't allow yourself to be distracted by ego trips or peer pressure.

- ◆ Always have a well-defined goal in mind.

RACIAL DISCIPLINE IN ACTION: HOW TO HANDLE A JOB INTERVIEW

Horace, a seventeen-year-old African American who recently graduated from high school, needed a summer job to help pay for college. The young man applied for a position in the customer service department of a large telecommunications company, and was invited to come in for an interview.

Horace and most of his friends wear baggy pants and earrings, imitating the style of some of their favorite hip hop performers. Horace's mother told him that he'd better remove his earring and wear a suit and tie for the interview. Meanwhile, Horace's friends teased him about going to work for "the white corporate system." One of them said, "Hey, man, I hope you're not gonna dress like one of them robots."

When Horace didn't answer, his friends started ribbing him even harder. Once the laughter died down, though, they all agreed that putting on a suit and removing the earring for the interview would make Horace a sellout. If you were Horace's parent, how would you advise Horace to handle the situation?

a. Refuse to sell out. Do what makes you comfortable. The notion of "selling out" doesn't apply in this context—even if it is an issue that young people often talk about. If Horace truly wants the job, his goal is to convince the interviewer to hire him.

"When you go on a job interview," we tell young people like Horace, "you only have a very short window to make the interviewer decide to hire you. People are only going to hire you if you get them to like you, and convince them that you can address their goals. Most interviewers want employees who will do the job well and conform to the rules. It's up to you to talk and dress in ways that meet or exceed their standards. If you decide not to do that, you have to be willing to live with the consequences—which in this case means not landing the job."

b. Turn down the interview. Unless Horace doesn't want the job or has a better prospect, this isn't a very smart strategy. Some jobs may have looser dress codes. But even when office or corporate positions have a casual dress code, you're usually expected to dress up for the interview.

c. Remove the earring, but dress the way you normally do. This is an ineffective solution. Halfway measures don't cut it. If Horace wants the job, he needs to go all the way and do what's necessary to achieve that goal.

d. Wear the suit and tie, and remove the earring. This is the only disciplined way for Horace to handle the situation. He doesn't have to worry about selling out, being a corporate robot, or anything else of that nature. Here's what we tell young people in Horace's position: "By giving the interviewer what he wants, you effectively manipulate that person to give you what you want. That makes you the one who is calling the shots."

Teach Your Child How to Win

Every encounter with a person of another race provides children with a testing ground for racial discipline. Through experience, a young person becomes more skilled at negotiating interracial encounters—and handling strong emotions that test one's resilience.

It's not always easy to define winning—especially in situations where racial bias comes into play. We see winning as generating a response that is most likely to help people achieve their goal in a given situation—even if that goal is simply avoiding trouble.

It takes a great deal of discipline to get past the feelings some interracial encounters provoke. Still, the essence of discipline lies in the ability to look beyond powerful feelings that may cause you to act in ways that are self-defeating.

It's important to help young people understand that the purpose of racial discipline isn't to provide an emotional outlet. Its purpose is to make you more effective so that you can turn interracial encounters in your favor.

Take the case of sixteen-year-old Sandra, who "sees red" when store security guards follow her every move while she's shopping. Store officials rarely admit it, but this kind of racial profiling is an all-too-common practice. Aside from being unfair and unpleasant for the person being profiled, studies show that African Americans are actually less likely to shoplift than other racial groups.

If you were Sandra's parent, what would you advise her to do the next time she's confronted with this kind of racial profiling?

a. Get in the security guard's face. Accuse him of being a racist. This approach might help Sandra vent her anger. However, she's likely to be detained or thrown out of the store. At the very least, her shopping experience wouldn't be very pleasant.

b. Walk out of the store and never shop there again. This approach constitutes an instant economic boycott. The question is, to what end? Unless the situation is extreme, Sandra might find herself confronted by the same kind of scrutiny at the next store.

c. Face the fact that you're living in a racist world, and there's nothing you can do to alter the situation. Allowing a troubling circumstance to sap your energy is never a good idea—whether or not race is a factor. Once you've determined what you want to accomplish, you always have options. At times, the strongest course of action may be to do nothing. But even then, it needs to be an affirmative decision on your part.

d. Use positive verbal and body language, and contain your underlying anger at store personnel. Instead of acting and speaking in ways that arouse suspicion and reinforce negative racial stereotypes, young people are likely to get much further if they are courteous and cooperative in their encounters with store personnel. This is the smartest approach, if Sandra decides that her main objective is to browse in peace or make a purchase. By using this strategy, Sandra has the best chance of deflating the suspicions and biases of the people who are scrutinizing her. This may not be an earth-shattering victory. Nevertheless, it's a disciplined way for a young person to take control of a difficult situation and get what she wants.

Racial discipline comes into play in any situation where racial profiling is a factor. However, it's absolutely critical for young people of color who are confronted by police. In this context, the definition of winning is simple indeed: Resolve the situation as quickly as possible, with a minimum of emotional and physical damage.

Among those who are remembered for their tragic encounters with cops are Johnny Gammons, whom police in Pittsburgh choked to death after a routine traffic stop took a tragic turn. There was also the 1998 case of five young men who were shot by state troopers on the New Jersey Turnpike. And while most traffic stops don't end violently, they can still be traumatic. Seventeen-year-old James found that out the hard way.

One Friday, a little before midnight, James had dropped off his date, and was driving home through the mostly white surburban neighborhood in which he lived. He was only a few blocks from his family's four-bedroom house when he saw the flashing red lights of a police car closing in on him. James later recalled that he took a little longer than he might have pulling over to the curb.

"License, registration, and insurance card, boy," the burly white cop growled.

James hadn't had much contact with the police, but he resented this officer's rudeness. After all, he was a law-abiding citizen, going the speed limit.

"What's this about?" James asked.

"Just sit there and keep your mouth shut," the cop replied.

The officer walked back to his car and took his time studying James's paperwork. James was getting impatient. It was late, and he wanted to get home. After a few more minutes, James stepped out of his car and was about to ask what was taking so long, when the cop pointed an angry finger and shouted:

"Who the hell told you to get out of your vehicle?"

In a flash, the cop ordered James to lie face down on the ground and spread-eagle. James was then subjected to a full body search, accompanied by a chorus of racial slurs. The cop finally let James go. But in the days and weeks that followed, the young man wouldn't eat and rarely came out of his room.

James is the oldest son of professional parents, who'd never schooled him or his two younger brothers on how to deal with everyday racial slights—much less such a harsh confrontation with the police. When James's mother tried to talk to him about the incident, the young man cried bitterly.

"Why did this happen to me?" he pleaded. "I didn't do anything wrong."

Anyone who has experienced this kind of treatment knows how degrading it is. But the lingering effects are infinitely worse for young people who haven't been prepared to handle such encounters. James's parents realized that their son needed help, and brought him to see us.

At first, James was so depressed and withdrawn he could barely talk about the incident. We helped James understand that what happened to him has happened to untold numbers of African Americans.

We explained to James that the first few seconds of eye contact, your tone of voice in addressing a police officer, and the way your hands move when reaching for your wallet can make all the difference in the world. Then we asked James to reconstruct the incident.

James told us that he was "pissed off" when the officer pulled him over and approached his car, and that he "didn't especially feel the need" to treat a cop with respect after he'd been called boy. It's quite possible that the cop wouldn't have searched him if the young man had pulled over immediately, not shown his anger, and employed the right kind of verbal and body language with the officer.

"It's natural to want to call that cop a racist pig," we explained. "But it takes discipline to control your emotions, and act in a way that helps you accomplish your primary objective. In this case, that objective is to safely remove yourself from the situation, with a minimum of negative interaction between you and the cop."

In time, James was better able to understand what he could do to make future encounters with the police go more in his favor. But he wouldn't have paid such a high price for this knowledge if his parents had armed him with racial discipline long before he was forced to face a dangerous, racially charged situation.

Racial profiling by police is an unfortunate reality in a system that often treats minorities unfairly. It's important to help a young person understand that fairness isn't the issue—especially when you're facing a potentially dangerous encounter. Rather, it's a person's ability to negotiate the encounter in a way that doesn't make a bad situation worse.

Reminder: Rehearse DWB stops with children before they get their driver's license.

It's especially important that boys be coached by their fathers or other grown men they respect. Confrontations between young black men and police often escalate, because males tend to become aggressive when they feel mistreated. It takes discipline for a young person to rein in his anger, and assume the kind of cooperative posture that minimizes the potential for causing a dangerous altercation.

Children achieve racial discipline when parents help them develop productive ways of thinking and smart ways of dealing with the race-related challenges life presents. As with all five disciplines, it's essential that you both talk to the child *and* show him what to do.

FIVE RULES OF THE ROAD

1. *Don't be sarcastic or condescending to the officer. Always be cooperative and polite. Address officers as sir or ma'am. Police usually like to be called "officer," while state troopers often prefer "trooper."*

2. *Use thoughtful, nonconfrontational body language. Don't stare or glare at the officer. Keep your hands in plain sight. Don't make any sudden moves.*

3. *Don't show anger—even if you've been provoked. Most police officers resent having their authority challenged. They may not like black people to start with, so don't throw gasoline on the fire.*

4. *Don't argue your legal rights. If you believe that a police officer has violated your rights, remember his or her badge or vehicle ID number. Legal recourse may be available if the circumstances warrant. However, at the point you are stopped, your task is to stay disciplined. That means maintaining control of your emotions and your behavior.*

5. *Always keep your goal in sight. The objective in most DWB encounters is to end the encounter as quickly as possible, and with a minimum of trauma. Getting stopped for no good reason is a drag. But being spread-eagled in the middle of the street and searched is a horrible experience that can give you nightmares. And there are far worse scenarios that can happen if you allow yourself to lose control of the situation.*

Caution: DWB stops are especially dangerous for groups of teenagers.

In such situations, the undisciplined behavior of any one of the teens can endanger everyone in the group. Please see Chapter Four for a complete discussion on handling the dangers of peer pressure.

RACIAL DISCIPLINE IN ACTION: HOW TO NEGOTIATE A DRIVING WHILE BLACK (DWB) STOP

Ron is a forty-six-year-old hospital worker who holds down two jobs. One of Ron's jobs is over an hour's drive from his home, along a highway that has a reputation for DWB stops. Nevertheless, when he is tight for time, Ron often drives at ten to fifteen miles an hour above the posted speed limit.

Even though many motorists ignore the speed limit, Ron knows that he's asking for trouble by speeding on a road where black drivers who go the speed limit are frequently stopped for suspicion of transporting drugs and firearms. Still, he needs that second job, and has decided to risk a higher probability of getting stopped by police. And while we don't endorse speeding, we have to admire the smart, disciplined approach Ron takes to minimize potential problems.

"The first step is to drive a car that doesn't attract attention. I drive a late-model Ford sedan, which I keep well-maintained. Cops are more likely to stop you in a high-profile speed demon or a car that looks like a wreck. Why look for trouble?"

Ron has also found a way to talk to cops that usually turns the encounter in his favor. "I'm always friendly, but respectful," he told us. "When the cop pulls me over, I immediately acknowledge that I was speeding, and apologize.

"I always keep my hands in plain sight, and ask if it's okay to remove my license and registration from the glove compartment," Ron continued. "Then, I explain that I have to work two jobs that are far away from each other in order to support my family, and that I can be fired if I'm late. I never use the excuse that I wasn't going faster than the flow of traffic, even if I was technically speeding.

"I tell the officer that I can't afford any more points on my driver's license, and ask if he'd consider issuing a ticket for an offense that wouldn't add more points. The officers usually either issue a warning, or write a ticket for a lesser offense. Sometimes they just tell me to slow down—and let me go."

Ron explained that most of these officers are white, and there's no way to tell how they feel about black people. But he can often see the initial tension dissipate as the two of them start to talk.

Both of Ron's sons have been with him when he has been stopped, and have had an opportunity to watch how their father handles these situations. Ron has also explained the dangers of DWB stops to his boys. He has told them that, as young black males, they have a good chance of being stopped just because of their age and skin color.

"Some of these cops may dislike—or even hate—black people," Ron has cautioned his sons. "If so, they probably have an ugly picture in their mind of how you're going to talk and act. Once a cop sees that you're not what he expects, there's much less chance of trouble."

Ron has explained that even hardcore bigots will usually acknowledge that there are "a few good ones" in any racial group. Ron has found a way to deflate whatever negative stereotypes an officer might be carrying. At that point, the white officer may well find himself thinking: "This guy might be black, but underneath, he's a lot like me—a hard-working family man, busting his butt to make ends meet."

Ron's sons have had the benefit of seeing their father demonstrate his own extraordinary racial discipline. And while they may still be too young to understand all the subtleties of their dad's approach, they are receiving an education that may one day save their lives. Still, young people don't acquire racial discipline overnight. Parents need to be consistent in their actions and willing to answer some tough questions from skeptical teens.

After a recent highway stop ended with a warning but no speeding ticket, Ron's sixteen-year-old son said: "I don't know, Dad. Looks to me like you're afraid to stand up to the man." Ron carefully explained that what really took place was him getting "the man" to do what he wanted.

"Think about it," Ron counseled his son. "I came out of that traffic stop the real winner. Not only that, but there was no loser. I didn't get a ticket, and the cop had a pleasant experience dealing with a black guy. This kind of thing won't eliminate racial prejudice, but who knows? Maybe the good experience this officer had with me will cause him to feel a little better about African Americans, and influence how he treats the next black guy he stops."

Summary

Ten Ways to Help Young African Americans Achieve Racial Discipline

1. Let young people know that race matters.

2. Encourage young people to embrace their rich cultural heritage.

3. Help young people understand that members of all races are more the same than they are different.

4. Teach young people to respect and support others.

5. Show young people how to clarify their main objective in every situation.

6. Help young people develop the discipline to think before they react.

7. Help young people develop the strength to generate a positive outcome from potentially negative situations.

8. Show young people how to deal effectively with those of different races and backgrounds.

9. Teach young people how to handle potentially dangerous, racially charged situations.

10. Make sure that young people don't use the racial prejudice of others to excuse their own shortcomings.

4

᪥

Emotional Discipline:
Saying No and Other
Strength-Building Strategies

*As parents, we must find ways in which to help children feel
special and appreciated without indulging them.*
—ROBERT BROOKS, AND SAM GOLDSTEIN
psychologists[1]

What's in This Chapter:

- Understanding the far-reaching impact of emotional discipline
- Giving children the strength to resist the quick fix
- Helping teens form positive peer relationships
- Showing girls and boys how to avoid the dangers of drugs, sex, and violence

EMOTIONAL DISCIPLINE IS the mechanism that gives young people the strength to say no to drugs and high-risk sex—even if that means losing the approval of "the crowd." Kids with emotional discipline are also less likely to become perpetrators or victims of violence or abuse.

We think of emotional discipline as a kind of buffer zone between the impulse that drives young people to participate in destructive, high-risk behavior and the thought process that enables them to delay gratification in favor of their long-term interests. With all of the physical, hormonal, and psychological changes adolescents experience, it's easy to see why exercising this kind of restraint is no day at the beach for many young people. Fortunately, there is a great deal *you* can do to make the road smoother and less treacherous.

In this chapter, we show you how to give young people the necessary strength to resist negative peer pressure, avoid dangerous risk taking, and steer clear of violence. We share proven techniques for helping teens develop a responsible approach to the temptations of drugs, sex, and negative peer pressure—and highlight those areas of special concern to black youth. As with all the disciplines, the sooner you start building emotional strength in children, the better equipped they will be to cope with temptations and stresses that come their way.

Fortify Black Children and Teens with the Discipline to Avoid Substance Abuse

Contrary to popular myth, African American teens are less likely to use alcohol and drugs than are their white and Latino counterparts. Nevertheless, substance abuse is an important concern for African American parents. This includes problem drinking, which is less prevalent among black high school and college students than among their white counterparts. Even so, alcohol abuse is one of the most serious health problems in the African American community as a whole.

Alcohol is both legal and socially acceptable, so it's easy for adults to ignore their own drinking problem (if they have one), and to pass along that attitude to their children. Using liquor in an attempt to relieve physical pain, anxiety, and social discomfort is a problem that cuts across racial and ethnic lines.

Studies show that the incidence of alcohol abuse is lower among affluent African Americans than among those who are less well off. However, the tendency to minimize the dangers of problem drinking cuts across socioeconomic lines. This kind of casual denial can send a message to children that drinking—and, by extension, use of other intoxicating substances—is okay.

In Chapter One, we talked about how important it is for parents to set a positive example for young people to follow. When it comes to using alcohol and drugs, your behavior and attitudes can make a critical difference. Children in families where parents regularly drink to get high or to escape reality are at elevated risk of becoming habitual drinkers themselves. Young people from such families are also more likely to mess with other drugs, because their parents have demonstrated that substance use is an acceptable way to deal with life's stresses.

The most harmful scenario is one in which parents not only get high, but also encourage their children to join them. Consider the results of the following recent survey of drug-addicted teenagers.

- Family members introduced 20 percent of the surveyed teenagers to drugs.

- Of those who used drugs with their parents, 76 percent used marijuana, 19 percent used crack, 16 percent used cocaine, and 6 percent used heroin.

- The percentage of parents who shared drugs with their adolescent children was pretty much the same (around 20 percent) for blacks, whites, and Latinos.

- Parent-teen drug sharing was only slightly more common in inner-city areas than in the suburbs (22 percent versus 17 percent).[2]

In some cases, drug-using parents actually believe they're doing kids a favor by encouraging them to try drugs in their presence. "I really thought that smoking pot with my son would show him that it's no big thing," eighteen-year-old Allen's misguided father told us. "That way, he'd be less likely to fall in with a bad crowd or become involved with drug dealers."

Allen recently completed a drug-rehabilitation program, and is recovering from his addiction to heroin and crack. His father's history of drug use put him at great risk for repeating that behavior. By condoning and putting his stamp of approval on drug use, that father effectively punched his son's ticket to the woeful world of drug addiction.

Although hard drugs are far from unknown among upscale black teens, the use of drugs like cocaine and heroin is more prevalent among poorer urban youths. Marijuana use, on the other hand, typically cuts across all demographic lines. Around 50 percent of African American teens will have experimented with marijuana before their senior year in high school, and one-third will have smoked a joint by the end of middle school.

Teenagers sometimes experiment with alcohol and marijuana to assert their independence from parents, or as a social lubricant that helps them feel more at home with their peers. The vast majority of adolescent experimenters don't go on to develop substance-abuse problems; but that doesn't mean parents should be indifferent to social or so-called casual teenage drug use.

Behavior that starts out as a way of getting comfortable with peers can mushroom into a serious problem if it's not nipped in the bud. Some adolescents begin using pot (and sometimes other drugs) because most of their friends are doing the same. After a while, getting high becomes the preferred way to relax and enjoy social interactions. Eventually, the young person also finds that the drug is also useful in times of stress, so he or she starts using the drug alone and taking it more frequently.

Young people who start out as social users may not have undergone any recent emotional trauma; nor do they necessarily appear to have any particular underlying psychological malady. This kind of drug use is quite common among black youth. It can also be tough to treat, because many adolescents who use drugs socially are not particularly unhappy—until they either become addicted or get busted.

There is an ongoing debate about the likelihood that social or occasional marijuana use will lead to experimenting with harder drugs. There is no hard evidence to support this contention. However, the potential legal dangers for black youth who smoke pot are well documented.

African Americans are twice as likely to be arrested for marijuana possession as whites. Young blacks who get busted are also more likely to receive harsher punishment than their white counterparts. Helping your child avoid an arrest record and possible jail time is reason enough to discourage any and all involvement with drugs.

WHY KIDS USE DRUGS

There is evidence that some individuals are at elevated risk genetically for substance abuse. Children from homes in which one or both parents have drug or drinking problems are the most vulnerable. That's why addiction specialists often counsel children from families with a history of substance abuse not to risk consuming a single beer or taking a single puff of pot. This isn't bad advice for any young person, even if it's sometimes ignored.

WHAT INFLUENCES CHILDREN
TO USE OR AVOID DRUGS?

- *Relationship with parents*
- *Parents' consumption of drugs*
- *Nature of peer relationships*
- *Degree of contact with peers who consume drugs*
- *Overall psychological health*
- *Recent loss or trauma*

There has been a long-standing disagreement about whether parents or peers have a greater impact on adolescent drug use. Although it's true that teenagers can easily be influenced by their peers, kids who experiment with drugs like marijuana often make the decision to do so on their own. Peers do play a major role in providing access to the drug, the setting, and the means for continuing to use the drug. Still, it's too simple to blame a child's drug use on his crowd.

In general, parents play the most essential and far-reaching role in the way children deal with drugs. The discipline and social skills boys and girls learn from their parents extend to every aspect of their lives, including the development of positive peer relationships. The bottom line is that loving parents who instill discipline provide a strong foundation for healthy relations with peers.

Parents who practice the basic strength-building principles we explore throughout this book greatly increase the chances that their children will be able to navigate the teen years without developing a substance problem. The following guidelines draw on these principles and are specifically targeted to prevent drug and alcohol abuse.

TALK FRANKLY TO YOUR CHILDREN ABOUT DRUGS.

It's important to make it clear that using drugs violates your standards of behavior. Naturally, it's a lot easier for children to internalize those standards when the words parents use are consistent with their actions. When it comes to drugs, parental attitudes play a key role. By the time most kids get to middle school, they are already aware that some of their classmates are getting high, so it makes no sense to pretend that drugs don't exist. The best approach is to help young people recognize why it's in their best interest to avoid drugs.

Parents would be wise to begin discussion of basic drug facts with children by the time they reach age ten or eleven. The following are questions parents need to answer—even if a child doesn't ask them specifically:

◆ *Why do people use drugs?* People use drugs to "get high." This means a temporary good feeling or release from pain. After a while, though, the high wears off, and users feel worse than they did before. This makes them want to take more of the drug. People who continue to use drugs to lift their mood often find that they have a hard time feeling good without taking something.

◆ *Why are drugs dangerous?* People who develop the habit of taking drugs often become addicted. That means that they must have the drug, and will sometimes lie and steal to get it. Drugs are also bad for your health.

Alcohol can cause permanent damage to the liver, kidneys, and brain. Marijuana can make your heart beat fast, cause you to lose your balance, and make you feel you can't control yourself. Drugs like heroin and crack are highly addictive and potentially lethal.

♦ *What are some different kinds of drugs to watch out for?* Aside from alcohol and marijuana, there is a wide spectrum of available drugs with an equally diverse array of effects. Some of these drugs are sold to patients by prescription from doctors; this doesn't mean they are legal for the general population—they are by definition controlled substances, to be used as directed by the prescribing physician only by the individuals for whom they are prescribed. Regardless of their bona fide use in medicine, these drugs are as dangerous as their completely illegal counterparts.

The most common illegal drugs, in addition to marijuana, are stimulants such as speed, cocaine, or crack, and narcotics such as heroin—all of which give the user a false, and usually fleeting, sense of well being.

Stimulants (uppers) keep you awake; that much is medically sound. Stimulants are also favored among street users for their apparent (though short-lived) energizing effect on concentration and stamina.

Methedrine (meth) is an amphetamine, an extremely powerful and dangerous class of stimulant that also takes users away from reality. Cocaine and its chemical cousin crack induce brief flashes of unfocused energy and a sense of well-being that seesaws quickly into depression, thereby prompting further (and frequent) ingestion.

Depressants (downers) include drugs that are supposed to cool you out, mellow you down, or help you relax. Narcotics and sedative-hypnotics are depressants that can put you to sleep in addition to their prescription use as analgesics (or painkillers) and tranquilizing agents.

Prescription painkillers in the opioid family (which means they are chemically related to opium) are called narcotics and feature such well-known names as heroin (which was initially developed as a prescription drug), morphine, and codeine, as well as more recent pharmaceuticals like Percodan) and hydrocodone (widely sold as Vicodin). All opioids are highly addictive.

Tranquilizers such as the brand-name items Valium and Xanax are prescribed by doctors for general anxiety, as well as insomnia, and are favored in the street trade by those who wish to "chill out." In this category is the so-called date-rape drug Rohypnol (a.k.a. "ruffies").

Barbiturates ("Barbies") are tranquilizers that include prescription drugs such as Seconal, Nembutal, and Fiorinal. All forms of tranquilizing depressants have dangerous and volatile interactions with alcohol and can be used as knock-out drugs.

Hallucinogens, such as ecstasy ("X"), LSD ("acid"), and certain varieties of mushrooms ("shrooms"), induce users to sense things in ways that vary enormously (and sometimes perilously) from conventional reality. Ketamine ("Special K") and PCP ("angel dust") are classed as dissociatives, because they cause severe dislocation of awareness—in casual jargon, they are the closest approximation of absolute oblivion this side of death.

Over-the-counter preparations commonly available in corner drugstores are also used as intoxicants, often eaten by the handful like candy to enhance their otherwise weak effect. Antihistamines containing chlorpheniramine (for instance, Allerest) are used as makeshift substitutes for downers, while anticongestants containing pseudoephedrine (such as Sudafed) can mimic cheap-and-dirty speed. People sometimes get high by inhaling everyday items like glue, refrigerant, gasoline, or household cleansers. All of these drugs can have dangerous or fatal side effects.

Keep in mind that the above listing is far from complete. Please also note that street names for the same drugs may vary from place to place, and new drugs periodically become popular among different types of users.

OFFSET DESTRUCTIVE MESSAGES FROM THE MEDIA.

The following statistics demonstrate the extent to which today's young people are bombarded with confusing images of alcohol and drug taking. As you look at these numbers, consider the messages contemporary films convey about drinking and taking drugs.[3]

- Alcohol is consumed in over three quarters of movies rated G or PG.

- One or more actors use alcohol in 94 percent of movies rated PG-13.

- Only 15 percent of characters who smoke marijuana in recent movies are portrayed as experiencing any adverse effects.

The next time you and your daughter or son watch a film, music video, or TV show that contains drug references, raise the following questions and topics for open-ended discussion.

- What is the actor or creator of the show or video trying to say about using drugs?
- How do the characters act and feel after they drink or take drugs?
- Would you like to feel and act this way?
- What about that appeals to you?
- What scares you or turns you off?

Parents have limited control over what teenagers do when they're out of the house and with their friends. That's why it's important to encourage young people to express their ideas without fear of punishment or rejection. Your show of affection and interest can serve as powerful preventive medicine. Make your position clear, but let children know that your love is unconditional—even if they do experiment with drugs or develop a substance problem.

HELP CHILDREN PRACTICE THE ART OF SAYING NO.

It's important to help children understand that they are likely to come into contact with drugs long before they enter high school. At some point they will be offered drugs and quite possibly be pressured not to refuse. The ability to say no and resist peer pressure is largely a product of the resilience and discipline parents have instilled. However, there are times when even resilient teenagers abandon their better judgment. One way to fortify children against this eventuality is to help them visualize the kinds of situations in which they're likely to find themselves, and develop effective techniques to handle them.

Most young people don't possess the experience or willpower of a mature adult, and are thus more vulnerable to negative pressure. Teens who pressure peers to join them in taking drugs may not be aware of their own motives, but teens who press others to use drugs can make it hard to say no. Teenagers who are socially insecure and want acceptance by a particular crowd will often succumb to this kind of manipulation.

It's your job to explain that boys and girls who find it necessary to pressure others to take drugs are usually the ones who are most needy and insecure. In some cases, they are drug dealers who have a financial interest in getting others to try their wares. Your main objective is to strengthen your son or daughter's resolve by arming them with the following tools.[4]

◆ *The right words.* So-called friends who try to convince others to take drugs can be as persistent as the peskiest salesman. In that case, a simple no may not be enough. Invite your son or daughter to try the following role-playing exercise with you.

Pretend that you are another teen who is trying to get your kid to use drugs, or ask your son or daughter to try to convince you to get high. Then reverse roles. Take turns sounding convincing as you use the following turndowns. Please note that all these words of refusal use "I" or first-person statements. They are not preaching or telling someone else what to do. Consequently they don't invite argument.

1. Thanks anyway. I'm going to pass.

2. I'm feeling really good. I can't see any reason to change that feeling.

3. No, I need to keep in shape for baseball (or another sport).

4. Drugs just aren't my thing. Please don't ask me again.

◆ *Connecting body language.* There are times when people say one thing, but manage to communicate something else entirely. For example, saying something in a quivering tone can weaken the message you're trying to send. That's why it's important to speak clearly and sound as if you mean what you're saying. The following are other body-language clues that let people know that your words are serious.

◆ *Standing (or sitting) up straight*

◆ *Looking the other person in the eye*

◆ *Walking away as soon as you've made your statement*

MAKE IT CLEAR THAT THE BEST HIGHS DON'T COME FROM DRUGS.

It's a parent's job to help children develop positive ways to release tension and feel good about themselves. Encourage girls and boys to participate in organized sports or to express themselves through art, music, or writing. If possible, find a way to participate in these activities with the child.

Plan a variety of fun activities as a family. Playing games together, taking walks or bike rides, or just hanging out and talking frequently have a more positive impact than expensive outings or events. Remember that there is no stronger drug prevention than your involvement with and affection toward your child.

BE ESPECIALLY SUPPORTIVE DURING TIMES OF TROUBLE.

Adolescents (and adults too) often use alcohol and drugs, hoping to relieve themselves of emotional pain. Therefore, parents need to be aware of life events that provoke behavioral changes in a young person. These can include the following:

- The death of a close friend or family member
- Being stopped and abused by the police
- Rejection by a love interest
- Being the victim of racial discrimination or bullying by peers
- Failing an important test or course in school

When young people experience one or more of these troubling events, they need to know that their parents are there for them. Kids may refuse to talk about what's bothering them. Still, a parent's genuine concern and affection can have more of an impact than most highly structured drug-prevention programs.

Sometimes parents are hesitant to get involved in a child's problems because they feel there's something specific they need to say or do. In most instances, you don't need to say or do anything. Just being available to your child as his or her primary source of protection and comfort is enough.

RECOGNIZE HOW YOUR OWN PROBLEMS AND ANXIETIES CAN UNDERMINE DISCIPLINE.

Parents sometimes become so absorbed in their own troubles that they overlook their children's pain and vulnerability. When mothers and fathers divorce, for example, they can get so wrapped up in their own battles that they forget how traumatic a broken marriage is for children.

We started counseling sixteen-year-old Brenda after her estranged parents asked us to help her overcome a serious substance problem. By then Brenda had crashed the family car and was found to be high on alcohol and cocaine at the scene. Brenda's mom and dad were both successful professionals who were so wrapped up in attacking each other during their dragged-out divorce that they were blind to what was happening to their daughter.

"I was coming home completely blasted almost every night," Brenda told us, "but my mom and dad never even had a clue. Before my parents' marriage began falling apart, I smoked grass occasionally or had a beer. But as their fighting got worse, I started getting seriously stoned. I don't know if I was trying to get their attention or just easing the terrible hurt of seeing my family fall apart."

It's essential that parents be sensitive to life events that are troubling to children. In some cases, outside intervention may be helpful. Seek out church and community-based groups that offer such services as divorce or grief counseling for youth. Remember, teens are sometimes hesitant to discuss matters that trouble them.

Although it's usually unwise and often fruitless to attempt to force children to reveal their feelings, it's essential that you make it clear that you are there if and when you're needed—and that your love is unconditional.

Be Aware of Unresolved Emotional Issues and Troubling Patterns of Behavior

Young people who develop chronic substance problems are sometimes trying to soothe deep-seated psychological pain. Research shows that teens who use mind-altering drugs habitually often suffer from depression and other psychological problems.

It can be difficult to tell the difference between a situational problem and a chronic psychiatric disorder—especially when substance abuse is involved. In some cases, young people are able to function in the face of emotional pain. Then something happens that launches them into heavy drug use, followed by an emotional breakdown.

Eighteen-year-old Thomas was the product of divorced parents, both of whom had substance problems. When Thomas was ten years old, his mother successfully completed a twenty-eight-day drug-rehabilitation program, and has been drug-free ever since. Unfortunately, Thomas's father, who had shared a marijuana joint with his son when Thomas was twelve, continues to drink and use illegal drugs.

Thomas used marijuana on a semiregular basis from the time he was fifteen and occasionally took pills to help him sleep. Though he was somewhat guarded, Thomas was a good student who had a fairly active social life. Then, toward the end of his freshman year in college, Thomas's girlfriend dumped him and began seeing one of his closest friends.

Thomas was extremely upset about the loss of his girlfriend. Still, he managed to finish out the school year. That summer, Thomas began using various combinations of painkillers, cocaine, and heroin on an almost daily basis. A few weeks before the new college term was to begin, Thomas stopped taking drugs. By that time, he was depressed, disoriented, and unable to return to school for fall classes.

We referred Thomas to a psychiatrist, who put him on a course of antidepressive drugs. We also suggested that the young man attend group therapy sessions and Narcotics Anonymous meetings to address his substance problems.

Caution: Untreated emotional problems can set the stage for substance abuse.

Teenagers with long-term psychological issues are extremely vulnerable to the ravages of drug abuse. Depression is a widespread problem among young people, and it can occur even in strong, loving families.

If you suspect your child is suffering from depression, you would be wise to seek professional help as soon as possible—preferably before the ravages of serious drug use compound the problem.

It's important to monitor your child's moods, particularly if you spot a pattern of troubling behavior. The following ten signs are warning flags that your child might be depressed. Some of these are also warning signs of substance abuse.

10 Warning Signs of Childhood Depression

1. A loss of interest in school, family, and daily activities
2. Difficulty sleeping or chronic oversleeping
3. Loss of appetite or chronic overeating
4. Chronic fatigue or bursts of unexplained and misdirected energy

5. Frequent headaches or digestive problems that have no apparent physical cause

6. Chronic sadness or pessimism about life

7. Withdrawal from social life

8. Being irritated or constantly stressed out

9. Crying spells that have no apparent cause

10. References to suicide

Teenagers who aren't clinically depressed can experience some of the above symptoms—especially if they've gone through one of the traumas or upsetting events we list earlier in this chapter. However, if a young person has a combination of two or more of these symptoms that lasts for more than a few weeks, schedule a complete physical examination with your pediatrician or family doctor to rule out the possibility that a physical illness may be causing the condition. Make sure the physician administers a urine test to see if there is evidence of drug use. Then ask the physician to help you formulate an appropriate treatment plan.

Treatment for substance problems typically includes psychotherapy, community-based programs, twelve-step programs like Narcotics Anonymous (NA) and Alcoholics Anonymous (AA), and inpatient rehabilitation programs. (Please see Chapter Ten for a listing of helpful resources in dealing with substance and accompanying emotional problems.)

WHAT PARENTS CAN DO TO HELP YOUNG PEOPLE OVERCOME SUBSTANCE PROBLEMS

- *Acknowledge that a problem exists and that changes in how the family functions may be necessary. Consider what you might be doing to contribute to your child's substance problem. Try to take a step back and figure out a different way to approach the young person.*

- *Encourage the young person to become more independent and work toward a substance-free life. Many young addicts haven't emotionally separated from their parents. They may outwardly reject their parents, but these young men and women are still dependent—on drugs. Participation in young people's Alcoholics Anonymous and Narcotics Anonymous groups can be very helpful, as can developing friendships with peers who are drug-free and successful at channeling their energies productively.*

♦ *Don't try to go it alone. Seek support and appropriate outside help for yourself as well as your child. Support groups of other parents whose children have drug problems can be helpful for parents who need to address unresolved family issues and to communicate more effectively with addicted children. In some instances, consultation and/or treatment by a qualified mental health professional may be necessary.*

Motivate Young People to Avoid High-Risk Sex

Early in adolescence, girls and boys experience rapid physical and hormonal changes; their bodies and newfound desires becomes areas of major concern. When these forces begin to converge with mounting pressure from peers, young people can have particular difficulty controlling their impulses to seek immediate gratification. Consequently, sex is an area in which a young person's emotional discipline faces an especially tough test.

Sexual urges are a natural part of growing up, and opportunities are likely to present themselves. Still, this is an area in which parents must help youngsters recognize the benefits of thinking about the future.

An adolescent may be physically able to have sex and conceive. However, it can be years before he or she is ready to develop genuine intimacy, understand the complex relationship between sex and love, and practice prudent birth and disease control.

Parents who convince their teens to stay away from drugs often have a much tougher time persuading them to exercise emotional discipline in the sexual arena. However, a single indiscriminate sex act can turn out to be far more devastating than experimenting with alcohol or marijuana.

Caution: Premature sex and pregnancy can significantly hinder young people's chances for success, destroy their health—and even lead to an early death.

In recent years, there has been a heated debate about whether sex is an appropriate subject for the classroom. And, if so, whether schools should be in the business of teaching safe sex and birth control, or only advocate abstinence. As a study conducted by *U.S. News & World Report* notes:

> Nine in ten Americans agree: Schools should teach children about sex. That, however, is the end of the consensus. Most adults fall into opposing camps on exactly which of the facts of life to teach. The "throw in the towel" crowd concedes, with value-free resignation, that having sex is normative teen behavior and the most that adults can do is teach young people how sperm meets egg, toss out loads of condoms and hope for the best. Meanwhile, the "stop it" forces call for scaring teens into premarital chastity with horror stories of shame and disease. Neither solution, however, works very well with today's sophisticated teenagers.[5]

Our own view is that parents need to take the lead in this aspect of a young person's development, and that schools can be expected to play only a supplementary role. Sex is an all-encompassing issue—one that involves adolescents' body image, life goals, and sense of competence—not to mention their physical and emotional health. These are serious issues that cut across racial and ethnic boundaries. But they are most pressing for black youth, who are more likely than their white and Hispanic counterparts to engage in and suffer the consequences of high-risk sex.

SEXUALLY TRANSMITTED DISEASE AND TEEN PREGNANCY: CRITICAL CONCERNS FOR AFRICAN AMERICAN PARENTS

Black teens begin having sex at an earlier age than do Hispanic and white teens, and are more likely to contract infection from human immunodeficiency virus (HIV), which can develop into full-blown acquired immunodeficiency syndrome (AIDS). In addition, such teens are at higher risk for other sexually transmitted diseases (STDs), including gonorrhea, syphilis, herpes, as well as urinogenital infections such as (in particular for young women) chlamydia. In addition, black girls get pregnant at a much higher rate than white girls. As you go over the following statistics, think about the dangerous picture they paint for black youth.

♦ Black teens are more likely than others to have had sexual intercourse. In a Centers for Disease Control (CDC) study of the risk behaviors of high school and middle school students, black students (71.2 percent) were significantly more likely than Hispanic and white students (54.1 and 45.1 percent, respectively) to have had sexual intercourse.[6]

♦ Black teens are more likely to have initiated sexual activity at an earlier age.

Percent of Teens Sexually Active
Prior to Age 13 by Racial Group

Black	20.9%
White	5.5%
Hispanic/Latino	9.2%

♦ Black teens are more likely to have had more sexual partners during their lives.

♦ White teens are more likely than their black and Hispanic counterparts to use contraception at first intercourse.

At every age level, black adolescents are more likely to become pregnant and bear a child: African American teens have higher pregnancy rates and higher birth rates than their white counterparts.[7] Both male and female adolescents experience the adverse social consequences of premature sex, including childbearing and sexually transmitted disease.[8]

Adolescent Pregnancy
Pregnancy Rates by Race/Ethnicity for
Adolescent Women Grades 9–12

White	Black	Hispanic
5.8%	14.1%	6.2%

Adolescent Childbearing
Live Births to Adolescents (per 1000 Adolescent Females)
by Race of Mother [National Vital Statistics Report,
Vol. 49, No. 10, September 25, 2001]

AGE RANGE (YEARS)	10–14	15–17	18–19
Total	0.9	27.5	79.5
White	0.3	15.9	57.3
Black	2.5	50.2	121.1
Hispanic	1.9	60.0	143.5

Black Adolescents and Sexually Transmitted Diseases (STDs)

♦ Among teens age 15–19 the chlamydia rate for black teens is seven times higher than the rate for white teens and three times higher than the Hispanic teen rate.

♦ Black teens account for 78 percent of all cases of gonorrhea among adolescents between ages 15 and 19.

♦ The rate of gonorrhea infection is two-thirds as high in black males as it is in black females.

♦ African American women aged 15 to 19 have a gonorrhea rate 19 times greater than that of non-Hispanic white females of similar age.

♦ African American men in the 15- to 19-year-old age category have a gonorrhea rate that is 52 times higher than the rate among 15- to 19-year-old white males.

♦ Black teens account for 81 percent of all cases of syphilis among adolescents between ages 15 and 19.

♦ Black female adolescents comprise 54.3 percent of all syphilis cases among adolescents and 83 percent of all female adolescent cases.

ADOLESCENT AIDS

Although African American and Hispanic teens account for only 15 and 13 percent, respectively, of the U.S. adolescent population, they account for 46 and 18 percent of the cases of adolescent AIDS.[9]

Adolescent AIDS
by Race and Risk Category

	White	Black	Hispanic
No identified risk	4%	22%	9%
Blood transfusion	62%	9%	26%
Intravenous drug use	6%	10%	17%
Heterosexual	9%	33%	19%
Men having sex with men	18%	26%	30%

The identified cause of the original HIV infection among the adolescents with AIDS varies by race and ethnic group. White teens were most likely to have been infected as the result of a blood transfusion. Hispanic teens were most commonly infected by homosexual sexual activity or blood transfusion. Infected black teens acquired the disease primarily through either heterosexual or same sex sexual activity.

The above statistics highlight the elevated risk factors that make it critical for black parents to take the lead in their children's sex education. There are two fundamentals about adolescent sexual behavior that highlight the key role you can play in helping your child develop the emotional discipline necessary to avoid high-risk sex.

- Teenagers want and need information about sex from their parents.
- Teenagers who have a high degree of communication about sex with their parents are less likely to engage in high-risk sexual behavior.

Taking the responsibility for teaching your child about sex is a major step in the right direction. Parents who avoid this responsibility increase the chances that their teens will learn about sex on the street or from the media. The sex education teens get from such sources does not build emotional discipline.

Your teenager's friends are likely to be both ill informed about sex and insecure about their own sexuality. Much of what adolescents say to each other is bragging or information seeking. The thought and values system behind these peer communications is unlikely to reflect the advice you might want to impart.

The images of sex as portrayed by the media can be more harmful than those painted by a teen's peers. Television shows are funded by advertisers whose sole interest is prodding viewers to spend money. "Sex sells" is a fact of life in both the entertainment and advertising businesses. And the kind of sex that sells has nothing to do with abstinence or safe practices.

WHAT MESSAGES DOES TV GIVE TEENS ABOUT SEX?

- *More than half of all shows and two-thirds of prime time shows contained either talk about sex or sexual behavior.*
- *Less than 10 percent of shows that contained sexual content included any reference to delaying sex, using contraception, or having safe sex. Only 1 percent mentioned the responsibilities or risks of sexual activity at any point in the show.*
- *Of the scenes that contained sexual intercourse, only half involved characters who had previous romantic involvement. None of those scenes contained even a passing reference to sexual responsibilities or risks.*
- *Premarital sex was depicted more than sex within marriage by a factor of 8 to 1.*
- *Casual sex was "almost always presented in a favorable light."[10]*

It's unlikely you will be able to prevent your teen from tuning into some of these misleading, potentially destructive messages. The high probability of such exposure makes it even more important that you counter those ideas and values with some of your own. Children are aware that parents have experience in the area of sex, and are eager to know what you think and feel.

We have designed the following guidelines to help you impart the emotional discipline that protects young people from the dangers of high-risk sex.

Lay the Groundwork Early—and Keep Building

Sex is a normal part of life, so it's never too soon to start educating children. Begin by using accurate words to describe body parts. When children ask about sexual matters, always give honest, age-appropriate answers. The sooner you and your child become comfortable talking about sex, the easier it will be to communicate your values effectively and impart accurate information.

Always answer the questions a child asks. When dealing with younger children, it's best to avoid too much elaboration. If you are unsure of how to answer, there are any number of books and videotapes that can help. (Please see Chapter Ten for a complete list of resources to help explain sexual matters to children of various ages.)

Reminder: The more accurate the information you provide, the better.

Don't fall for the line that, by providing your teens with information about birth control and sexuality, you are encouraging them to become sexually active. Young people who are armed with accurate information about sex are more likely to be careful and selective in their sexual behavior. Parents who are willing to talk openly are in the best position to deliver such information.

Tips for Talking to Kids About Sex

◆ **If you feel nervous or embarrassed, admit it.** Some of us grew up with parents who, for whatever reason, didn't talk about sex. If discussing sex with your child is uncharted territory, don't be ashamed to say something like: "I'm a little nervous about this, but I think it's something important for us to talk about. I always want you to feel that the two of us can talk together about anything, even if it's a little uncomfortable." If even that is too much for you, ask another relative or your pediatrician to fill the gap.

◆ **Take a positive approach.** It's important to convey that sex is natural, and not a taboo area that's shrouded in mystery. Remember that your child may not want to talk about sex, even though you're ready. If your son or daughter seems uptight or uninterested, don't force the conversation. Wait until a time when the subject comes up naturally. If the child seems to be hesitant to discuss sex with you, he or she may be more comfortable with your spouse—or with another adult.

◆ **Be a good listener.** Children and teens frequently complain that parents don't listen to them—and they often have a point. Make sure that you spend at least as much time listening to what your son or daughter has to say as you do talking. This simple rule of thumb will help you assess what children do and don't want to talk about. Whenever you run into a gap in communication, try repeating what the other person has said and asking if you've heard them correctly.

◆ **Arm young people with the information they need.** Sex is a multifaceted topic. As children develop, they require information about various issues. For example, you may have a wide-ranging discussion about sexual development, but that doesn't address other crucial topics, such as masturbation, condom use, pregnancy, and sexually transmitted diseases. Each of these issues requires separate but interrelated discussions.

Remember that sex education is an ongoing process. It's important to help children understand that sex is about a lot more than plumbing and childbearing. Sex is an important aspect of human relationships, one that involves intimacy, power struggles, decision making, and the ability to recognize future consequences.

BE AWARE OF WHAT YOUR TEEN IS GOING THROUGH.

Keep in mind that adolescence can be a confusing time for young people, as they experience strong, unfamiliar physical and emotional changes. As much as anything else, adolescents need parental help to understand what's happening. Teens have sex for all sorts of reasons. These include the following:

◆ The need for closeness or communication

◆ Replacement of lost affection

◆ Lack of alternatives for meeting emotional and social needs

Boys who experiment with high-risk sex are often propelled by a misguided sense of invincibility—an "it can't happen to me" attitude. When we ask boys who've impregnated their girlfriends or contracted HIV why they didn't use condoms, the answer often is: "I figured that this kind of bad stuff may happen to other people, but not to me."

Girls who get pregnant at a young age are sometimes overwhelmed by the desire to please or hold on to a partner. It's not uncommon for girls in this position to report that they were out with an older, more experienced boy who demanded sex or committed date rape.

Parents who provide information, guidance, and understanding can help their teens anticipate the consequences of sex and avoid being pressured. The more you know about the forces that are pushing and pulling at your kid, the better equipped you'll be to offer help and guidance.

UNDERSTANDING WHY YOUR INFLUENCE MAKES A DIFFERENCE

- *Mothers and fathers who arm their teens with discipline, support, and information about sex give them the strength to overcome potentially dangerous peer pressure.*

- *Open and ongoing parent-teen communications about sex can serve to reinforce your values about sex and life in general. This increases the chances that your teen will behave in a manner consistent with those values.*

- *Teens get practical information and improve their sexual decision-making skills when parents communicate openly with them. Young people who are strong enough to make their own decisions are better able to resist the temptation to have unprotected sex—or to have sex at all.*

BE PATIENT AND ACCEPTING.

When you talk to your child about sex, don't come on too strong. You'll get further by creating a friendly, conversational atmosphere. Parents who act as if they know everything and talk to children as if they know nothing can cut off communication before it begins. If your son or daughter wants to have a talk about sex, begin by asking what they know.

Listen carefully; don't censor or correct what they say. Teenagers don't like to admit that there are things they don't know, so give them credit by complimenting them for whatever knowledge they do possess. Then try to add to that knowledge in a gentle and constructive way. Keep in mind that the timing and tone of your communication can have a great bearing on how effective you are in getting your message across.

Caution: Moralizing about sex usually doesn't work.

Telling adolescents that having sex is wrong or immoral can make it seem more tempting than it already is. Loving parents who raise children in a home where discipline and morality are valued often find that teens have internalized these standards and are willing to postpone gratification. That is much different than trying to give a seventeen-year-old a lecture on the most moral way to approach sex.

STATE YOUR POSITION, BUT ALLOW FOR DISAGREEMENT.

There is no one right way to discuss sex with a child, just as there is no one morally right approach to this complex issue. Nevertheless, children need to know where their parents stand—so it's up to you to bring up the subject, even if your son or daughter doesn't.

If you feel strongly that teens ought to abstain from sex until they marry, don't be shy taking that stand. Your position might be a matter of religious conviction, or it may be based on health and safety concerns. Whatever the case, you need to make your stand crystal clear—without fear that your child will argue or reject those views.

Once children know how parents feel, they may agree or disagree. Mothers and fathers need to support areas of agreement, and to encourage open discussion around areas of disagreement. In any case, you need to communicate through words and deeds that your love is not based on the child's accepting and complying with your position. Young people will have numerous decisions to make about sexual activity throughout (and beyond) adolescence. We've said this before, but the point can never be overstated:

A young person needs to know that a parent's love is always there, wherever the road may lead.

Practice What You Preach.

The influence parents have on the sexual behavior of their children has at least as much to do with the way the family operates in general as it does with giving specific sexual advice. Teens often make inferences about sexual values by observing how parents behave in a variety of situations. As a group of researchers who conducted a recent study on parent-teen communication concluded:

> What parents do [often] speaks louder than what they say. Informal messages communicated via role modeling may be more influential than the formal communication that occurs. Such informal messages may include: how parents behave toward significant others, how parents behave toward members of the opposite sex, the examples parents set in the home regarding their own sexual behavior and values, types of films parents take their children to see and permit to be viewed in the home, other types of media parents allow in the home, and the type of comments parents make to friends in front of their children.[11]

Be Aware of Family Problems That Can Trigger Risky Behavior.

Adolescents who are sexually promiscuous or careless are often reacting to a problem within the family. Young people sometimes become sexually active in order to get their parents' attention or because they fear that their family is falling apart. For example, seventeen-year-old Rodney is a star athlete who has resisted numerous opportunities to have sex. That all changed after Rodney's father got laid off from work and his parents started having loud fights almost every night.

"I've talked to Rodney about the dangers of having sex before the time is right," his mother told us. "All these girls were running after him, talking about how fine he looks. I was afraid that he'd get someone pregnant and destroy his future. I also worried about AIDS, and warned Rodney that, in today's world, sex can kill. We talked about this a lot, and he paid attention. Rodney always had a good social life, but he knew better than to mess with sex.

"My husband has been very uptight since he lost his job. He's angry and frustrated because he can't find work, and we've been fighting all the time. A few weeks ago, I noticed Rodney doing stuff he never did before. Last Thursday, he brought a girl to the house for sex at a time when he knew I'd walk in. It's like he wanted me to catch them in the act. Later on, I tried to talk to Rodney about it; he just shrugged his shoulders and walked out of the room. Suddenly, my son doesn't want to hear what I have to say—and it hurts."

Rodney's change of behavior was both a plea for help and an attempt to get his parents' attention. It's as if he was saying: "Look how badly you're hurting me. Maybe if you stop thinking about yourselves and look at what it's doing to me, things could go back to the way they were."

It was clear that Rodney's sudden outburst of risky sex was a reaction to his parents' problems. Even though his breach of emotional discipline wasn't about sex, he was now actively courting the very dangers he'd been resisting for years. We advised Rodney's parents to seek marriage counseling—for both their sake and their son's. We also cautioned them to contain their arguments, and to do whatever they could to re-create a more stable and peaceful family environment.

Keep Children and Teens Safe from Violence and Abuse

Today's kids are vulnerable to violence in a variety of circumstances. In urban communities, gang violence poses a very real danger to innocent citizens. And while teenage gang violence is often portrayed as a feature of African American urban neighborhoods, the problem is far more extensive than that.

There are street gangs in 94 percent of all U.S. cities with populations over 100,000. Gangs are active in over 800 cities nationwide—including some 100 cities with populations under 10,000. Today, there are Mexican, Vietnamese, Chinese, American Indian, and various white-ethnic gangs.[12]

WHAT ARE STREET GANGS?

*S*treet gangs have been described as an aggregation of youths who
perceive themselves as distinct, who are viewed as distinct by
their community, and who call forth a consistently negative image
of themselves through their actions. American street gangs have historically been ethnically based. Early American street gangs were
Irish, Polish, or Italian. In the 1950s and 1960s, African American,
Mexican, and Puerto Rican gangs became prominent. While gangs
have traditionally been male dominated, female involvement in
gangs and all-female gangs are not uncommon.[13]

Gangs develop their own identity and gang culture, which are identified by "street" nicknames, tattoos, and certain gang colors. Pop music
videos have glamorized these stylings—some of which have been picked
up by the broader adolescent culture.

In general, parents don't need to be alarmed when children favor
particular clothing or hairstyles. Still, many of the media images of gangs
have furthered negative racial stereotypes, and made it more difficult
for the public to understand the real nature of this major threat to our
youth.

That so many schools now use metal detectors and security guards
demonstrates the extent to which gangs and a pervading fear of violence
have upset the educational environment. Although all adolescents are affected by violence, the threat is far greater for black youth.

Homicide is the leading cause of death among African American adolescent males aged fifteen to twenty four years. In the state of New
Jersey, where we practice medicine, homicide accounts for 28.5 percent
of African American male and 12.7 percent of African American female
adolescent deaths. Contrast these numbers with those of their white
counterparts, for which homicide accounts for only 4.2 percent of male
deaths and 6.3 percent of female deaths.

The death rate for African American males in New Jersey is 150 per
100,000 versus 85 per 100,000 for Caucasian males. Sixty percent of mi-

nority male adolescents in New Jersey report that their lives are significantly affected by violence.[14]

Families, especially those living in urban communities, should consider a child's membership in a street gang as a deadly serious matter. Studies show that gang members have a 60 percent greater chance of violent death than teens who manage to steer clear of gangs.[15]

Teenagers often join gangs as a way of protecting themselves in a violent world and to be part of what they describe as "a family." There are a number of risk factors that predispose kids to gang membership, including poverty, unemployment, and a lack of educational opportunities, and having an older sibling in a gang. Even under the most trying economic conditions, parents can continue to be successful in helping their children avoid gangs by fostering positive values, taking advantage of community and mentoring programs, and using the parenting principles we stress throughout this book.

SEVEN WARNING SIGNS THAT YOUR CHILD MAY BE INVOLVED IN A GANG

1. *A new group of friends*

2. *New nicknames or street names*

3. *A decline in school performance and attendance*

4. *Refusal to talk about comings and goings*

5. *Alienation from other family members*

6. *Suddenly showing up with same tattoos as new friends*

7. *Wearing jackets and other clothing with particular colors and logos*

In Chapter Ten, the Selected Resources section, we list a number of resources designed to help parents of children who are currently in gangs or are at risk for becoming gang members. The stronger the presence you and other positive adult role models provide, the greater the chances your child can avoid gang involvement. We suggest that parents who are concerned about gangs take the following steps.

- Find out about gangs in your neighborhood and nearby communities.
- Talk to your children about gangs and their dangers.
- Help children develop the strength and discipline to avoid negative peer pressure.
- Encourage boys and girls to join teams and supervised clubs that foster a feeling of belonging.
- Monitor your child's comings and goings.
- Encourage scholastic achievement.
- Discuss long-term career and lifestyle goals.
- Become involved with school and community gang-prevention groups.

MAKE SURE CHILDREN DON'T BECOME BULLIES OR VICTIMS.

As more black Americans move out of poorer urban areas to more affluent suburbs, they are often shocked to learn that their kids have not escaped the culture of violence and abuse that exists in virtually every American community. For today's middle school and high school students, bullying has become a prime concern. Even if your child is not hurting—or being hurt by—others, we urge you to give this matter serious attention.

Young people who become bullies or victims are lacking in resilience and discipline. In both cases, their behavior reflects emotional insecurity and an imbalance of power in the way they deal with peers.

To some extent, the power struggles in which children and adolescents engage reflect those of adult society. Racially prejudiced individuals are often driven by real or imagined threats to their power. As is the case with all power struggles, there are stronger and weaker players—and extremes on both ends of the scale. In recent years, we've seen a growing problem in the way this jostling for power is played out among young people.

UNDERSTAND THE BULLY.

Children become bullies for any number of reasons—all of which reflect emotional insecurity. Some bullies may appear to have high self-esteem. In reality, they often lack social skills, and intimidate others as a way of making friends and gaining respect. Other bullies are themselves victims of abuse, neglect, or harsh parental discipline, who take their frustrations out on less powerful peers.

Research shows that boys generally threaten or inflict physical aggression in order to bully a peer, whereas girl bullies favor psychological tactics such as social exclusion, belittling, and spreading hurtful rumors. Bullying may or may not have a racial basis. Regardless of their race, gender, or size, all bullies seek power by hurting or demeaning other people. Bullies have trouble empathizing with others, and tend to be indifferent to the hurt they inflict on their victims.

Parents often have trouble accepting reports from teachers and other parents that their kids are bullies. In some cases parents believe it's better that their child is in what appears to be the more powerful position. As far as these parents are concerned, it's the parent of the weaker child who needs to worry. This casual attitude toward bullying should come as no surprise—considering the high value our culture places on competition and dominance.

In the social hierarchy of middle school and high school, bullies are sometimes considered cool, whereas their victims are seen as social outcasts. In reality, bullies are no less at risk than their victims.

Recent studies show that being a bully can be hazardous to a young person's emotional and physical health. Teenage bullies are more likely to experiment with alcohol, drugs, and sex. They are also at greater risk of dropping out of school, becoming depressed, and entertaining suicidal thoughts.

WHAT TO DO IF YOUR CHILD IS HURTING OTHERS

If you get a call from school or other parents accusing your child of being a bully, try not to get defensive. Instead, ask the caller to describe what happened, and try your best to listen to what that individual is saying. If there's a problem, your goal is to take corrective action as soon as possible.

Start out by talking to your son or daughter about the incident or be-havioral pattern that has come to your attention. Give the child a fair hearing, so that you understand his or her point of view. Don't interrupt or criticize—even if you're not satisfied with the explanation.

Rather than focus on the past or a single event, let your son or daughter know that bullying is unacceptable under any circumstances. Then shift the focus of discussion to the kinds of troubling issues that can provoke bullying behavior. Ask, "Is there something you'd like to talk about? Maybe I can help."

Reminder: Faulty parenting often leads to bullying.

We often find that bullying is a product of parenting-style problems. Children who are treated with respect by their folks rarely become bullies. However, we have seen well-meaning parents bully their children without even knowing it.

Do you come down on your children physically or verbally as a way of getting them to comply? If so, you may be creating a bully.

Do you often yell at your children, ignore them, or severely punish them for minor breaches of discipline? Parents who use this approach send a message that bullying pays off.

Too much permissiveness on the part of parents can also lead to bullying. Mothers and fathers who don't create discipline, and let themselves be manipulated by overly demanding children, also send a message that intimidation is the only way to get what you want.

In our discussion of parenting styles in Chapter Two, we endorse an authoritative approach to parenting, one that strikes a balance between demanding rote obedience and giving in to a child's every demand. This is a flexible system that allows parents to set the rules while still considering a child's opinions and viewpoints. Young people who come from homes where parents set high standards that motivate (rather than force) them to meet those expectations are unlikely to become bullies.

FIVE WAYS TO STOP CHILDREN FROM BULLYING

1. *Establish a zero-tolerance policy. Let children know that bully-ing is unacceptable under any circumstances. Explain that racism is a particularly serious form of bullying, and that it's a matter of pride for African Americans to avoid inflicting pain on other human beings.*

2. *Be consistent in applying discipline. When you make a rule, stick to it, so that the child is clear about what you expect. Kids who are unsure of the rules sometimes bully as a means of feeling more secure and gaining control.*

3. *Spend time together. Bullying and other troublesome behavior tends to occur when parents don't spend enough time with their children. Many parents are so concerned with providing for their families or moving up the economic ladder that they effectively leave their children to raise themselves. Children need to be close to their parents, both for reassurance and to develop the emotional resources to maintain mutually nurtur-ing relationships.*

4. *Show children how to manage conflicts. It's important that your child sees you using patient dialogue and reason—not force—to get what you want, while motivating others to cooper-ate. The more effective you are in that approach, the greater the chances your child will follow suit.*

5. *Encourage young people to walk a mile in the other guy's shoes. Bullies often have a problem empathizing with the pain and discomfort of others. Have children project themselves in a variety of situations and to come up with solutions in which nobody is hurt. If the child bullies, don't just let him blow off those actions or tell you it's not a big deal. Point out that vic-tims of bullying suffer a great deal of pain, which can some-times haunt them for years.*[16]

Reminder: Bullies gain courage when others stand around and watch.

Most bullies like to do their work in front of a crowd, hoping to look cool and gain social acceptance. By standing around and becoming part of the audience, other kids give tacit approval to the goings on.

Encourage young people to be proactive in stopping the bullying, without putting themselves in harm's way. If the bully is a friend, encourage the child to talk to him in private. If not, consider embarrassing the bully by shouting out, "Stop it, we're not impressed," and encouraging others to do the same. Calling a teacher, a parent, or a cop is another possibility—though such actions have to be undertaken with care.

At the very least, it's essential that parents instruct kids to never just stand around and watch a bully hurt someone else. Doing that only makes things tougher for the victim, even as it bolsters the actions and reputation of the bully.

UNDERSTAND THE VICTIM.

Over the last few years, there have been a number of tragic, high-profile incidents that involved a form of victimization known as nerd or geek bashing. Kids who had long been socially ostracized and victims of bullies suddenly vented their frustrations by bringing guns into school and murdering classmates and teachers. Thankfully, such incidents are rare. These tragedies have, however, brought the issue of teen abuse to the fore.

Every young person has problems with peers at one time or another, and there have been serious incidents of student hazing in both poor and wealthy neighborhoods. However, there's a big difference between one-time or occasional victims of peer abuse and kids who are regularly selected as targets by bullies. Some of those kids are obese or small for their age. Others are targeted because of race or cultural background. Many kids are able to handle these differences in ways that discourage bullies. Those who continue to be chosen as targets often have the following characteristics in common.

+ Poor self-image
+ Low self-confidence

- Social anxiety or insecurity
- Tendency to cry or become emotionally flustered
- Inability to stand up in a fight

Boys and girls who are victims are often embarrassed to discuss their problems at home. That's why parents need to be sensitive to the following warning signs with respect to their children.

- Fear of walking home from school or getting on the school bus
- Coming home with torn clothes or books and refusing to explain
- Asking for extra lunch money (a sign he might be paying someone off)
- Acting depressed, anxious, or tearful
- Feigning illness to stay home from school

WHAT TO DO IF OTHERS ARE HURTING YOUR CHILD

Some targets of bullying tend to be quiet and shy. These kids need parents to encourage them to express their feelings and show them how to manage their anxiety when confronted. Other victims have a way of mouthing off and egging bullies on. Girls and boys who fit this description need to think before opening their mouths. In addition, parents need to encourage such children to find safer outlets for expressing their frustration and anger.

Parents can help by showing children how to spot and avoid bullies. A course in karate or another martial art can sometimes work wonders. Fourteen-year-old Patrick is a former victim of bullying who was recently awarded a green belt in tae kwon do.

"Before I studied martial arts, I couldn't even hold my own in a fight," Patrick told us. "Now, if someone tries to take a punch at me, I block it in a skillful way that lets people know that I'm not someone to mess with. Come to think of it, it's been a while since anyone has tried to bother me."

Patrick's story is not unusual. Young people who learn a disciplined way of defending themselves actually increase their chances of avoiding fights. Their training gives them the confidence to stand their ground when confronted and to resolve problems in an effective, nonphysical way.

In addition to helping instill physical confidence, parents are well advised to encourage boys and girls to build on their strengths and talents—whether in sports, the arts, or mechanical, technical, and academic pursuits. By encouraging children to improve their skills and concentrate on the things they're good at, you help them become stronger and more resistant to bullies. You might also consider helping your child develop new friendships with peers who share common interests. This can help them improve their social skills and further increase their level of confidence.

"3 Ps" That Help Kids Cope with Bullies

Terrence Webster-Doyle, author of two books on bullying, recommends that parents help children develop the following "bully busting" skills.

- **Prevention.** Understand the causes of conflict and know how to avoid it.

- **Preparation.** Use role playing to teach effective verbal skills that can often resolve conflicts before they escalate.

- **Protection.** Learn to defend yourself so that you have the confidence not to fight.[17]

Help Black Teens Resist Peer Pressure to Choose "the Street" Over Success.

In Chapter Five, we briefly touch upon a particularly troubling kind of peer abuse that is all too common among African American students: namely, the abuse heaped on boys and girls who do well in school. High-achieving middle and high school students report getting ridiculed, having their books torn, and being beat upon by peers who accuse them of selling out their race and attempting to be white.

"My boys are always pressuring me to keep it real and be 'down' [street smart], and forget about my grades," sixteen-year-old Antoine confided. "Sometimes they call me a nerd or an Oreo cookie because I get all As and Bs in school. One time, all my books were stolen. They deny it, but I'm pretty sure it was my crew messin' with me. They say they want me to be black, but what does that mean anyhow? I want to go to college, get a good job, and raise a family. Does that make me some sort of sell-out or race traitor?"

African Americans who haven't moved up the economic ladder have sometimes accused those who moved forward of acting white or selling out. At one time, such insults were aimed at those who were perceived as turning their backs on their community. But when today's black youth talk in those terms, they're essentially rejecting all the trappings of what most Americans (including boys like Antoine) consider success.

This kind of abuse is a type of nerd bashing, one that many bright students experience regardless of color. But it is especially troubling in the black community, because it creates another obstacle for our youth and works to further the interests of those who would keep us down. As a *Time* magazine article once observed:

> It is a sad irony that achievement should have acquired such a stigma within the black community. Hard work, scholarship and respect for family values have long been a cornerstone of black identity.
>
> In the years before the Civil War, many black slaves risked their lives learning how to read. In 1867, just four years after the Emancipation Proclamation, African Americans founded Morehouse and Howard universities. . . . Between Reconstruction and 1910, the literacy rate among Southern blacks climbed from 20% to 70%.[18]

African Americans have long valued educational achievement and upward mobility. It's crucial that you use the disciplines we describe in this and other chapters to give your children the strength to resist negative peer pressure and help them stay on track as they work to achieve their goals and realize their dreams. We implore you to continue reminding your sons and daughters that, by achieving for themselves, they enhance the well-being of their community, as they turn their lives into an object lesson of what it really means to be black.

Summary

Eight Ways to Build Emotional Discipline

1. Give young people the strength and discipline to avoid substance abuse.

2. Help children and teens understand the causes and dangers of substance abuse.

3. Talk frankly to your children about sex.

4. Help young people recognize the dangers of high-risk sex.

5. Be aware of family and personal problems that can trigger risky behavior.

6. Protect children and teens from gangs and other forms of violence.

7. Make sure your son or daughter doesn't become a bully or victim.

8. Help your son or daughter choose positive peer relationships.

5

Practical Discipline: School Days

We have aspirations for a better world that will benefit all young people, inspiring them, supporting them, allowing them to intellectually soar. Let's hope that, unlike racial and religious tolerance, such dreams are not so elusive.

—REVA KLEIN
journalist[1]

In This Chapter:

♦ Motivating children to do their best

♦ Finding mentors to help your child succeed in school and in life

♦ Handling school problems before they take root

♦ Helping African American children overcome the inequities of the educational system

♦ Making the best educational choices for your child

♦ Understanding your child's educational rights

♦ Dealing effectively with teachers and school administrators

FOR AFRICAN AMERICAN CHILDREN, doing well in school is a particularly strong predictor of success—especially economic success. But black children face a variety of obstacles in school that can undermine their chances. This disparity has come to be known as the *achievement gap*. The following are some of the inequities that affect black students and their parents.

The Achievement Gap:
Racial Disparities to Look Out For

- African American children (especially boys) are disciplined at a higher rate than whites, especially in high school.

- Black students are more likely to encounter subtle biases based on group expectations. They are more likely to be recommended for special education classes and remedial courses, labeled as behavior problems and diagnosed as having attention deficit hyperactivity disorder (ADHD).

- Black parents are much less successful than their white counterparts at prodding school bureaucracies to address their children's needs.

- Black parents have less access to administrators and teachers than white parents do.

- Black parents are less likely than white parents to be given access to information about gifted and other accelerated programs.

- Black parents are given tours of schools less often than are white parents.[2]

Trying to motivate your child to do well while working to overcome problems that are endemic to many school systems takes skill and determination. As with most complex issues, there is no quick fix. However, we've broken the process down into the following manageable steps designed to help you help your child.

Help Your Child Develop the Discipline that Fosters School Success

It's up to parents to make sure that children comply with the basic rules of school success. That means attending all classes, completing all homework assignments, working hard in school, and staying out of trouble. Children also need to focus on tasks that might seem boring or meaningless—and that too takes discipline. It's a parent's job to explain the importance of doing well in even the most boring subjects—and to help the child understand the connection between scholastic achievement and success in life.

UNDERSTANDING THE REAL PURPOSE OF HOMEWORK

In his book *The Good Enough Child*, psychologist Brad E. Sachs makes the following perceptive observations about homework:

> Homework is one of the first things children need to learn to be responsible for on their own. Because of this, it is not surprising that there are frequent family fights around homework—fights that may echo previous ones having to do with bedtime, toilet training, and feeding—as parent and child struggle to determine who's really in control. . . .
>
> The primary goal of homework is. . . . [for children to acquire] the skills that will enable [them] to autonomously manage their lives. Making choices about how much and how hard to study, where and when to study, how to balance academic responsibilities with social life and extracurricular activities—this is where the real learning occurs . . .

> *The objective [for parents] is to gradually cultivate and*
> *stimulate [a] child's internal motivation and intellectual cu-*
> *riosity, and his capacity to persevere on his own without being*
> *able to count on instant success or gratification. . . . This can-*
> *not happen overnight; it takes years of modeling, appropriate*
> *supervision, and advice.*[3]

Reminder: Students don't automatically understand why success in school matters.

Children sometimes ask, "Why do I have to learn this?" These questions can be tough for parents to answer. In some cases, you can offer a practical explanation of how a subject relates to everyday life. For example, you can tell grade school students that they need math skills to go shopping and keep track of their money. High school students may recognize that it's important to learn a foreign language if you explain it in terms of the growth of global markets and the increase of ethnic diversity in our country.

When you're unable to offer a particularly good or practical reason for learning something, you can cite the benefits of accumulating as much knowledge as possible. At times, the most honest answer is: "You're going to be tested on it, and it's important to do well on tests."

There's no doubt that the curriculum and teaching methods in many school districts leave a great deal to be desired. Still, there is much to be said for stressing the need for children to try hard in even the most boring subjects taught by the most uninspiring teachers. You can help your child succeed in school by taking the following steps.

- Talk to your child about his or her schoolwork on a daily basis. More often than not, children complain most about the subjects in which they're weakest—and parents need to be attuned to these potential difficulties. When students complain about how boring or meaningless work is, they are often crying out for help. If, for example, your child constantly tells you that he hates math, the first thing to do is to make sure he's not having trouble with the work.

- Praise and reward success. When a child brings home good grades, be generous in your praise. Let the child see how proud this makes you feel. If the good work continues, consider setting up some kind of reward, perhaps a special meal at a restaurant of her choice.

◆ Make sure your child uses proper speech. Trying to prevent adolescents from using street slang and various X-rated expressions among themselves is usually a waste of energy. However, it's essential that black children use correct English in school. If your son or daughter accuses you of asking them to hide their "real selves," explain that teachers and other people with power over their lives are likely to judge them by how they speak.

Black kids who curse or use street slang only hurt their chances of success in a situation where the cards are already likely to be stacked against them. One way you can help is by monitoring your own use of inappropriate language, and setting a good example.

◆ Don't let your child fall behind. As soon as you notice that your child has a problem with schoolwork, respond swiftly. The sooner you take action, the better the chances of pinpointing and correcting the problem. (More about how to do this later in the chapter.)

◆ Make sure that your child associates with peers who recognize the value of academic achievement. If you can't find those contacts in your child's school, seek them out through the kinds of religious and social organizations we discuss in Chapter Three.

Caution: Don't allow your child to be pulled down by the taunts of poor students.

One reason black parents have an especially tough time convincing children to value scholastic success is that it's often regarded as a negative among their peers—a sign that they're selling out to the pressures of a white world. In some communities and schools, high-achieving children are isolated and ridiculed by their peers. This kind of negative peer pressure has been used to explain why black students don't perform up to their potential.

Help Your Child Negotiate Racial Barriers in School

Too often, school administrators and teachers are sorely lacking in their knowledge of diversity issues—even if they are required to teach diversity and create the appearance of racial equality. It's not at all uncommon for even well-meaning professionals to demonstrate racial insensitivity or undermine a student's academic potential. Malcolm X, in his autobiography, recalls an incident in high school that was all too common in the past:

> I happened to be alone in the classroom with . . . my [white] English teacher[. I] had gotten some of my best marks under him, and he had always made me feel that he liked me.
>
> I know that he probably meant well in what he . . . advise[d] me that day. I was one of the school's top students but all he could see for me was the kind of future "in your place" that almost all white people see for black people.
>
> He told me, "Malcolm, you ought to be thinking about a career. Have you been giving it thought?"
>
> . . . I told him . . . "I'd like to be a lawyer."
>
> [The teacher] looked surprised. He kind of half-smiled and said, " . . . a lawyer—that's no realistic goal for a nigger. You need to think about something you can be. You're good with your hands. Why don't you plan on carpentry?"
>
> The more I thought afterwards about what he said, the more uneasy it made me. What [really disturbed me] was [that teacher's] advice to [the white students] in my class. . . . Most of them had told him they were planning to become farmers. But those who wanted to strike out on their own, to try something new, he had encouraged. Yet nearly none of them had earned marks equal to mine.
>
> I realized that whatever I wasn't, I *was* smarter than nearly all of those white kids: But apparently I was still not intelligent enough, in their eyes, to become whatever I wanted to be.[4]

This incident took place in the 1930s, and white Americans might argue that such a scenario is unthinkable today. But we continue to counsel youth who have been discouraged from reaching their goals by "well-meaning" educators.

Today, it's less likely (though not impossible) that a teacher would use the N word in advising a student. If the use of such language could be established one could expect that the teacher would certainly be taken to task—if not fired or sued. Still, as the following recent incident shows, schools are still capable of covering up even overtly racist language and behavior on the part of staff, and turning the arrow of blame on the complaining students.

During her junior year in a racially mixed high school, a former patient named Vanessa complained to her parents that her physical education teacher seemed prejudiced against minorities. This teacher sometimes made disparaging remarks, many of which seemed designed to insult the five African American girls in the class.

At one point, the teacher actually used some racial epithets in describing the behavior of black people. The five African American girls were so outraged by the remarks that they stood up as one, walked out of the class, and headed for the dean's office. The dean knew all of these girls to be A- or B students. He listened attentively to their complaints, and asked them to wait as he conferred with the principal. A few minutes later, the dean returned, and calmly told the girls to go home and to bring their parents to school the next day.

The parents were advised that the girls had left class without permission and would have to be punished for this violation of school rules. The punishment consisted of a week's detention, three additional sessions of physical education to make up for the lost time, and the loss of one half a grade on their final phys. ed. marks. Nothing was said about the teacher's racist remarks or what sanctions she might face.

Fortunately for Vanessa, her mother was an attorney, who was not intimidated by school bureaucrats. She walked into the principal's office, looked him directly in the eye, and said: "If you take a single point off my daughter's grade, I will sue you, the teacher, the school, and the board of education."

In the end, the girls were given two days of after-school detention; all other punishments were dropped. The parents never found out if the teacher was reprimanded for her racist remarks.

This incident is instructive for several reasons. First, it shows how far some school systems will go to cover up discriminatory behavior. This is part of the cover-your-behind mentality students and parents are likely to encounter when they complain.

In a more perfect world, the principal would have told the girls that he admired their courage in walking out of class and reporting the teacher. Perhaps he would have mentioned that they should have waited until the class had ended, but he would have acknowledged that their action was understandable. Then he would have promised to speak to the teacher and get to the bottom of these serious charges. Unfortunately, we all must deal with the imperfections of the world in which we live—even as we strive to make things better.

Several months after this incident occurred, an organized group of minority parents complained that the principal often turned a blind eye to allegations of race discrimination. As a result of this group action, the principal was forced to take early retirement.

There's no question that Vanessa's mother, who was one of the leaders of this parent group, handled the situation correctly. School administrators will do almost anything to avoid a racial discrimination lawsuit—and you don't have to be a lawyer to indicate that you're prepared to take legal action if it's warranted. If the powers that be don't respond to your personal complaints, join with other parents who've had similar experiences and take action as a group.

If you're going to make certain that your children's interests are protected, you need to know how to deal effectively with teachers and school bureaucrats. You also must teach your children what to do when they encounter overt or covert racism.

Whatever else it may be, succeeding in school is a game that black children must know how to play if they are going to reach their potential. All children face a variety of struggles in the course of their school years. But black boys and girls must also know how to deal with racism that is sometimes so deeply ingrained that it's invisible to the perpetrators. Certainly it's important to teach children to stand up for themselves and fight their own battles. But when it comes to dealing with the subtle biases of the educational system, parents have to be at the forefront of the fight.

Help Your Child Deal with the Pressures of Being Black and a Good Student

One reason racial issues are the most baffling of all school-related problems is that there are many subtle and complex nuances involved. For example, some studies suggest black students underachieve on standardized tests; some commentators and pundits with political agendas attempt to interpret this controversial statistic to imply that black students are genetically less intelligent than their white counterparts. Therefore, they contend, it makes no sense to pour money into social and educational programs that benefit African Americans.

The idea that some racial groups are intellectually inferior is nothing more than politically motivated intellectual racism. Furthermore, such stereotypes don't take into consideration any of the underlying pressures that black students encounter in schools. What's even more troubling is that many programs that are (at least theoretically) designed to include black students are just as blind to the needs of these young people.

High-achieving black students must walk a treacherous tightrope to navigate all the pitfalls, mixed messages, and indignities they are likely to encounter in their school career. The situation is often more difficult for bright or gifted minority students.

As we have noted, black adolescents who are high scholastic achievers are often accused by peers of playing a white man's game and selling out their culture. Very bright black students have often expressed fears that doing well academically means losing their cultural and racial identity. Such students will sometimes hide their academic gifts by playing the class clown or channeling those gifts into sports, which is a much safer way to gain acceptance by both peers and the school community.

For young people of color, success in school—and in life—requires the ability to negotiate in two worlds and balance two identities that are sometimes at odds with each other. Research shows that some black students succeed by acting as if race is not a factor in their lives. But real life has a way of exposing this fallacy.

In a *Newsweek* article, Sylvester Monroe, now a successful African American journalist, described the pain he experienced when he was plucked out of an urban neighborhood and given a scholarship to St. George's Academy, an almost exclusively white private school in New England:

> One of the greatest frustrations of my three years at St. George's was that people were always trying to separate me from other black people in a manner strangely reminiscent of a time when slave owners divided blacks into "good Negroes" and "bad Negroes."

Somehow, attending St. George's made me a good Negro, in their eyes, while those left in [the Chicago housing project where his parents lived] were bad Negroes or, at least, inferior ones. . . . Looking back on it, I was pleased to show what black boys were capable of. Yet, there was a faint disquiet. What bothered me was that some people found it easier to pretend I was something else [other than black]. "We're color-blind here," a well-meaning faculty member once told me. "We don't see black students or white students, we just see students." But black was what I was; I wasn't sure he saw me at all.[5]

We have worked with many students who shared Mr. Monroe's sense of isolation and frustration. These youngsters often represent the fulfillment of their parents' dreams. When emotional and social problems begin to surface, these same parents tend to feel that these are minor sacrifices that youngsters should make willingly, given the potential rewards. But we know any number of bright African American students who dropped out of top private schools—not because they couldn't keep up with the work, but because they couldn't handle the isolation and emotional strain. The pressure is often greatest on poorer urban adolescents.

One such teen, who was tragically shot by police in Harlem, is the subject of the book *Best Intentions: The Education and Killing of Edmund Perry*, by Robert Sam Anson. One of Perry's friends and fellow students at the elite Phillips Exeter Academy described the kind of stress black students often encounter in primarily white private schools:

You are caught up in a situation where everybody says you should be happy, where you think you should be happy, and instead of being happy, you find there are tears in your eyes because you are so angry. . . .

Personal racism you can deal with. Someone calls you nigger and you can smack him in the mouth, and if you are bigger than him, he's gonna know not to call you a nigger again. Edmund [Perry] had dealt with that kind of racism all of his life—we all do—but before he went to Exeter, he had never, ever in his life dealt with institutional racism. That was something he couldn't fight against. How do you fight an assumption? How do you tackle history? How do you get your hands on an environment? You can't even begin to come to grips with it. That's what makes it so . . . hard to deal with. And the thing is, it's never personal. It's just there.[6]

It takes a mature and disciplined adolescent to take the kind of long view that makes such a situation tolerable. Parents can help by understanding the pressures these young people face, and carefully considering whether their child is equipped to handle what may seem like golden opportunities.[7]

Reminder: The highest-rated school may not always be the best choice for your child.

If the child is having social or emotional difficulty adjusting to any school situation, seek out professional counseling. Whatever the circumstances, it's important to develop an ongoing support system of family, friends, teachers, clergy, and other adults to help young students develop the necessary strength to succeed in school. This kind of support is especially important for girls and boys who are going through some kind of emotional upheaval, such as divorce or the death of a loved one.

Keep in mind that there are many reasons why children and teens have academic problems, some of which have little or nothing to do with school. As we point out in Chapters Four and Eight, there are any number of medical conditions and emotional circumstances that can make it almost impossible for children to achieve anything close to their academic potential.

Expose Your Child to a Variety of Mentoring Experiences—Both In and Out of School

One reason children often have a hard time seeing school as being relevant to their lives is that many of the professional athletes and entertainers they emulate were not particularly good students. Celebrity worship is an even bigger problem in the African American community, because there are fewer positive, nonglamorous role models for young people to emulate—especially when they're at school.

Black teachers make up less than 10 percent of the profession, including administrators and guidance counselors. It's not unusual for some black students to go through their entire scholastic career without ever having a black or other nonwhite teacher.

There are, of course, instances of concerned white teachers playing positive roles in the lives of black students. Still, there is a glaring need for adults who have firsthand experience overcoming the challenges black students face to provide instructional support and mentoring.

Children of all ages need opportunities to have regular contact with adults, other than their parents, who can support them and become constructive influences. When schools provide mentoring opportunities, whether by staff or outside volunteers, parents should make certain that children take full advantage of them. Unfortunately, even the best schools can't be counted on to give children of color the full range of mentoring experiences they require. That's why it's important to seek them out on your own.

Research shows that isolation of black youth has many negative consequences, including a high instance of academic failure. According to the National Dropout Prevention Center, students who don't complete high school often cite the lack of a single person who cared about them as a primary reason for dropping out. These students feel little or no attachment to their school, and have no close bonds with teachers and other educational staff.[8]

Caring adults who step in to fill that gap can make an enormous difference in the lives of young people—and not just those who are in danger of dropping out of school. Average and gifted students also need mentoring if they are to reach their potential. A mentor's influence doesn't always result in immediate or profound changes in a student's attitude or grades. However, mentors are often effective in helping students identify problems that impact academic performance and devising workable solutions.

There are many mentoring opportunities available outside the school setting that can inspire children to succeed in school and in life. Mentoring can occur through one-to-one contact or in groups. The process can take place either formally or informally—and its impact can extend to every aspect of a young person's life.

Thomas W. Dortch, Jr., is president of the national 100 Black Men of America, Inc. Today he leads an organization that provides mentors for over 100,000 young African Americans each year. But when he was growing up in Georgia, Mr. Dortch found mentors in the local barbershop.

[In that barbershop], you found the men of the community playing checkers, debating the talents of ballplayers, re-telling the latest jokes and reporting the news that occurred in the neighborhood. More than 30 years later, those encounters remain strong. I learned many lessons in the barbershop: lessons about personal conduct, humor, success, morality, self-respect, and manhood. Simply put, I was being mentored. Back then, though, we didn't call it that.[9]

This kind of informal mentoring was once a regular feature of African American communities. Although these opportunities may be somewhat harder to find today, informal contact with adults in the community can supplement the guidance and resilience parents provide.

ONE-TO-ONE MENTORING RELATIONSHIPS

The role of a mentor is to provide support, guidance, and encouragement to students by role modeling a variety of attitudes, skills, and effective ways of negotiating life's challenges. Mentoring is not a series of lectures. It is, rather, an ongoing opportunity for a child or teen to observe an older, more accomplished person, and to see how that individual handles various situations. Conversations are part of the process, but they are less important than the lessons a young person learns by looking. As with effective parenting, it's not what a mentor says, but what he does that counts.

In addition to our teaching schedules, medical rounds, and formal counseling, we both do a good deal of one-on-one mentoring of urban adolescents. When possible, we arrange for after-school jobs, in which the young person spends most of those working hours in close quarters with one of us. Naturally, there are conversations about what's going on in the teen's life. But, again, the most valuable lessons are not given verbally.

For example, we feel that it's especially important for young black men to learn to treat women with courtesy and respect. There's surely no harm in telling a young man to be courteous. But it's far more effective for a male mentor to demonstrate what that means.

Recently a sixteen-year-old named Jack, who was participating in a mentoring program at our medical school, barreled ahead of three women who were waiting to get on an elevator. Jack's mentor always made it a point to let women go first, but apparently the young man hadn't gotten the message. So, the next time Jack attempted to precede several women onto the elevator, his mentor physically blocked him by putting a raised arm in the young man's path. After that, Jack began treating women with greater courtesy.

Mentors can also communicate good work habits and positive attitudes toward school in a similar fashion. The young people we mentor get to see how hard we work, as well as some of the rewards we reap from our efforts. These adolescents come in contact with students, doctors, and patients of various races and backgrounds at the medical school, and this helps them develop a broader view of the world and an understanding of what it takes to be successful in this world.

While it's not absolutely necessary that all adults who mentor black adolescents share the same racial background, it is important that at least some of those mentors be black. As we've noted, most black youth have not had a great deal of exposure to successful African Americans outside of the sports figures and entertainers they've seen on television.

It's a given that white people can succeed in business and the professions. Firsthand contact with successful black adults is the most convincing way to show black adolescents that these possibilities are also available to them. An equally important lesson comes from watching successful African Americans invest their valuable time helping young people.

Mentors can be accomplished in a particular field of interest. For example, youngsters with musical talent can benefit from the guidance of older musicians who recognize and want to nurture their talents. This kind of situation is based on the traditional master-apprentice relationship, where the older, more experienced person profits emotionally and spiritually from passing his skills on to the next generation.

Other mentoring situations are not based on the sharing of a particular artistic or vocational interest. For example, the vast majority of young people we mentor do not necessarily envision themselves as doctors, teachers, or writers. Similarly, successful black businesspersons who participate in mentoring programs are not primarily interested in encouraging young people to enter their specific career or field. The keys are demonstrating an active interest, and setting an example of how high black students can climb, if they are motivated and willing to work hard.

Mentors don't need to be professional counselors or leaders in their fields to be effective. As one author on the topic explains:

[Mentors] can be confidants or friends who are able to guide, challenge, and encourage the child on a fairly regular basis. Mentoring has been compared to "having an uncle that cares for you . . . and wants to see you do well. He is not your competitor: he is there to support you, not to compete with you or discourage you. He is not your critic as much as he is your cheerleader."[10]

WHAT MAKES AN EFFECTIVE MENTOR?

1. *Mentors invest time and energy fostering a young person's success—both in and out of school.*

2. *Mentors help a young person make a successful transition to adulthood by teaching them specific skills, or by role modeling effective and appropriate behaviors. Sometimes mentors can serve both of these functions.*

3. *Mentors voluntarily take responsibility for one or more members of the next generation.*

4. *Mentors of African American youth have a commitment to the ongoing interests of the community.*

Mentors who work on a one-on-one basis with young people have to decide on the best use of their limited time together. Typically, in formal mentoring relationships, the adult and youth spend at least some of their time engaged in structured activities. These can include the following:

♦ *Tutoring.* Mentors can review homework, class work, or test papers; they can then follow up by discussing opportunities for improvement in study skills and time management. Mentors can also supervise or assist students on assignments or school projects.

♦ *Reading.* A visit to the library or media center to select reading material or to research a selected topic. The mentor and student can also both read a book, story, or newspaper article and share ideas about it.

♦ *Field trips.* Mentors can arrange outings to places of cultural interest and sporting events—as well as to businesses and college campuses. Some field trips can emphasize enjoyment, while others can focus on goal setting or possible career choices.

♦ *Leisure activities.* Playing catch with a baseball, throwing a football, or kicking a soccer ball can provide a bonding experience and reinforce such social skills as fair play, and balancing competitiveness with cooperation. More sedentary games like chess, checkers, and cards are also useful.

♦ *Talking.* One-to-one communication is something a mentor and student can do in the course of any of the above activities. Conversations can focus on sharing experiences, exchanging opinions, discussing areas of special interest or mutual concern. Verbal exchanges can be lighthearted or serious, casual or goal oriented.

FIND THE "RIGHT" MENTOR.

Some mentoring occurs naturally, such as the positive relationships students establish with teachers, coaches, relatives, neighbors, or older peers. These informal contexts are just as important as more formal mentor-student relationships, even if they lack a formal structure. A high school teacher, for example, may see a hundred or more students in any given term, but form no mentoring relationships. When such relationships do occur, they are not part of a teacher's formal job description. Nevertheless, the impact of such relationships can transcend that of any academic instruction.

Brent Staples, a distinguished black author and journalist, has a Ph.D. in psychology from the University of Chicago. Staples had been taking a commercial course in high school, and was on track to become a secretary or an administrative assistant. During his school years in the early 1960s, that was considered a path to success for black students. Staples never even thought about going to college. Fortunately, an English teacher (who happened to be white) recognized the young man's potential and helped him secure admission to a special college program. This teacher wasn't a formal mentor, yet he made all the difference in the young man's life.[11]

The late Congresswoman Barbara Jordan related a similar story about a junior high school teacher who encouraged her to excel to her fullest capabilities. "She was concerned about what she perceived to be a lack of self-confidence in me," Congresswoman Jordan told Bill Moyers in an interview. "[The teacher] said, 'You have got a first-class mind. You don't know it, but you have. And if you don't develop that mind further, you're gonna lose it. And I don't want to see that happen.' . . . For me, that was a beginning for thinking differently about myself."[12]

Wise parents always encourage and support this kind of informal mentoring. Still, they know better than to count on it. We strongly recommend that you put some thought into assessing your child's needs before deciding on the best kind of mentoring situation.

In formal mentoring relationships, it's important to match the mentor and student carefully. Just as some teachers elicit better performance from certain kinds of students, some mentors are more effective with different types of children. For example, a gifted African American student attending a primarily white private school is likely to have different needs than a poor student with behavioral problems attending a public school in an urban area.

There are many mentoring programs available to African American youth. Some are offered by local churches, others by groups like Big Brothers Big Sisters of America and 100 Black Men, Inc. In recent years, corporations and social organizations have become increasingly active in promoting employee and member involvement. Similarly, a growing number of colleges and universities now require students to participate in mentoring and other volunteer community-based programs. You can find a complete list of mentoring programs in Chapter Ten.

BENEFITS OF GROUP MENTORING

Providers of mentoring services have long debated the relative benefits of the one-on-one versus the group approach to mentoring. Our feeling is that both can have positive results, and that, in general, there is no better or worse way to mentor. That said, it's important to recognize the advantages of group mentoring in order to make an informed choice. These include the following:

- ◆ Groups help give members a sense of belonging. Each member has an opportunity to recognize that others share his or her problems.

Likewise, when one member solves problems successfully, others can be inspired to do the same.

♦ Groups foster discipline, respect, and empathy for others—qualities that often spark positive changes in attitude and behavior.

♦ Many of the problems young people have are at least partially based on group or peer issues. Therefore, it makes sense to try to resolve them in a group context.

♦ Groups buffer the youth from the potentially negative effects of a bad one-on-one match or a mentor who unexpectedly leaves the program. Under these circumstances, groups can provide a safety net of support.

Whichever type of mentoring program you select, it's important that you look for the following features:

♦ Positive nurturing

♦ Well-defined goals

♦ High expectations

♦ Objectives that are tailored to the child's individual needs

♦ Long-term commitment

Take an Active Role in Your Child's Education

While mentors can do a great deal to help a child succeed, it falls on parents to tend to the small day-to-day details—and to oversee the general direction of their children's education. Too many parents send their kids off to school and hope that all will go well. More often than not, this approach amounts to wishful thinking. No parent can completely trust a school to meet a child's individual needs. Black parents would do well to keep a close eye on every step of a child's school experience, and be prepared to speak up at any phase of a process that begins before a child enters the school building.

CHECK OUT THE SCHOOL.

Make an appointment with the school principal before your child enters any new school. Tell him that you'd like to tour the building and observe classes in session. This step serves two key purposes:

+ Your active interest lets the principal know that you will not brook any violation of your or your child's rights.

+ Your firsthand view gives you an opportunity to draw your own conclusions about the school.

Set up a time when the principal is able to accompany you on the tour. Spend at least a few minutes in several classes. See if the children appear to be motivated and involved in their work. Observe the way the teacher interacts with the class. Ask the principal about the racial diversity of both the curriculum and the educational staff.

Principals will sometimes try to shove you off to a secretary or other subordinate. Unless the principal is on leave or otherwise unavailable, don't allow yourself to be passed down. If necessary, insist on rescheduling the appointment for a time when the principal can attend to you.

BECOME A FAMILIAR VOICE.

Attend all meetings to which parents are invited, including parent-teacher organizations and board of education meetings. Feel free to ask questions, and don't be intimidated. You have a right to know what's going on at your child's school and to state your opinion.

BRING UP RACE WHEN IT HELPS YOUR CAUSE.

If you perceive differences in the way children of different races are treated, speak up. This is not to say that you should cry racial prejudice without both just cause and the ability to back up those charges. If, for example, your child has a learning disability or other special need, take advantage of all available services, and make sure they are being offered on a nondiscriminatory basis.

Similarly, if you feel that your child qualifies for an accelerated or gifted program, let the powers that be know how you feel. For example, we know several black high school students who moved into another district and were immediately placed in a lower-track class than the one for which they were qualified. When the parents became aware of the error, they asked that it be corrected. The school administrators complied in every case. All of them claimed that it was a simple administrative mistake. Um-hmm!

Don't hesitate to ask about the racial breakdown of any class or program that interests you. If you feel your child is being excluded on the basis or race, don't be afraid to speak up. Sometimes just implying that racial discrimination is at play can get you what you want. However, it's important to make sure that your child is well suited for the particular class or program you're lobbying for.

Try To Pick Your Child's Teachers.

There's no question that, in every school, some teachers are more competent and caring than others. Furthermore, certain teachers are better able to get their message across to certain types of students. For example, an impatient teacher might be effective teaching youngsters who catch on quickly, but disastrous for students who need a bit more time to grasp things. Still, more often than not, schools place children in classes without giving much thought to where they are most likely to succeed. As a concerned parent, it doesn't make much sense to accept a class assignment automatically when it's usually made on a more or less random basis.

It's an open secret that, in many schools, parents who are active in parent-teacher organizations are allowed (unofficially) to select their children's teachers. In racially mixed or primarily white schools, black parents often don't choose to take an active role in school activities. In some cases, the parents are working, and don't have much spare time. In other instances, black parents don't feel comfortable participating in what some mothers have described as white-only cliques.

Whether or not you're involved in school activities, you can try to pick your child's teachers—or at least request that your child not be placed with a teacher with whom you're not comfortable. This is somewhat less feasible in the higher grades, where children generally have a different teacher for each subject. Even here, it's sometimes possible to request or decline a given teacher in a particular subject area.

Most school principals cringe at the thought of parents coming to their office, or demanding that their child be placed with a particular teacher. "If I do it for you," the usual line goes, "I'll have to do it for everyone." That may be an understandable administrative concern—but it's not your problem.

As your child's advocate, your goal in this situation is to place your child with the best possible teacher. At the very least, you want to avoid teachers who are known to be incompetent, or who have negative attitudes toward children of particular racial groups.

It's a good idea to talk to various teachers and to solicit opinions of parents whose children have been in those classes. However, the most accurate way to judge is to sit in on the various classes in your child's grade level for an hour or more. Public schools are often legally bound to accommodate such requests. The following guidelines are adapted from those author/educator Muriel Karlin Trachman uses to help parents appraise and select teachers.[13]

Ten-Step Checklist for Evaluating Teachers

1. *Find out who the teachers are in your child's upcoming grade, and how other parents feel about them. When a parent expresses an opinion about a specific teacher, ask for her reasons. Teachers whom some parents describe as strict or demanding can be top-notch educators who provide the structure your child needs.*

2. *Ask yourself if there's a good environment for learning in the classroom. Good teachers know how to control the class without invoking fear. Children are constantly testing the limits to see who is in control. In a well-run classroom, the teacher is the person in charge.*

3. *Observe whether the teacher is constantly fighting for control. Does she often have to shout at the class? A good teacher should have an easy rapport with the children, and not constantly be forced to scream and to assert her authority.*

4. *Ask yourself if the students appear to be learning. What looks like play can sometimes be part of a well-conceived lesson. On other occasions, the teacher may have scheduled some time for play. If you spend enough time in a classroom, you'll get a sense of how hard the students are working.*

5. *Observe whether the teacher seems to show favoritism toward a few children, while ignoring the needs of other students.*

6. *Observe whether the teacher appears to treat children of all races and ethnic groups in an evenhanded way. Note any signs of either overt or covert racism.*

7. *Ask yourself if most of the students seem to be comfortable in their environment.*

8. *Be watchful of whether students are permitted to fight in class or verbally attack one another.*

9. *Notice whether the children address the teacher with respect and with warmth.*

10. *Take note of how the teacher deals with disruptive and inattentive students.*

After you've spent time in various teachers' classrooms, go into the principal's office and politely express your preference. The principal may simply listen, but not make a commitment either way. Make it clear that you plan to persist. School administrators don't want to deal with unhappy parents on a daily basis, and will often try to avoid problems by giving you what you want.

STEPS TO TAKE IF YOU'RE UNHAPPY WITH YOUR CHILD'S PROSPECTIVE TEACHER

◆ If you feel strongly that your child has been placed with an unacceptable teacher, do everything in your power to change that placement.

◆ If it's simply a matter of avoiding a particular teacher, ask the principal to transfer your child to any other teacher's class. Principals are less resistant to such requests than those expressing a specific teacher preference. If, on the other hand, you have your mind set on a particular teacher, your task is likely to be more difficult. Still, that doesn't mean you should stop trying.

Schools are designed to deal with large numbers of students, and special requests are usually discouraged. That's no reason to give up—even if a principal insists that under no circumstances will he allow parents to pick their children's teachers.

◆ Make an appointment with the principal as soon as possible—preferably before the beginning of the new school year. Some schools try to discourage requests by not revealing class assignments until a day or two before school begins. Such administrative ploys shouldn't prevent you from trying to get what you want.

Reminder: Always take your requests and complaints to a decision maker.

Don't accept a conference with a dean or assistant principal. As with any negotiation, it's essential that you deal with the person who has the power to make decisions. In most schools, that's the principal.

When you meet with the principal, don't criticize the teacher. In general, principals are well aware of why parents select particular teachers over others, so it usually isn't necessary to get into specifics. Just say that you know your child and have carefully observed the various teachers. Let the principal know that you feel strongly that your child would do much better if he were placed in a particular teacher's class.

Some principals will promise to consider your request. However, don't be surprised if you get a response that goes something like this: "All the teachers in this school are capable educators. We can't let one parent choose his or her child's teacher, or we will have to do the same for every other parent who prefers another teacher. With so many children, that simply would not be possible."

The best way to counter this kind of statement is by continuing to politely assert your position. Don't let yourself get angry or frazzled. Point out that you are only talking about your child—and that you just want what's best for him or her.

If the principal is still unwilling to grant your request, let him know that you are prepared to go to the superintendent of your school district. Add that you hope you won't have to resort to this step, and that you're confident the two of you can resolve the matter. Most principals don't want to rock the boat, and having parents running to the superintendent demanding changes in class assignments is something they'll try to avoid if possible.

Whether you're talking to the principal or superintendent, make sure you get your point across in the most effective way possible. Consider saying something like: "I know you're very busy, and the last thing I want to do is upset your procedures. However, I know my child, and I'm sure he will do much better in Ms. Thomas's class. I hope you understand that it's my job as a parent to make sure my child does as well as he can in school."

If the administrator you're dealing with is white and you think it's appropriate, consider pushing the matter a step further by bringing up the issue of race. The mere hint that you are alleging racial discrimination is something no school district wants to touch. At that point, the principal or school superintendent may be thinking, "What a pain in the butt. The last thing I want is to listen to this parent's complaints all year. Someone like this might start making waves with other minority parents. That's just what I need."

In the end, the administrator is likely to give you what you want, partly because he or she respects you for showing such extraordinary concern for your child's education.

Monitor Your Child's Academic Progress Every Step of the Way

It is important that you meet with your child's teacher soon after he or she enters the class, and that you make it clear that you intend to cooperate. Say something like: "Please let me know if there's any way I can help you. Also, I'd appreciate it if you would let me know how my child is doing—particularly if he seems to be having problems."

Many parents overlook this important step, but a good teacher will appreciate your show of interest. However, if a teacher seems indifferent or discourages your participation, take this as a sign that you will have to monitor the situation even more closely.

To a large extent, parents can judge a child's progress by test grades, written work, and verbal communication. Kids sometimes resent their parents asking too many questions about schoolwork—even if they're not having problems. If you start your monitoring early in your child's academic career, he or she is more likely to experience your involvement as genuine concern and not an intrusion.

Most teachers insist that parents sign all tests, so that there will be no surprises when report cards come. If a child rarely brings home tests or often claims that there's no homework, be sure to confirm that with the teacher. Some schools have found that it's more effective to give fewer tests and less homework, so you would do well to obtain that information early in the school year. In addition, author/educator Muriel Karlin Trachman suggests that parents ask children the following questions after each school day:

- Did you learn anything new or interesting today?
- Is there any work you don't understand or need help with?
- What is your homework for tomorrow?
- Did your teacher check and return yesterday's homework?
- What tests do you have coming up?
- Is there anything else that happened at school that you'd care to talk about?

Checking tests and written work are good ways to monitor what's going on in class. Make sure you know when a test is coming up, and always find out how well your child did. You can write off one poor test score to a child's having a bad day. However, a second subpar grade may be a red flag, and you'll want to find out what's going on as soon as possible.

First, ask the child, "Was there something you didn't understand?" If you can't identify the problem or provide the necessary help, make an appointment with the teacher. A concerned teacher will be happy to meet with you, and can often give advice on how to help the child.

"The customary bureaucratic means of communication from a child's teacher to the parent consist of four report cards and perhaps two parent-teacher conferences during the course of the school year," notes Muriel Karlin Trachman. "A concerned parent, however, wants to have a sense of how the child is doing on an ongoing basis."

If you suspect your child is having difficulty, meet with the teacher immediately. Whenever you do meet with a teacher regarding your child's performance, you should always ask the following questions:

- Do you feel the child is working up to his potential?
- Is he participating in class?

- Is he well behaved and cooperative?

- How can I work with you to help my child's performance?

These questions set a cooperative tone and make it easier for you and the teacher to work together to foster the child's best interests. The important thing is to identify problems as soon as possible, and try to come up with the most effective solution.

THREE KEY REASONS STUDENTS MAY NOT BE PERFORMING TO THEIR POTENTIAL

1. *The teacher isn't adequately getting the concepts across, and the student is having trouble understanding the work. Sometimes this is a question of poor teaching. In other instances it may relate to the particular teaching method a school district is using at a given time.*

2. *The student is upset about something unrelated to school-work—such as a death or illness in the family, divorce, or a broken romance. For the most part, schools are ill equipped to deal with such problems.*

3. *The student has a perceptual or learning problem that has not been adequately diagnosed.*

Make Sure Problems in School Are Properly Identified and Corrected

Not long ago, children with dyslexia were often misdiagnosed as mentally retarded or learning disabled. Dyslexia is a perceptual impairment that has nothing to do with a student's intelligence—even though it can have a negative impact on school performance and test scores. Researchers continue to uncover many other learning problems, though schools are often years behind in recognizing and dealing with them. Consequently, students with problems that are not acknowledged or understood by the school system can easily get mislabeled, which then produces a raft of other problems.

Caution: Misdiagnosed learning disabilities can destroy a child's academic career.

When parents first become aware that children are having difficulties in school, they often feel upset. Even if your child does have a learning disability, it isn't a sign of low intelligence or diminished future prospects. In many instances, it is a relatively mild problem that is primarily a product of poor teaching or a style of teaching that is difficult for your child. With younger children, the problem may be an undiagnosed perceptual problem that's easy to correct. We have designed the following steps to help you identify problems, and then take appropriate measures to eliminate and manage them.

◆   If it appears that your child is not working up to her potential, immediately schedule hearing and vision tests. Schools sometimes administer these tests, but a school nurse is more likely to overlook or mislabel problems than your family doctor or pediatrician. If the doctor does discover a problem, he can prescribe glasses or a hearing aid, or send the child to the appropriate specialist.

If it turns out that your child does have a vision or hearing problem, inform the principal and teacher immediately. Some schools offer special programs to help children with these difficulties. Minor problems can often be easily corrected. For example, students with vision problems can be assigned seats closest to the blackboard, while those with hearing deficits can be assigned teachers with relatively loud voices. Of course, these steps are in addition to the eyeglasses or hearing aids a doctor may prescribe.

◆   Have a conference with your child's teacher. If the teacher can't immediately pinpoint the problem, ask the following questions:

Is my son or daughter paying attention in class?

Is he or she doing the homework assignments?

Does the child seem to be interested in the work and trying hard?

♦ If the child needs more help than you can provide at home, ask the teacher what kind of help is available either during or after school hours. Some schools provide tutoring during lunch hours or after school. You can also ask the teacher to give you some material so that you can do some extra work at home.

If you are unable to provide help yourself, hire a private tutor. If at all possible, seek out a licensed teacher who has tutoring experience. If money is tight, find an older student in the neighborhood who excels at that subject. Offer a modest fee, or some kind of exchange of services.

♦ If tutoring doesn't result in improved performance, set up a conference with the school principal to discuss your options. Most school systems offer free testing. However, if you can afford it, we would strongly suggest seeking testing from an outside source.

There are several reasons for this strategy. A school system's testing procedures may not be as thorough or as objective as those of an outside agency. School districts sometimes receive extra money for each child who is diagnosed with particular disabilities. On the other hand, they may be obliged to spend money to help children overcome other learning problems.

When children are mislabeled by school systems, parents can find removing those labels next to impossible. So if an incorrect diagnosis is made, it's much less problematic to have it made by someone other than your school system.

When you receive any sort of diagnosis, always ask questions and seek out at least one other opinion. While it's unwise to automatically reject an evaluation you may not agree with, you should make it a point to carefully review all recommendations before accepting them.

Two school-related problems are of particular concern to parents of African American students—placement in special-education classes and being diagnosed with Attention Deficit Hyperactivity Disorder (ADHD). In case you are told that your child falls into either of these categories, we offer the following suggestions to help you understand your rights and plot an appropriate course of action.

SPECIAL EDUCATION

In theory, special-education classes are designed to offer struggling students extra support to help them improve their academic skills through a plan tailored to their particular needs.

Special education programs are costly, and some school systems have intentionally overapplied the special-ed label to give borderline students access to smaller classes and more individual attention. But in some school districts, the tendency to label more children as special education students appears to be a way to pour more dollars into the system without providing the extra help students need to improve.

In one major east coast city, for example, there is approximately five times as much money spent on a special-education or special-needs student than is spent on each "normal" child. As a result, there are some children placed in special-education programs who don't belong there. Despite the dollars that are supposedly being poured into providing additional services, many of these misdiagnosed children suffer as a result of this labeling. And a disproportionate number of these students are black.

Recent studies by The Civil Rights Project at Harvard University, which looked at educational and legal issues in the nation's special education system, reveal the following disturbing statistics:

◆ Black students are about three times more likely than whites to be labeled emotionally disturbed or mentally retarded.

◆ Black students are much more likely to be removed from a mainstream public school classroom and placed in an isolated special-education class than white students with similar problems.

◆ Despite the tendency to link placement in special education classes with poverty, the studies show that minority students (especially males) are more likely to be placed in special-education classes in more affluent neighborhoods.[14]

If you believe that your child has a disability, like autism, mental retardation, or cerebral palsy—and this has been confirmed by an appropriate medical and/or psychiatric diagnosis—don't hesitate to take full advantage of the additional services. If, however, your child has less serious intellectual, physical, and emotional difficulties, you may be better off forgoing the special-ed label.

With the ever-increasing emphasis on standardized testing, students placed in special-ed classes are likely to find themselves at a severe disadvantage. In many special-ed classes, students are faced with lower expectations and a less demanding course of study that leaves them poorly prepared for high-stakes exams that often determine whether they can graduate.

Another problem is that the tests that determine whether students will be placed in special-ed classes are highly subjective. These tests, which are administered by school psychologists, are unreliable and easily influenced by the attitudes of the person giving the test toward the cultural background and personality of the student being tested.

Caution: Don't agree to special-ed testing unless you're convinced it's appropriate.

Once a child of color is sent for a special-ed evaluation, there's a very good chance that he or she will be given that designation. Once students are so classified, it's extremely difficult to get rid of a label that can become part of their permanent academic record and stigmatize them for many years to come.

Even if you feel that your child will benefit from being labeled a special-ed student, be sure to visit his or her proposed class, and to obtain a full description of the services that will be provided before making a decision.

Reminder: There are lots of reasons why children have trouble achieving in school, and no one all-encompassing solution for any of them.

Educators have made progress in recognizing and diagnosing learning disabilities, but there is still a very long way to go. Parents have to walk a fine line between trusting their own assessment of their children, understanding the way their particular school system works, seeking out the best professional advice, and utilizing those recommendations in ways that are in the child's best interest.

Attention Disorders (ADHD and ADD)

There are two main types of attention deficit disorder: attention deficit hyperactivity disorder (ADHD) and attention deficit disorder without hyperactivity (ADD). According to *The Diagnostic and Statistical Manual of Mental Disorders* of the American Psychiatric Association (DSM), the primary characteristics of ADHD are "developmentally inappropriate degrees of inattention, impulsivity, and hyperactivity. The onset is before the age of 7 years, with at least eight of the following fourteen criteria occurring for at least 6 months":

Characteristics of ADHD

1. Often fidgets with hands or feet or squirms in seat
2. Has difficulty remaining seated when required to do so
3. Is easily distracted by extraneous stimuli
4. Has difficulty waiting turn in games or group situations
5. Often blurts out answers to questions before they have been completed
6. Has difficulty following through on instructions from others
7. Has difficulty sustaining attention in tasks or play activities
8. Often shifts from one uncompleted activity to another
9. Has difficulty playing quietly
10. Often talks excessively
11. Often interrupts or intrudes on others
12. Often does not seem to listen to what is being said
13. Often loses things necessary for tasks or activities at school or at home
14. Often engages in physically dangerous activities without considering possible consequences[15]

Characteristics of ADD

Attention deficit disorder without hyperactivity (ADD) is more difficult to define than ADHD. Diagnosis of the condition usually requires an observation of no less than seven of the nine following behaviors for a period of six months or more:

1. Has difficulty with sustained attention (reading, homework)
2. Fails to concentrate unless in one-to-one or low stimuli environment
3. Is unable to complete activities or work on independent projects
4. Doesn't appear to be listening
5. Is messy, disorganized
6. Daydreams or stares blankly
7. Has trouble following instructions or directions
8. Is apathetic or unmotivated
9. Is unable to shift from one activity to another[16]

   Lists of symptoms can help parents and teachers spot children with possible attention deficit problems. However, there is great debate about using the above behaviors to make any sort of diagnosis. Consider the revelations of a large-scale study that compared the conclusions of thirty-nine journal articles describing children who had been labeled as having ADHD and ADD.

- There were sixty-nine different characteristics used to describe children labeled ADHD and ADD, with little agreement among researchers regarding these characteristics.
- Many of the cited characteristics were subjective in nature and, at times, contradictory.
- Studies comparing the characteristics of children labeled ADHD and ADD to the characteristics also produced confusing and contradictory results.

◆ Children labeled ADHD and ADD were not found to have characteristics different from those of children with other handicapping conditions.

◆ Some studies examining attention factors failed to find significant differences between children with and without ADHD and ADD.

◆ A review of twenty-five papers addressing possible causes of ADHD and ADD turned up thirty-eight possible causes for these conditions. Little agreement was found among those authors regarding the numerous and diverse causes addressed, and little solid evidence was found to support any of the causes.[17]

Caution: Be aware of racial bias in diagnosing attention problems.

When teachers become more concerned with controlling behavior than teaching, they tend to overdiagnose attention deficit hyperactivity disorder (ADHD). That's because hyperactive students can disrupt a class. There are, however, many disruptive children who don't have ADHD, even if the drug most commonly used to treat that disorder does sometimes temporarily calm them down.

On the other hand, children with attention deficit disorder without hyperactivity (ADD) simply have problems focusing, and this often impairs their ability to learn. But because they are not disruptive, these students and their problems tend to receive a lot less attention from teachers and school systems.

These are hot-button issues for black students, because many school systems are overvigilant in spotting behavioral problems, especially with boys. At the same time, schools often don't expect much from black students when it comes to academic performance, and may be slow to look for appropriate remedies to these kinds of difficulties. Parents need to recognize these tendencies, and to become proactive in dealing with problems as they arise.

Typically, when a child is diagnosed with ADHD, a doctor will prescribe a stimulant drug—most typically Ritalin. However, some researchers believe that psychiatrists are often too quick to medicate problems that are rooted in a child's anger and frustrations that get acted out in a classroom setting. This is especially true for black male students who are frequently given Ritalin soon after they are labeled as being difficult or unmanageable. In reality, many of these young people are suffering from conduct disorders, conditions that are often confused with ADHD.

The Diagnostic and Statistical Manual of the American Psychiatric Association describes conduct disorder as "a repetitive and persistent pattern of behavior in which the basic rights of others or major age-appropriate societal norms or rules are violated." Children are diagnosed with conduct disorder if they display at least three of the following behaviors over a twelve-month period.[18]

1. Often bullies, threatens, or intimidates others

2. Often initiates physical fights

3. Has used a weapon that can cause serious physical harm to others (e.g., a bat, brick, broken bottle, knife, gun)

4. Has been physically cruel to people

5. Has been physically cruel to animals

6. Has stolen while confronting a victim (e.g., mugging, purse snatching, extortion, armed robbery)

7. Has stolen without confronting a victim (e.g., car theft, shoplifting, forgery)

8. Has forced someone into sexual activity

9. Has deliberately destroyed the property of others

10. Has broken into someone else's house, business, or car

11. Often "cons" others by lying in order to obtain goods or favors or to avoid obligations

12. Often violates school and parental rules and codes of behavior

Reminder: Conduct disorders may or may not be accompanied by ADHD.

Conduct disorders are treated with counseling—not Ritalin—if they are not accompanied by ADHD. Students who are diagnosed with ADHD as well as conduct disorders are generally given Ritalin and referred for counseling.

The use of drugs like Ritalin often does result in better classroom behavior; however, some mental health professionals who specialize in treating ADHD have raised the following concerns.

◆ Drugs like Ritalin address the symptoms, not the causes of behavioral problems. That means the emotional distress causing ADHD remains unchanged.

◆ A child can come to view taking medication as a badge of helplessness. Some physicians and mental health professionals worry that it may be difficult for children who are constantly medicated to develop resilience and self-control.

Before you allow your child to begin taking Ritalin or any other drug, make certain you are receiving a correct diagnosis. If possible, get an independent evaluation from a qualified professional who is not employed by your child's school system. We also recommend that you take the following issues into consideration before letting your child begin any course of medication.

◆ Have you ascertained that your child's problem is not a conduct disorder?

◆ Is the child going through an emotionally trying period? If so, that may explain behavior that appears to be ADHD.

◆ Does the child have an inexperienced or intolerant teacher who can't handle "difficult" children? Such teachers may push for a quick diagnosis and a chemical solution.

◆ Is there anything you, as the child's parent, can do to lessen the child's anxieties? Setting more effective behavioral limits can help some children gain better impulse control. Increasing trust through more open parent-child communication can also have a positive impact.

◆ Have you considered counseling or psychotherapy? These solutions may require more time and energy, but they can have far more favorable long-term effects than taking drugs like Ritalin.

Should you decide to opt for Ritalin or some other kind of drug therapy, please keep the following in mind:

◆ Drug therapy can be greatly enhanced by appropriate professional counseling.

◆ Drug therapy is most effective when there is cooperation and communication among the parents, school staff, and the prescribing physician.

- It's critical that parents and teachers understand the basic effect of the medicine being used and note how the medication and dosage interact to provide the best results. Any changes in the child that might be related to the drug therapy should be noted and reported to the child's pediatrician or primary care physician.

- Keep in mind that each child is different. Therefore, his or her reaction to medication will vary.

Summary

A Seven-Step Formula for Academic Achievement

1. Help your child develop the discipline that fosters school success.

2. Be prepared to help your child negotiate racial barriers in school.

3. Help your child deal with the emotional pressures of being black and a good student.

4. Expose your child to a variety of mentoring experiences—both in and out of school.

5. Take a proactive role in your child's education.

6. Monitor your child's academic progress every step of the way.

7. Make sure problems in school are properly diagnosed and corrected.

6

~

Practical Discipline:
To College and Beyond

African Americans have always found ways to gain access to education: Even under slavery, when severe punishment was inflicted on enslaved African Americans who could read—not to mention those discovered educating others—the ability to read and write was valued highly and passed down, where possible, through generations. It should be no surprise, then, that the actual number of African Americans entering college, receiving degrees, and going on to graduate and professional schools [is] at an all-time high.

—CATHY J. COHEN AND CLAIRE E. NEE,
behavioral scientists[1]

In This Chapter:

- Helping young people grasp the importance of attending college
- Understanding and explaining the true meaning of success
- Planning to pay for college
- Assessing your child's readiness for college
- Deciding on the college that best fits your son or daughter

Why Higher Education Is Especially Important for African American Children

IN CHAPTER ONE WE CITED research showing that African American parents are now 50 percent more likely than their white counterparts to rank a college education as the most important ingredient in their child's success. These lofty educational aspirations apply to the entire black community, including families who live in poor urban areas. However, there is often a great disparity between what parents want for their children and the knowledge they need to make certain those goals are achieved. The information and tools we provide in this chapter help you close that gap.

It would be a stretch to insist that parents should require all children to attend college. Clearly there are some young people who lack the academic skills; others simply don't possess the temperament for academic work, even if they have the intelligence. There are also people with certain technical, artistic, or entrepreneurial skills who attain great success without a higher education. Still, for the majority of African American children, college is well worth the required time and financial investment.

Studies show that a college degree can mean over a half million dollars of additional earnings during a lifetime in the workplace. However, attaining a college degree can do a lot more than simply increase a young person's earning potential.

Researchers at Washington University in St. Louis found that black students who graduate from college increase their IQ scores more than four times as much as white students during the course of their college careers. These researchers attribute the changes in black students' IQs to the relatively poor quality of elementary and high school education many of these students experience. They contrast this to the higher quality of education colleges generally offer all students, regardless of their race.[2]

These results put another nail in the coffin of politically motivated social scientists who claim that blacks are genetically less intelligent than whites. Studies like this also explain why so many African American parents believe that the decision to attend college is key to a young person's success. For many African Americans, a college education truly is the great equalizer. It is the gateway to both career success and forward movement of the African American culture.

Today we run into few minority parents who don't understand the value of a college education. There are still some who question whether it's worth spending four or more years out of the workforce or who fret about the rising cost of funding a college education. To these mothers and fathers, we can only say that we don't know a single college graduate who regrets getting a higher education—nor do we know a single parent who looks back and doubts that the costs of putting a child through college are worthwhile.

Understandably, educated parents are more likely to encourage their children to pursue a college degree. We also know many parents who didn't have that opportunity but are determined to make it available to their sons and daughters. Whatever your own educational background, it is becoming increasingly clear that a college degree is as necessary today as a high school diploma was in previous generations.

NINETEEN OF AMERICA'S FASTEST-GROWING OCCUPATIONS

1. Systems analysts

2. Computer engineers

3. Physical therapists

4. Residential counselors

5. Human services workers

6. Occupational therapists

7. Paralegals

8. Medical records technicians

9. Special education teachers

10. Corrections officers

11. Operations research analysts

12. Speech and language pathologists and audiologists

13. Private detectives and investigators

14. Surgical technologists

15. Dental hygienists

16. Dental assistants

17. *Nursery and greenhouse*   19. *Sales representatives*
    managers

18. *Securities and financial*
    services workers

(Note: Most of these careers require a college degree.)
(Source: Bureau of Labor Statistics)

As recently as the 1960s it was possible for a relatively uneducated worker to support a family at a reasonable level. Innovations in communication and technology have fueled a new economy—one that demands more sophisticated workplace skills, greater intellect, and a broader social perspective. As psychiatrist and educator James P. Comer notes in an article directed at black college students:

> This is the first time in the history of the world that it has been necessary to have a reasonably high level of education to successfully meet adult life tasks . . . working, living in the family, rearing children, and serving as a responsible citizen.[3]

As a concerned parent, you want to be certain that your child has both the discipline and the resources to meet and excel at those tasks. This is part of the legacy you are passing on to future generations—a legacy of education that has long been an integral part of African American culture.

During slavery, most African Americans were not permitted to read and write. Still, many found a way to educate themselves in secret—often at great risk. We've certainly come a long way since then. Still, despite all the progress over the past decades, African Americans continue to encounter race-based obstacles. When your sons and daughters are out in the world competing for a job or a promotion, you'd best assume they will have to be better—not just as good as—their white, Asian, or Hispanic counterparts. In order to get that leg up, they are going to need that college degree. Here are the steps you need to take to make that a reality:

1. Instill in your child the desire to go to college.
2. Start planning now to pay for college.
3. Select the right college environment.

Instill in Your Child the Desire to Go to College

In general we advise parents to talk to their children in terms of *"when you go to college"* rather than *"if you go to college."* We take this approach because we firmly believe that a college degree is a tool young people need to succeed in the workplace and mainstream society. Moreover, we believe that education is key to the progress of African Americans as a community.

The idea that college is a must doesn't always sit well with young students. Some girls and boys aren't enamored with school, and don't see why they have to continue any longer than absolutely necessary. In many states, a child is legally required to attend school up until age sixteen—a year or two before most students finish high school. It would be short-sighted to allow a young person to leave high school without a diploma, even if it's not against the law. And it is quickly becoming almost as short-sighted for parents to convey the message that college is an option rather than a necessity.

Reminder: If you tell children they don't have to go to college, they probably won't go.

In talking to children about college, you want to help them develop the foresight and motivation to stay on track in school. The message should never be, "This is something we're forcing you to do." Instead you want young people to understand the connection between getting a good education and attaining things that they value. These include the following.

A Brighter Economic Future

By the time they reach kindergarten, children are well aware of the advantages material possessions can provide. They can see that some people live in bigger houses, drive newer cars, wear nicer clothes, and take more elaborate vacations. By their early teens, many children are intensely status conscious about material things—though they often have distorted ideas about both what it takes to obtain them and the amount of satisfaction that accrues from having them.

Many urban youth, for example, have been lost to drugs, gang violence, and prison because they perceive drug dealing to be a fast way to make big money. When a youngster believes he can make over a thousand dollars a week as a drug runner, it can be hard to sell him on the benefits of a part-time job flipping burgers so that he can start saving for college. The discipline to resist the lure of fast money starts in a home where the parent or parents emphasize the importance of education and teach a strong work ethic.

Young people from more affluent families can also have false impressions about money. Those who've grown up in a financially secure environment may not understand the sacrifices and hard work involved in maintaining the lifestyle. They may also feel that their higher socioeconomic status makes them better than their less affluent brothers and sisters.

It's essential that parents help children understand that a college education opens the door to a richer life—in terms of financial and intellectual wealth. But, as Coretta Scott King, widow of the Rev. Dr. Martin Luther King, once told graduating seniors at Illinois College in Jacksonville:

> Just because you are a member of an elite group, that doesn't mean you
> have a license to start acting elitist. On the contrary, God made it possible for you to get a good education so you could use what you have learned, not only to have a good income and a comfortable life for yourself and your family, but also to help other people have a better life. You are here today because you have been called to serve.[4]

These are extremely important words, because young people sometimes have trouble understanding that financial wealth is only a step on the path to achieving their full potential.

A MORE SATISFYING AND MEANINGFUL LIFE

In the 1950s the psychologist Abraham Maslow developed a motivational model called *The Hierarchy of Needs*.[5] This model remains a useful way to show how motivations change as different levels of needs are satisfied. We have adapted Maslow's model to help parents visualize and explain the pyramid of motivations that make a higher education so meaningful to young African Americans. In our version of the model, we envision more fluid boundaries between the five levels than in Maslow's original hierarchy.

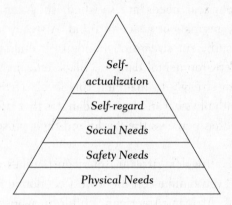

LEVEL 1: PHYSICAL NEEDS—HUNGER, THIRST, SHELTER, REST, WARMTH

Until people can satisfy these basic needs, nothing else matters. Survival depends on seeking ways to fulfill these physical requirements. As psychologist and author Na'im Akbar notes in a message to African American college graduates, African Americans have always had a knack for doing more with less:

> Each generation of African Americans has had an array of special challenges. During [slavery], the primary challenge was basic survival: maintaining food, shelter, and clothing and protecting ourselves from the savagery of our predatory masters.
>
> This preoccupation consumed the mental activity of the majority of our ancestors. Many of them were still able to rise above the subsistence conditions and strive for psychological ascendancy and an intellectual grasp of the meaning of our condition. Those who sought transcendence . . . often had to drag many of those who were preoccupied with survival issues to the higher vision of freedom from captivity. . . . Their persistence opened the door for our presence here today.[6]

In theory, there is supposed to be a safety net that protects people from the ravages of physical deprivation. Even when it fulfills this task, government does little or nothing to provide coverage on the next level.

LEVEL 2: SAFETY NEEDS—SECURITY, PROTECTION FROM PHYSICAL AND EMOTIONAL HARM

Once people's physical needs are satisfied, they can concentrate on achieving a more permanent peace of mind. A steady job, for example, that provides a sufficient stream of money to live above a subsistence level, safe from environmental dangers. Black citizens who live in poor urban areas often struggle to maintain this level. Their neighborhoods can be fraught with physical and psychic dangers that affect the way both parents and children perceive the world and their prospects for the future.

Despite these struggles, African American families always have valued education—even families on the lowest economic rungs. A remarkable number of African American children whose parents were uneducated and unskilled have managed to achieve a higher education.

Rather than credit black families for persevering in the face of formidable obstacles, some critics have unfairly accused African Americans of promoting cultural values that hinder young people's educational development. In perpetuating this stereotype, these critics have made it even more difficult for black youth to progress.

LEVEL 3: SOCIAL NEEDS—BELONGING, ACCEPTANCE, FRIENDSHIP, AFFECTION, LOVE

African Americans have found ways to develop strong social bonds even under extremely difficult circumstances. The harsh realities of slavery and the race-based difficulties that linger to this day have often served to bring people together through extended families, community involvement, and church-based groups.

On the other hand, a young person's need for belonging and acceptance can lead to gang involvement and other forms of negative peer pressure. (For a full discussion of this issue, please refer to Chapter Four.) Some researchers contend that children—and especially teens—are generally more influenced by their peers than by their parents. We find that when parents provide discipline and a strong set of values early in life, children are far better able to resist negative peer pressure—including pressure to not excel in school. As Charles, a seventeen-year-old high school senior from an urban community, told us:

> My friends have zero interest in college. They are into hangin' out, or whatever. When I ask them, "What are you going to do when you graduate from high school?" they don't really have an answer. If I say, "Well, what about college?" they either laugh at me or change the subject. They might figure that college is just for white kids, or maybe their parents never told them that it's something they might be able to do. My parents always let me know that they expected me to go to college, and that's exactly what I'm planning to do.

Young people like Charles need peer relationships as much as their less-disciplined counterparts. It's just that teens who've been reared with a balance of love and discipline have the strength to risk being rejected by peers who don't share their outlook. In reality, it's teens like Charles who are doing the rejecting. They are willing to take a calculated social risk because they can see something better and more valuable waiting for them down the road.

LEVEL 4: SELF-REGARD—
INTERNAL: SELF-RESPECT, AUTONOMY, ACHIEVEMENT
EXTERNAL: STATUS, ATTENTION, RECOGNITION

In addition to the achievement of financial wealth, these fundamentals of our identity are the primary rewards that motivate African American students to attend college. These are relatively long-term goals that require discipline and the ability to delay gratification. For example, young people can often begin earning money right away by going straight into the job market after high school graduation. It takes long-term vision for young people to recognize that their job opportunities and financial prospects are likely to be far better after they graduate from college.

In general, children are more likely to pursue a higher education if at least one parent has attended or completed college. But studies show that the influence of family often takes on an additional dimension for black students.

These students often cite as motivation parents who encourage them to achieve beyond the parents' own level. Albert, a scholarship student at an Ivy League university, explained his family's influence this way:

> My parents are hardworking people with very little formal education. From the time I was little, I remember them saying that they wanted me to do better than they did. I was the first in my family to go to college. I am the oldest of four children, and I think my parents were counting on me to be a role model for my younger sister and two younger brothers. Anyhow, I never could have gotten this far without my folks' help and encouragement.

Students like Albert often talk about the potential to earn more money and the desire to make life easier for their families. But most are equally interested in the prestige and recognition of family and peers, as well as a sense of fulfillment and accomplishment. As Sandra, who is about to enter her first year of medical school, told us:

> I've wanted to be a doctor ever since I was a little girl. But my experience in college has given me a much broader understanding of what it would mean to realize that goal. There are so few black women doctors. By joining those ranks, I can actually help change the character of my profession and work with others who share that desire.

Sandra's thoughtful remarks touch on a long-standing debate about the primary purpose of a college education. The worldview Sandra developed during her four-year career seems to have made a stronger impression on her than the biology and other courses that are more technically relevant to an aspiring doctor. Is this ultimately what colleges are supposed to do? Or are they supposed to be in the business of arming students with workplace skills?

On one side are those who contend that a person ought to come out of college with at least some specific career skills. Others believe that intellectual development should be the sole purpose of a higher education. Our own approach combines both these viewpoints.

Bobby, a college freshman who was planning to become an engineer, wondered why he was required to take courses in English literature and foreign language. The answer is that college is not a technical school.

Part of its purpose involves developing students' minds, broadening their perspective, and giving them a sense of how they might make a contribution to society. Nevertheless, we believe that, by the time students graduate, they ought to at least have some sense of what the future holds—whether it's in the workplace or in some sort of advanced or graduate program.

LEVEL 5: SELF-ACTUALIZATION—
FULFILLMENT OF PERSONAL POTENTIAL, SELF-KNOWLEDGE, GOING BEYOND THE SELF

We consider self-actualization to be the strongest drive human beings possess in becoming the best people they can possibly be. Self-actualization makes it possible to fulfill our unique destinies. The drive to achieve that unique destiny is a big part of what motivates people to move forward, overcome obstacles, master the world, and, hopefully, make a meaningful contribution to it. The love and discipline parents impart to children are essential to this process.

In developing his hierarchy, Maslow assumed that every person has an intrinsic potential for self-actualization. There are no guarantees, however, that this potential won't be stifled in one way or another. In order to reach this full potential, children must receive positive regard from others, which in turn helps them learn to think positively about themselves.

Parents are a child's earliest and most significant influences, so they play a major role in this process. The strength and discipline mothers, fathers, and other primary caregivers impart can go a long way in determining how children see themselves—and the ultimate course their lives will take.

Maslow described people who reach this level as possessing the following traits: spontaneity, resilience, receptiveness to new ideas and experiences, ability to solve problems, a democratic attitude, and a well-thought-out system of values. To this list, we would add the following characteristics: inner freedom, a balanced perspective on the importance of money and material possessions, an appreciation of nature and spiritual feelings, and a desire to be connected to both the past and the future. This final attribute has special meaning for African Americans.[7]

The opportunities that are available to current generations exist largely because of the sacrifices of others. In the same way, the prospects for coming generations depend on the foundation others build for them. Maintaining this sense of connectedness is especially important for young African Americans, because of the nature of our people's past, and the lingering uncertainty about our future.

It's up to parents to help children understand the importance of being *for* their race, and not simply *of* their race. As more African Americans graduate from college and achieve affluence, it's essential that they never lose sight of their cultural values and traditions.

You can move to a mostly white suburb, send your children to private schools and Ivy League universities, and make your mark in a world where white remains the gold standard. Still, when you lose connection with your people, you lose an important part of yourself—and you deny your children an important part of their heritage.

As we discuss later in this chapter, a disturbingly large percentage of African American college students drop out before they earn a college degree. Often the reasons have less to do with the difficulty of the course work than with social and emotional issues, many of which are based on race.

As we stress throughout this book, discipline is the key to raising strong children who will grow up to be successful adults. For black Americans, that strength and success require maintaining an ongoing link with the African American community.

Carol Moseley-Braun, the first African American woman elected to the U.S. Senate, in 1992, put it succinctly when she delivered the following message to African American college students:

> With personal discipline, there are no limits on what you can achieve. You need [discipline] in the classroom, and you need it outside of the classroom. . . . College is a lot of work. . . . However, your education doesn't end with graduation. . . . Just as you demonstrate discipline in obtaining [a college degree], you must demonstrate discipline in using it. . . . You must get involved. . . . You must lead by example.[8]

TALK TO CHILDREN ABOUT COLLEGE.

The way you view success plays a major role in shaping what you expect from your children, and how they react to those expectations. Before you can convince your child of the importance of attending and completing college, you need to examine your own notions, feelings, and ideas, and how they translate into what you want for your son or daughter. We've designed the following questionnaire to help you do just that:

- Do you feel your child has the ability to attend and complete college?
- Does your child express a desire to go to college at this time?
- Do you talk to your child in terms of when (not if) he or she will go to college?
- Have you discussed with your child why a higher education is especially important for African Americans?
- Who are your child's role models for success?
- Did most of your child's current role models attend and complete college?
- Do you facilitate contact between your child and peers who are college bound?
- Have you exposed your child to college graduates or students— whether inside or outside the family—who can serve as mentors or role models?
- Have you talked to your child about the true meaning of success—and how a higher education can help make that possible?
- Have you talked to your child about the positive impact his or her success can have on future generations?

Plan Now to Pay for College

The cost of college is something most families need to consider. These costs have been rising at a far faster pace than the rate of inflation, and they can be an intimidating prospect for a family of modest means. Still, the fact that over half of African American undergraduates come from the poorest quarter of American families (compared with less than 25 percent of white students) demonstrates that a higher education is within the reach of virtually every family. The process of funding a child's college education takes planning and discipline. The earlier you start, the easier the process will be. Here are some steps to follow.

Begin Saving for College as Early as Possible.

If your budget permits, start putting some money away for college each month—even if it's only a few dollars. If it appears you don't have any money for this purpose, create a budget. Look at where your dollars go each month, and try to find a way to cut down on something else to begin saving for college. Once you come up with the money, look for a systematic way to begin saving.

There are bank accounts and mutual funds designed for parents who are trying to save for college, as well as bonds that mature when your child is ready to start school. Find a bank officer or financial adviser who can help you put this kind of plan in motion, and stick with it.

Caution: Don't count on an athletic scholarship to fund your child's college education.

A recent study found that two-thirds of African American males between the ages of 13 and 16 believe they can earn a living playing professional sports, compared to around one-third of their white counterparts. It's easy for parents to get caught up in the dreams of wealth and glory that come with a child's success in sports.

Most high school athletes will not land college scholarships. Even parents whose sons or daughters have exceptional athletic ability need to proceed with caution. No matter how great a young person is at sports, it's essential that parents help him understand that good grades are far more valuable than success on the playing field.

We've worked with a number of top high school athletes who received college scholarships, even though their academic skills were well below par. Many of these students flunked out of college—with shattered dreams and without any workplace skills.

It may appear that achieving success in sports is a more attainable goal than reaching the top in any other field. Black players make up 80 percent of the team rosters in the National Basketball Association and nearly 70 percent in the National Football League. Black baseball players have won 41 percent of baseball's Most Valuable Player titles over the last twenty-five years, though they account for just 17 percent of the players. These statistics conceal the reality that the odds of a high school athlete playing any professional sport are 10,000 to 1. Playing in the NBA is a 50,000-to-1 shot.[9]

GET YOUR CHILD INVOLVED IN COLLEGE PLANNING.

By the time children enter high school, it's wise to bring them into the financial-planning picture. Talk to them in general terms about the cost of college. Consider discussing the possibility of your high school student getting a weekend or summer job, and put part of those earnings toward tuition, books, or room and board.

Even if money for college is not an issue, it's usually a good idea to encourage high school grads to help pay for their education. Even if you're planning to pay for tuition, let them pay for something—be it books, clothes, or eating out. If they need to work part-time in order to contribute, that's fine. However, it's not a good idea for students to work too many hours. Studies show that students who work twenty hours or more after school each week are at significantly greater risk of dropping out than those who work ten hours or less. Many of the students who work these long hours do so to pay for clothes and other status items at the expense of the kind of grades good colleges require.

Some affluent parents—especially those who came from humble beginnings—don't want their children to struggle. That's understandable. However, it's important to remember that your children are growing up in a different environment, and their needs are not the same as yours were. Sometimes your attempts to do everything for them can have a negative impact on their competence to do for themselves. Without responsibility, young people can't develop the discipline they need to succeed.

LOOK INTO A VARIETY OF FINANCIAL AID OPPORTUNITIES.

There are a wide variety of options for financial aid available. Parents who become informed and investigate the range of possibilities are likely to find they can overcome the financial hurdles of putting a student through college. Sources of financial aid include scholarships and grants (which involve money that doesn't have to be repaid), work-study programs, and student loans (which sometimes carry hefty repayment responsibilities). Advantages in one student's situation can be disadvantages in another instance, but when considering these opportunities please take into account the following.[10]

Scholarships and grants: This is the most desirable kind of financial aid, because these monies are gifts that don't ever have to be paid back. Scholarships and grants are available from a wide variety of sources, including churches, community groups, private foundations, federal and state governments, and the universities themselves. You or another family member can also inquire about financial aid or scholarships that may be available through your (or the relative's) company.

High school guidance counselors can offer information about scholarship opportunities, and there is a wealth of constantly updated information available on the Internet. In Chapter Ten, we offer a listing of scholarship Web sites, publications, and helpful organizations.

If your son or daughter is a high school senior, he or she needs to fill out a Free Application for Federal Student Aid (FAFSA) form, preferably no later than January or February of the senior year. The form is issued by the Department of Education to determine how much financial aid students are eligible to receive. High school guidance counselors often have the FAFSA forms, but the fastest route is to visit the Web site http://www.fafsa.ed.gov/ and get the forms online.

On the FAFSA form, students are asked to list the colleges they are interested in attending. Once a student is accepted for admission, the school will outline the kinds of grants or aid for which a student is eligible. The schools will also specify what they require the student's family to contribute, above and beyond the aid package. Keep in mind that students are required to reapply each year, and the amount of aid versus what the family is required to contribute is subject to change.

Students who don't qualify for scholarships, grants, or work-study programs (which provide money and credits in exchange for work on campus) can finance their education through loans. There is a wide variety of loans available to both students and parents. The most desirable loans are those that don't have to be repaid until after a student graduates and is generating income. Some loans provide a total or partial interest subsidy while the student attends school. Loans to parents who wish to help finance a child's college education generally require a repayment plan that begins as soon as the loan is issued.

Studies show that African American students who receive debt-free financial aid are much more likely to complete their college studies than are those who take loans. In fact, almost 70 percent of black college dropouts cite high loan debt as the major cause of withdrawal.[11] This should be reason enough for parents to start putting a financial plan in place as early as they can.

Reminder: *If possible, take off the financial pressure during a student's freshman year.*

More African American students drop out during their freshman year than during any other stage of college. The reasons for this have to do with psychological and emotional factors, as well as the need to adjust to academic work that is likely to be far more difficult than what the student was required to handle in high school. Holding down a job simultaneously can be the straw that breaks the camel's back.

If you can possibly afford it, try to structure a first-year environment in which the new student can devote productive hours to academics. Once students become acclimated to college-level work, they can often add a part-time job to the mix and maintain their grades. One possible approach is for the parents to provide more financial support during the first two years, and then let the child contribute more during junior and senior years.

Reminder: *Don't overlook any possibility to gain admittance or financial aid.*

There is sometimes special help available for families with limited financial resources. In certain instances there are allowances made for families with specific hardships. For example, children of single mothers whose husbands don't fulfill their child-support obligations are sometimes able to qualify for reduced tuition and even relaxed academic requirements at top-notch colleges. And although there are a number of organizations that don't charge for matching families with scholarship opportunities, there are also individuals and companies that charge a modest fee and have a record of getting good results.

There are situations in which being a minority can put you at a distinct advantage. For example, after Sharlene graduated from an Ivy League school with a 4.0 grade-point average and an almost perfect score on her law boards, many top law schools were clamoring for her to attend. All the schools offered full scholarships, and a few hinted at some additional off-the-record perks. There's no question that a white or Asian student with Sharlene's qualifications would have also been considered desirable. Still, it's clear that her being African American gave Sharlene a leg up in this situation.

"I'm a little uncomfortable about all these schools sucking up to me because I'm African American," Sharlene told us. "I'd really prefer it if they wanted me strictly on the basis of my qualifications."

We respect Sharlene's position; nonetheless, we urged her to use every advantage to gain entrance and financial aid. We extend that advice to all college applicants and their families.

It would be nice if the world ran strictly on merit, but it's unrealistic to think in those terms. Admission to college can hinge on any number of factors, including a family's wealth or history with a particular institution, a student's extracurricular involvement, the color of her skin—even the kind of impression an applicant makes on an admissions officer.

Given the current racial climate, you can never be certain if your race will provide a positive edge or put you at a disadvantage—whether you're seeking university admission, a scholarship to law school, or another kind of financial aid. So, if you suspect that mentioning color will be a hindrance, don't feel under any obligation to do so. But if using your race can potentially put you at an advantage, don't think twice. Just do it.

Reviewing the Financial Aid Process

- *Make financial planning for college a family project.*

- *Design a spending plan that lets you save on a regular basis.*

- *Use all available resources to learn about opportunities for financial aid.*

- *Start making contacts and applying early.*

- *If you must take a loan, understand your options and read the fine print.*

- *Utilize every available advantage at your disposal.*

Select the Right College Environment

One of the questions parents of college-bound students often ask is, "What kind of college is best for my child?" Another is, "Will they be better off in a historically black college or university (HBCU) or in a traditionally white institution?"

These are important questions, because the ability of students to fit into an institution is a key factor in determining whether they graduate, transfer to another school, take a temporary break from college, or drop out completely. We strongly advise you to work closely with your child to evaluate the college-bound student's particular talents, skills, and background as well as the prospective college environment and culture. In making this assessment, it's important to consider the following factors.

THE YOUNG PERSON'S READINESS

This includes a student's academic history, level of emotional maturity, and social skills—as well as the ability to deal with new and challenging situations.

For example, young people who come from protected but mostly black environments may not be prepared for the kind of discrimination they're likely to encounter at some primarily white institutions. Those who have grown up in affluent, mostly white communities may feel out of place at a historically black university.

Interestingly, students from tough urban neighborhoods often make better social adjustments than their more affluent counterparts, because they've had more experience deflecting the slings and arrows of racism. This has made them stronger and more resilient—at least in this regard.

On the other hand, affluent black students who've excelled at mostly white private schools are less likely to have problems making the academic adjustment. Nevertheless, a troubling percentage of these students leave college during or immediately after their freshmen year because of emotional or social difficulties.

Caution: Never discount the importance of race in a black student's adjustment to college.

Although the dropout rate for all students is highest during the first year of college, African American students have to deal with a number of race-related issues that put them at higher risk. A new college student from an all-black community who has little experience interacting in a mostly white environment often feels alienated on campuses where minorities aren't especially welcome in all-white fraternities and sororities. Such discriminatory practices are almost never officially acknowledged, but there is a wealth of anecdotal evidence to confirm such bias.

This kind of racism can blindside young people who lack the experience and resilience to deal with it. Instead of interpreting such racial bias as ignorant, stereotypical responses to skin color, they take it as an indictment of their self-worth. First-year students living away from home and without the protection of their family for the first time can quickly become depressed and overwhelmed by this sudden exposure to overt and covert racial bias.

Black college students who've grown up and attended schools in primarily white neighborhoods often look forward to socializing with other African Americans in college. However, these students sometimes have problems fitting in at racially mixed or largely black campuses, because they have little experience dealing with peers of their own race. We have helped many students who've returned home during or after their freshman year to put their emotional issues in context before resuming their college careers. But many of these problems could be avoided if parents took steps to instill the strength and racial discipline young people need to negotiate unfamiliar environments before they go off to college.

It's important for parents to recognize that children benefit from a wide range of experiences and diversity encounters. It's natural for parents to want to shield and protect children, but young people who are too insulated from the larger world often lack the tools to deal with new and unfamiliar situations. We strongly suggest that parents take the following steps to help young people successfully negotiate encounters with people of their own race and those of other races. These skills are part of the racial discipline that underlies success both during and after college.

- Make sure your child has opportunities to interact with people of different racial groups. If those opportunities don't exist in your community, make it a point to find them elsewhere. This is especially important for families who live in primarily black neighborhoods.

- Make sure your child develops a sense of belonging in the black community and an appreciation of the African American heritage. This is especially important for families who live in primarily white neighborhoods.

- Let your child know that racial prejudice is a reality of life—but that it's an obstacle that can and must be overcome.

(Note: Please see Chapter Three for a complete discussion of racial discipline.)

THE COLLEGE ENVIRONMENT AND ITS CULTURAL CLIMATE

It's clear that some students who drop out of a particular college would have a much better chance of succeeding at an institution with a different kind of atmosphere. For example, we know many college freshmen who've returned home depressed because they felt isolated on campus. Such isolation can occur at mostly white institutions that are insensitive to the social and emotional needs of minority students. It can also happen at all-black colleges, if the incoming student has been around mostly whites, and feels uncomfortable around peers and faculty of his own race.

The following steps can help you anticipate and avoid these problems.

Visit the schools your teen is considering: Just because a student can get into a school that has a high academic standing doesn't necessarily mean it's the right choice. Rasheed, who has always wanted to be a lawyer, was admitted to a Big-Ten school—one that was reputed to have a top-notch prelaw program. "If you can get good grades there," Rasheed's guidance counselor told him, "it's your ticket to a good law school."

This was an important plus for Rasheed. However, the young man and his parents had decided that they would spend a weekend at each of the schools he was considering. Here's what Rasheed told us after his visit to the Big-Ten school:

> The campus was very pretty, and the people who took us around were nice. But I hung out a little, and I got to see how the students act after class. Most of the students were white, and I got the impression that many of them weren't real comfortable around black people. There were

also very few minority professors and administrators, and that kind of turned me off. I know it's a great academic school, but I'm just not sure.

We strongly encouraged Rasheed and his parents to look elsewhere—and, if possible, to talk to current students and alumni before making final decisions. Rasheed had considered attending several traditionally black universities, but he also had some concerns about that alternative. "The world we live in isn't all black—just as it isn't all white," Rasheed observed. "I think I might be better off in a setting where I can deal with different kinds of people."

Rasheed wound up attending a school in the northeast, one that had a much larger percentage of minority students than the Big-Ten school he was considering. During his freshman year, Rasheed lived in an all-black dormitory. By the end of that year, he'd made a wide variety of friends, and felt comfortable moving into a racially mixed dorm. Rasheed is doing extremely well both socially and academically.

Look for colleges with formal mentoring programs: Research shows that a student's ability or inability to succeed in college is often determined during the first six weeks of the freshman year. Some colleges have sought to increase the odds of success by assigning formal mentors who begin working with new students as soon as they enter the institution. These programs can be especially helpful to African American males, who are at far greater risk of dropping out than their female counterparts. Consider the following statistics:

- Since the 1970s, the number of black women receiving baccalaureate degrees has increased 55 percent, versus just a 20 percent increase for black men.

- In first professional degrees, black women have had a 21 percent increase versus 5 percent for black men.

- In master's degrees, black women have had a 5 percent increase versus a 10 percent decrease for black men.[12]

As is true in many other areas, concerns about the retention of African American young men in colleges are greater than with their female counterparts. For parents with sons about to enter college, a formal mentoring program can be a big plus.

Ideally, these mentors should be compatible with regard to race and gender to the students who are assigned to them. This is often hard to arrange at primarily white institutions. Still, the individual attention one-to-one mentoring provides has proven to be useful, even if the mentor is of a different race or gender. Also, colleges and universities that institute these mentoring programs demonstrate an interest in attracting and re-taining more minority students.

Deciding If a Historically Black College (HBCU) Is Best for Your Son or Daughter

The answer to this question depends on a combination of factors, in-cluding your child's background, educational history, and personal pref-erence. Lawrence Otis Graham, an attorney who has written a number of books on race-related topics, recalls the deliberation he went through before he chose to attend Princeton University.

Graham was aware of this Ivy League school's checkered racial past—and that the police in the town of Princeton had a reputation for racial profiling. Although he could have gotten into any number of highly rated colleges, Graham explained his choice of Princeton as follows:

> I had no hard proof to substantiate Princeton's rumored history [of racial bias] when I decided to attend. . . . I only knew I wanted the best. I wanted the stereotypical pastoral setting. And I wanted a place that his-tory had recognized: I thought that the college of [Woodrow] Wilson, [F. Scott] Fitzgerald, Adlai Stevenson, and Bill Bradley was it.
>
> I had my reasons for not applying to one of the many top black colleges, including the fact that they were not listed in the "Most Competitive" cat-egory in the *Barron's Guide to America's Colleges,* and because my need for white approval at that time was extremely important. The only people I so-cialized with in my high school were white honors and advanced place-ment students. Beside myself, there was only one other black guy in the group. My black friends outside of high school were also honors and AP students. We were all terribly ambitious and all planned to attend a school in the [Ivy] League. . . . My parents knew not to suggest a black college to me. They knew that at age seventeen I cared about doing only those things that that were considered to be "the best" in the broadest sense.[13]

There is a temptation for the reader to substitute the word *whitest* for the author's *broadest* sense. Nevertheless, Graham doesn't seem to regret choosing Princeton, even if he didn't have a particularly comfortable social and emotional experience there. It remains unclear if Mr. Graham would counsel his own children to follow his lead.

At the end of the day, the key to choosing a college comes down to determining the best fit between student and institution. We know many African American professionals who've gone to historically black colleges; As parents, they will often do everything in their power to discourage their children (especially their sons) from going to primarily white schools. To parents with this mindset, the choice between Harvard and Howard is a no-brainer.

Neither of us attended historically black colleges. Still, we're well aware of the advantages these institutions offer. In many cases, being in an all-black environment strengthens a young person's cultural pride. Students who attend schools like Spelman, Morehouse, and Howard draw strength from their involvement in black fraternities and sororities, and from their contact with black faculty and administrators. In a sense, the kind of group involvement students experience at historically black colleges is comparable to the benefits of belonging to a black church. It's hard to put a value on that kind of bonding and sharing of common experiences, but it can never be minimized.

On the other hand, most people have to function in a world of diversity. Some would argue that a racially mixed (or even mostly white) college renders students better prepared to face that reality. Whatever choice students ultimately make, the key to their success depends more on what they do with their education than where they obtained it.

Reminder: Success as a freshman opens many doors.

Once students get through their freshman year, they can think about whether they want to remain in their original school or apply for a transfer elsewhere. We know students who start out in historically black universities and choose to transfer to racially mixed schools after their initial year. We also know students who leave mostly white colleges, transfer to all-black schools, and successfully complete their degrees. Again, there is no one surefire formula for college success. However, by taking a thoughtful and disciplined approach to college planning, you can greatly improve the odds that your son or daughter will succeed.

Summary

Seven Ways to Help Young African Americans Succeed in College

1. Recognize the many reasons why a higher education improves a young person's prospects.

2. Instill in your child the desire to go to college.

3. Begin saving for college as early as possible.

4. Get your son or daughter involved in every aspect of college planning.

5. Explore a wide variety of financial aid opportunities.

6. Help your son or daughter select the most suitable college environment.

7. Prepare your high school student for the social and academic pressures of college.

7

❧

Practical Discipline:
Money and Careers

You will need to be the best you can be in whatever career you pursue. The only thing worse than the denial of opportunity for African Americans by white-controlled institutions is the denial of opportunity for Black people by African Americans who are poorly prepared, undisciplined, and unwilling to perform at the highest level possible, providing role models of Black excellence.

—JAMES P. COMER, M.D.[11]

In This Chapter:

- Helping children develop financial discipline
- Demonstraing a goal-oriented approach to the future
- Creating a vital connection between work and money
- Helping children develop career-success skills
- Negotiating interracial encounters in the workplace

THE EARLIER YOU START TEACHING children about money, the better off they will be. Even before they start school, youngsters can be given opportunities to begin earning money, and to make choices about spending and saving. Children develop financial discipline progressively as they get older and increase their understanding of the relationship between work and money.

In this chapter, we help parents explain the connection between work and money to their children. We describe a number of practical steps to help parents instill in their children an understanding of that critical relationship. We discuss the difference between jobs and careers, and show parents how to help children recognize the importance of finding work they feel good about and that provides a comfortable lifestyle.

Parents must assume the primary responsibility for teaching financial discipline and career skills. It's unrealistic, for example, to expect schools to play more than a supplementary role when it comes to getting students to appreciate the value of a dollar. Studies show that high school students know less about financial topics than their counterparts did a generation ago. In addition, parents must often counter the destructive messages about money that young people get from the media and on the street.

Mothers and fathers need to teach children to recognize the impact of making positive financial and career choices while helping them develop a positive attitude toward work. This is especially important for African American parents, who must prepare their children for the very real possibility of encountering racial discrimination both as consumers and in the workplace.

Truths and Myths About African Americans and Money

Teaching children financial responsibility is clearly not an issue that's important only to a particular group. Still, until recently, there has been less than a major concerted effort to teach black families the techniques of productive money management. As Kelvin Boston, author of *Smart Money Moves for African Americans,* observes:

> Black families shy away from money discussions, even though ignorance of money-management techniques may have contributed to a cycle of debt they battle today. One of the biggest problems we've had in dealing with finances is that [our people] don't teach children about money.
>
> [Many African American] parents didn't talk about it at the table, so children have wrong ideas about how we live. A lot of youngsters, for example, might go into a house thinking God turned on the lights and pays for the heat and TV. The sooner we get around to talking about finances, the sooner they will understand it's not just important to have access to money but to manage it wisely.[2]

African Americans have been hampered by a number of negative stereotypes about their work ethic and their handling of money. The portrait has been one of a lazy people who spend far above their means. This attribute is symbolized by what is sometimes called the "red Cadillac" syndrome. In this piece of prejudicial profiling that goes back to the 1940s and 1950s, the stereotype is that of a poor, urban black man driving around in a big red Cadillac that he's purchased "on time," and with no concern about how he's going to pay for it.

This stereotype conveniently ignores the millions of African Americans in all generations who've worked hard, sacrificed, and stretched limited financial resources to achieve better lives for themselves and their children.

Today Americans of all colors suffer from staggering credit card debt—the result of people spending far more money than they earn. It would not be going too far to say that the sports utility vehicle (SUV) syndrome has become to contemporary white suburbia what the red Cadillac once was to the black urban ghetto. This out-of-control consumerism is fueled by an advertising industry that's well aware that many of today's kids see almost five hundred television ads in the course of an average week.

African Americans continue to suffer financial penalties based strictly on race. They are routinely charged more for automobiles, bank loans, and home mortgages. At the same time, black workers are usually paid less than their white counterparts for similar jobs. There's no question that the economic picture has gotten substantially brighter for African Americans in recent years. But, unfortunately, blacks still aren't doing as well as whites. Consider the following numbers, which were cited in a *Newsweek* cover story about the social and economic standing of African Americans.

- The incomes of African Americans are at a record high level, but they continue to lag far behind white income. One set of statistics showed the average income for a family of four at around $35,000 compared to an average income of around $56,000 for a white family of comparable size.

- Unemployment is lower than it has been since the mid-1970s. Still, more than twice as many black workers (around 9 percent) are unemployed compared to white workers (around 4 percent). The differences are even more lopsided among workers ages 20 to 24 (16.8 percent for blacks versus 6.5 percent for whites).

- Only 40 percent of black males between the ages of 16 and 19 are in the labor force, compared to almost 60 percent of white males in that age group.[3]

The above statistics are from America's most recent stretch of virtual full employment and economic prosperity. Such imbalances tend to get worse in slow economic times. Downturns and upturns in the economy are cyclical. However, the need to instill financial discipline has special meaning for black parents who would do well to assume that the coming generation will continue to suffer similar economic disparity.

Teach Financial Responsibility at Any Age

There are some who believe that American society is intentionally trying to keep some minorities at an economic disadvantage. Regardless of whether or not you agree with this theory, there's no question that financial responsibility and smart career planning are key issues for African American families. Here are the tools to help young people achieve discipline in those areas.

SET A GOOD EXAMPLE.

Children can begin to grasp the concept of money as early as three years of age. By the time they enter school, girls and boys should have some sense of how money is generated and managed. Your children will be observing how you handle money. And, as is the case with many other issues, they will be influenced far more by what you do than by what you say.

If, for example, you tell your teen not to squander her money on things she really doesn't need while you blow your paycheck on frivolous items you can't really afford, your words are likely to fall on deaf ears. When children have the opportunity to observe parents handling money the right way, they are far more likely to follow suit.

GIVE AN ALLOWANCE.

One way or another, either you're going to wind up buying things for your kids or you're going to give them the money to buy those items. Common sense would dictate that giving children regular amounts of money each week is a more effective way of promoting financial discipline than handing out money as things come up.

There is no exact formula for determining the appropriate weekly allowance to give a child. Some experts believe in giving children a dollar per week for each year of their age. In determining how much of an allowance to give, take the following factors into consideration.

- Your family's financial situation
- The cost of living in your area
- What other girls and boys your child's age are receiving—assuming you consider that amount to be in line with the first two factors
- The child's age and ability to handle money

It's a good idea to make the amount of any allowance large enough for a kid to buy something tangible—be it a fast-food lunch or a small toy. That way, a young child begins to understand what the weekly sum he receives can buy.

Reminder: An allowance is a learning tool—not just dollars and cents.

Once you begin to give an allowance, it's best to continue doing so without interruption. This will help the child learn to balance the desire to buy and the need to save. The question of whether to pay children for chores around the house is open to debate. Our own view is that children ought to contribute to the running of the household, and that no compensation is necessary. Beyond that, there are any number of options.

One approach that works well is requiring certain chores and offering money if the child completes additional tasks. For example, ten-year-old Tempest is responsible for helping clean off the table at breakfast and dinner. However, for the past year her parents have been giving her an additional two dollars a week for making all the beds every day.

Recently, Tempest used the extra money she earned to buy a new bicycle. She takes far more pride in her new possession than the girl next door, whose new bike was a gift, not the product of work. Children who can buy the things they want with the money they've earned usually feel better about their possessions. Most important, they receive a valuable lesson in connecting work with money.

Encourage Saving.

By the time children are in grade school, they ought to be saving part of their allowance for goals you've discussed with them in advance. It's important to talk to children about the difference between long- and short-term goals. For example, a ten-year-old may be able to buy a CD after only a few weeks of saving. On the other hand, he may have to save for a year or more to buy a PlayStation that costs several hundred dollars.

Setting goals that have different time frames is a good way to help children develop discipline and patience—tools they will need to succeed at virtually anything they try.

There's nothing wrong with saving money in an old-fashioned piggy bank. However, a savings account at a local bank is usually a better idea. Many savings banks allow children of any age to open accounts with no minimum deposit. Children can make deposits on their own—either in person or by mail. However, the presence or signature of a parent is usually required to withdraw money.

Although the interest on savings accounts tends to be quite low, children have a chance to calculate and watch interest build up in their accounts. If you can afford to do so, think about matching every dollar a child places into a savings account. This provides an incentive for younger children.

HELP CHILDREN DEVELOP A PRACTICAL APPRECIATION OF MONEY.

The more you can relate money to tangible things in children's lives, the better they will be able to process the information. For example, saying that a particular toy is too expensive may not have a lot of meaning to a seven-year-old. But when you say something like "This video game costs as much as a week's worth of groceries," you're communicating in terms children are more likely to understand.

Once children reach their teens, consider showing them some of your bills and explaining some of the factors that make these expenses go up or down from month to month. Young people are always at an advantage when parents teach them to value self-discipline and hard work. That's why it's better not to buy everything children ask for—even if you can afford it.

When your fourteen-year-old son comes home and insists that he must have that $200 pair of running shoes, or your sixteen-year-old daughter demands that you buy her a $400 outfit she saw on her favorite actress, you are under no obligation to say yes. For families of more modest means, such requests may be out of the question. But even if you're fabulously wealthy, it's never advisable to let children have everything they ask for.

The vast majority of mothers and fathers are not in a financial position to indulge a child's every whim. Even if you eventually reach that point, your children will need to work in order to have full and useful lives, if not to survive. Consequently, financial discipline and career skills are a necessity, not an option.

Helping Children Understand Money

The following are tips for teaching financial responsibility to children at different stages of development:

- **Children under age 5:** Explain what money is and where it comes from. Show them how to identify the various bills and coins. Explain the concept of trading money for things. Ask your child to guess which items at the supermarket cost more or less.

- **Children ages 6 to 8:** Structure activities that focus on money skills. For example, help them set up a monthly savings goal. Work with them on managing their allowance. Help them to open a savings account and encourage them to make regular deposits. Exchange different amounts of money, and ask them to make the correct amount of change. When at the store, discuss which items are better buys. Ask the child to estimate the total of your purchases.

- **Children ages 9 to 12:** If the child doesn't have a savings account, have him or her open one as soon as possible. Get children involved in understanding and paying the family's bills. Show them how to write checks and make out deposit slips. At this stage, youngsters are better able to identify long-term goals and begin saving for them. Discuss the amount of their allowance, and possible ways to supplement those monies.

- **Teenagers:** Teach them about compound interest and basic investment possibilities. Involve them in making financial choices. For example, ask your teen to do the research for major family purchases and help you choose which product to buy. Give them full or partial responsibility for grocery shopping. Have them set up a spending plan to help them reach their goals.

- **College students:** The summer before college and every summer thereafter, require your son or daughter to work in order to contribute to some aspect of the educational costs. If you get them *a credit card primarily for emergency use, take time to explain the benefits and dangers of this financial instrument. Make sure you set a spending limit you can live with. Help the child understand that credit is not a gift, but a loan that has to be repaid— sometimes at a high rate of interest. Make it clear that you will withdraw this privilege if it is abused.*

Reminder: Children tend to imitate their parents.

Talking to children about financial responsibility can make a difference—especially if you practice what you preach. Girls and boys who are most likely to acquire financial discipline are those who observe their parents handling money responsibly. Parents who pay their bills on time, stay out of debt, don't use credit cards irresponsibly, and regularly save a portion of their income are likely to see their sons and daughters mirror those good habits.

Explain Jobs and Careers

By introducing the concept of careers early, children begin to grasp the idea that people must work to earn a living—and that someday they will too. As the child grows, it will become clearer that the various careers tend to produce different lifestyles.[4]

By seven or eight, most children are starting to become aware of status. For example, Denise was in the third grade when she asked her mom the following question: "How come we live in a big house with a pool, while cousin Michael lives in a small apartment?"

Denise's mom wanted to help her daughter understand the connection between the kinds of work people do and how they live. "Your dad and I are both attorneys," she explained, "while Michael's mother is a single mom who supports her family by working as a teacher's aide. Lawyers make more money than teacher's aides because that profession requires a lot more education; plus, there are two of us working."

This mother wanted her daughter to understand that you don't define people solely on the basis of what they do and how much they earn. Denise's mom had affluent acquaintances who told their children that people who make more money are better than those who earn less. Some had even told their sons and daughters not to associate with people they deemed unworthy because of a lower socioeconomic status.

Denise's mom believed this to be an unfortunate and destructive point of view, especially in the African American community. That's why she added the following words to her explanation:

"Michael and his mom may live in a small apartment, but they are just as good as people who live in the biggest mansions. Michael's mother is a smart and caring person. She's a hard-working woman who is going to college at night for her teacher's license so that she can make a more comfortable life for herself and her son. It's important to have a good career so that you can have a comfortable lifestyle. But don't ever measure a person's worth by how much money they have or the size of their house."

This is the kind of balanced message we encourage parents to impart. What people do for a living and how much money they earn are important only when framed within a more complete system of values. At the end of the day, it's what you do with your money that matters—not only in terms of how comfortably you live, but also in terms of how much you contribute to the lives of others in the community who are less fortunate.

EXPLAINING THE DIFFERENCE BETWEEN JOBS AND CAREERS

In general, a job is labor for which people receive a set dollar amount in exchange for hours worked. Careers are work to which people usually have a greater commitment. Many careers require a higher education and/or extensive training.

It's important to explain that the jobs school-aged kids do—be it mowing lawns, delivering papers, or flipping burgers—help them develop fundamental workplace skills and prepare them for their future careers.

Reminder: Career education is an ongoing process.

As children continue to develop a sense of what different careers entail, they begin trying them on for size. One way they do this is by announcing their intentions to family and friends.

One evening, seven-year-old Arif told his dad he wanted to be a baseball player. Two days later he announced he was planning to work at Burger King when he grew up. It turned out that Arif had been watching the World Series, and he became excited about watching the players hit home runs. When Arif's dad asked why he wanted to work at Burger King, the boy started talking about how great it would be to eat those delicious fries whenever he wanted.

It's best not to be judgmental—especially with very young children. Instead, ask questions about why the child is interested in a particular career, and listen carefully to how he answers. It is rare for a child to pick a career at a young age and stick with that choice. Most youngsters will change their minds countless times as they grow and develop new interests. Still, youngsters should always be encouraged to express interest in careers—even if some of their early choices sound totally unrealistic.

When youngsters talk with excitement about a particular career or profession, parents should respond positively to this interest in the future—and be ready for more career pronouncements in the years to come.

In rare cases, young children focus on an area of interest early in life and carry it through to a career. But in general, such excitement is sparked by the newsworthy accomplishments of well-known personalities and celebrities. In other instances, a young child is responding to the heavy-handed influence of parents who've determined that he or she is going to be a professional athlete, a performer, or a surgeon—sometimes before the child is even born.

Such aspirations on the part of children may represent the ambitions of parents who want to live through their children, or who fantasize their sons or daughters will become so rich and famous that they themselves will never have to work again. Too often, a child's interests and potential aren't even considered.

Occasionally children demonstrate extraordinary talent at an early age, and their careers take off from there. However, the vast majority of children don't choose their field of interest while in grade school or even in high school. Still, most children are aware of the world of work on some level—even if many of their ideas are unrealistic.

Reminder: Don't be seduced by the lure of celebrity.

It's especially important that African American parents help children find career role models that are both positive and realistic. Unfortunately, most of the black people in the media are either criminals being dragged off by the police or superstars in sports and entertainment. We meet many African Americans in their thirties and forties who've never previously seen a black doctor. So, it's not hard to understand why minority parents often point to celebrity superstars as symbols of success, while paying little or no attention to more positive role models in less glamorous fields. We strongly advise you not to take this approach.

No matter how great an athlete or singer your child may be, the chances of him or her becoming the next Michael Jordan or Whitney Houston are next to zero. This doesn't mean that you should discourage children who show talent in these so-called glamour fields. However, in such cases, it's essential that the motivation to pursue that goal come from the child, and not an overzealous parent.

All children of color should be encouraged to meet and emulate African Americans who are successful in areas like medicine, law, business, and education. These are careers that hold out both the promise of a comfortable lifestyle as well as a realistic chance for success. They are also areas that offer young people the opportunity to make a difference in the community.

A parent's job is to encourage children to become informed and to develop the career skills they need to become successful. The key is stimulating children's curiosity about careers and encouraging them to start thinking about and exploring the kind of work they might enjoy. The following steps can help you give your child a well-rounded understanding of what careers involve.

SHOW A POSITIVE ATTITUDE TOWARD YOUR OWN WORK.

It's often a good idea for parents to take children to the workplace. If, however, you're going through a particularly stressful time on the job or truly dislike your work, you may want to consider having the child accompany a relative who can create a more positive experience. But remember, a humble job is nothing to be ashamed of; doing something well always imparts a valuable lesson. It can also be instructive to let a child understand what you do relative to other career options.

Tom, who is about to graduate from medical school, recalls going to work with his father when he was eight. "My dad was a longshoreman. It was very hard physical work, and it caused him many health problems. I recall the first time my father took me to the docks, and I watched him lifting those heavy crates. He kept talking about wanting something better for my younger sister and me. My father wasn't ashamed of what he did for a living, but he wanted his children to get a good education so they could have it easier. Whenever I was tempted to screw up in school, I always thought about the strain on my dad's face as he lifted those crates. I definitely wanted an easier life for myself. I've always been proud of my dad, and wanted to make the most of the opportunity all his hard work made possible."

DON'T PRESSURE CHILDREN TO CONFORM TO YOUR CAREER EXPECTATIONS.

It's important not to limit your child's view of the workplace to your particular situation or field of interest. You may be highly successful in a particular career and want your child to follow in your footsteps. Such aspirations can backfire, especially when children don't have the same skills and capacities as their parents.

Arthur is a successful accountant who always envisioned his son Jim taking over his thriving business. Arthur started taking Jim to his office when he was very young and giving him little jobs to do. Jim enjoyed helping his dad, but he wasn't good with numbers. By the time he was ten or eleven, Jim knew that an accountant was the last thing he wanted to be.

Jim was fourteen when he came to see us. He was an average student who came right out and said he had no intention of going to college. He was, however, an extremely mechanical person who could fix anything. Unfortunately, his father put no value on those skills.

"What would you like to do for a living?" we asked Jim.

He answered, "I don't know; maybe repair cars or even airplanes."

"No way!" his father said, in a firm tone of voice. "I will not have my son working at some dirty, greasy garage."

We explained to this father that trying to put square pegs into round holes is an exercise in futility. Pressing children too hard to go in directions they hate invites rebellion and family strife.

We advised Tom to encourage Jim to discuss and pursue his own dreams. It was tough at first, but after a few months the young man's grades began to improve.

Jim is now seventeen and entering a local community college, though he's not considering accounting as a career option. Tom still feels disappointed. However, he now understands that if he kept rejecting his son's career goals, he would be setting the stage for bigger problems down the road. And who knows? Maybe Jim's interest in cars and planes will expand to an interest in becoming an automotive or aeronautical engineer, careers that require a four-year college education.

Help Children Develop Critical Career Skills

As children develop, it's important to expose them to a variety of workplace settings to help them expand their vision of future career options. It has been well documented that today's high school graduates will potentially have three to five different careers during their working years. So it doesn't make a lot of sense to get bent out of shape if your kid starts talking about a career goal that makes you uncomfortable. What matters most is that a young person is giving serious thought to career options and developing the skills that underlie success.

Many of today's most successful men and women had summer jobs throughout their teenage years—including internships and other career-related work experiences in their field of interest. Some had year-round paper routes while still in elementary school. A large percentage had a strong sense of where they wanted to go prior to graduating from college and rose to the top in a relatively short time.

The vast majority of African American success stories are not set in family backgrounds of great wealth, nor are they about those who've been handed an important position in a lucrative family business. Most successful black men and women got where they are through hard work and discipline.

Successful people usually share a number of common attributes—all of which can be taught. Despite the fierce competition that exists in most

fields and the additional obstacles black people must face, there are opportunities for those who know how and where to find them.

Success in life is primarily a product of skill—not luck. It's up to you
to begin teaching the following skills early, so that your child has the
foundation and discipline to become a success.[5]

SELF-PRESENTATION

The way one presents oneself to others is a key factor in every aspect of
life. When you present yourself, you have a very short time to make the
right impression—and the right impression depends on your goal in the
particular situation.

In Chapter Three, we talked about the importance of staying focused
on your goal and not getting sidetracked. We used an example of a recent
high school graduate who was being pressured by friends to wear an earring and baggy pants to a job interview. The young man's friends told him
that, by dressing in a suit and tie, he would be selling out both himself
and his race.

Young people are often concerned about "selling out." We try to show
them that the real power rests with the person who knows what he wants
and is smart enough to take control of the situation.

The purpose of a job interview is to get what you want, we tell people
like our high school senior. For that to happen, you have to make the interviewer like you. The way to do that is to give him what he wants—
which is a picture of an employee who'll be cooperative and who
understands the rules and conventions of business without being told.
This is a self-presentation choice that's likely to wind up with you getting
what you want—the job. Creating the appropriate presentation puts you
in charge of the situation.

Conformity issues can become more complex when young people are
asked to subdue their black identity to deal more effectively with white
customers. Consider the case of Jack Hardy, a forty-year-old African
American sales manager who earns a six-figure income selling pharmaceuticals and medical products.

When we asked Jack how he counsels young African Americans who
are thinking about pursuing sales careers, he gave the following answer:

> Some have accused me of being a race traitor, but I really believe that a
> salesman's name is very important. I tell young black men that if I had

an Afrocentric name like Rahim or Atiba, I would either use an initial or change it in order to conceal that fact.

Young men sometimes resent this kind of advice. They accuse me of asking them to sell out or hide their "real selves" by acting and speaking white. I tell them that a salesperson needs to get his foot in the door, and that people are often looking for a reason to deny you entrance—especially if you're black.

If a potential client is white, you'd best assume that race is likely to be used as a conscious or unconscious excuse for that person to say no instead of yes. By presenting yourself in a way that emphasizes a black image, many white customers are going to feel uncomfortable, and give their business to someone else.

We're not telling you to encourage your children to hide their African American identity. However, it is important to make them aware of some of the complex self-presentation issues African Americans confront in the workplace.

Self-presentation is a multilayered skill that goes well beyond the basics of dress or the name you use. There are specific abilities, like talking on the phone and writing letters, that can be developed through practice. But less tangible qualities like enthusiasm, versatility, and sensitivity come from dealing with people in a variety of real-life situations. Here are some tips parents can use to help young people develop outstanding self-presentation skills.

Encourage children to become involved in as many activities as possible. This is the best way to develop the skills and the personal courage that are so important throughout life. There are always opportunities for young people to get involved in areas in which they have an interest. And if opportunities do not present themselves, help your child understand that it is his or her responsibility to seek them out.

Talk to your children about getting involved in school and community activities. High school students should be encouraged to get an after-school job in a business, industry, or professional area of interest. If your teenage son expresses an interest in journalism, for example, suggest that he write a column for the school newspaper, or offer to do a free piece for a small local paper.

Encourage resourcefulness. There are usually multiple ways to accomplish a goal. If, for example, your aspiring journalist can't interest the local newspaper, maybe he can start a self-produced online newsletter. This kind of step takes energy and courage. But the only way young people learn to do is by doing for themselves.

POSITIONING

There are a lot of familiar sayings that stress the importance of good timing, including: "I'd rather be lucky than good," and "He was at the right place at the right time." There's no doubt that luck is important, and timing is a big part of being lucky. The old bromides about good timing imply that people have little or no control over their own luck. However, a careful look at successful people shows that there are many things that can be done to help luck along.

As career coach and author Adele Scheele observes: "For the most part, people who find themselves in the right place at the right time also had experiences being at the right place at the wrong time, at the wrong place at the right time, and at the wrong place at the wrong time. They learned how to get ahead from being in different situations. It's not only that they hang in and try again. Somehow, successful people learn how to try again in different ways."[6]

Reminder: Career success is a process, not a one-shot deal.

Nobody has ever devised an exact formula for achieving success. Still, you can greatly increase a child's chances by encouraging him or her to pursue a wide variety of experiences and to continue to learn from each one.

CONNECTING

Have you ever heard the phrase *It's not what you know but whom you know?* There's no question that people often get jobs through their families and friends. Since the majority of powerful people in this country are white, African Americans often find themselves at a disadvantage. Part of the resilience you must pass on to your children involves coming to terms with the fact that life often is not fair.

The odds are great that your son or daughter is going to need contacts to get ahead in this world. This does not mean that your family has to be rich or influential. By encouraging children to do the following, you can help them hone their contacting skills.

Encourage young people to make contact with those they wish to emulate. If, for example, children express interest in a particular field or profession, urge them to find a mentor. Talk to the child about the need to keep trying, and not to take rejection personally. If your child approaches a few people and they reject him, discuss how he might alter his strategy.

Teens need to be reminded that successful people are likely to be very busy. So teens are going to have to pursue the relationship. If a young person is having no luck approaching people who are too well known, suggest trying someone with a lower profile who may not receive so many requests. There are many prominent women and men who enjoy mentoring up-and-coming youth, but it's the responsibility of the young person to keep up the pursuit and to maintain a positive attitude.

People sometimes don't pursue contacts because they are shy or are afraid that people will feel used. But connecting with others involves using people in the best sense of the phrase. Teens should be reminded that the same person who helps them with their career today might look upon them as a valued contact ten years from now. Indeed, we have been around long enough to see this come to pass with some of our former students and mentees who now occupy prominent positions.

Encourage children to practice and refine their connecting skills. The best way to accomplish this is by speaking to people in a variety of situations. One technique is to interview people in whom you have an interest. If your child expresses admiration for a prominent person in a particular field, suggest that she try to interview that person for the school paper—or for a term paper. Some people may say no, but others will be glad to find time for such interviews.

Another technique high school and college students can use is joining the programming committee and organizing an assembly. If, for example, a young person is interested in a particular career, perhaps she can put a panel together of interesting people in that field. The next step in the connecting process is to follow up by selecting the person on that panel who is of most interest, and continuing to stay in contact with that individual.

Reminder: Many prominent African Americans enjoy helping young brothers and sisters.

This may be less true in glamour fields like entertainment or sports, where stars are barraged with requests for interviews or appearances. In less visible professions, however, highly regarded African Americans often feel honored to help those who share their professional interests and cultural heritage.

FIVE CONTACT TIPS PARENTS CAN IMPART

- *People you meet by chance can sometimes turn out to be valuable contacts—so get out there and talk to a lot of people.*

- *Once you establish a contact, keep in touch with that person. Let him know how you are progressing by writing, e-mailing, or calling from time to time.*

- *If one of your contacts helps you, do something to show your appreciation. Send a thoughtful gift or a thank-you note.*

- *Keep a file of all your contacts so that you can refer back to them months or even years later.*

- *Don't be afraid to reach out to those people who are in a position to help you. Remember, they probably needed the help of others to get where they are today.*

RACIAL INTELLIGENCE

The ability to deal with an increasingly racially diverse workplace has become an essential skill in today's world. Ten years ago, corporate America was predominantly white and male. It still is today, but there's one major difference—companies are being forced to diversify.

The U.S. Department of Labor projects that, by the year 2010, only 20 percent of new entrants to the workforce will be white American males. The remaining 80 percent will be people of color, women, and immigrants. There are other good reasons for companies to promote racial and gender diversity. These include:

- More cooperative and productive work environments that make innovation more likely
- Increased opportunity to take advantage of the largest talent pool
- Greater potential to broaden the customer base
- Good public perception that can enhance the bottom line.[7]

Despite this apparent need for increased diversity, African Americans still have a tough row to hoe. Harvard Business School professor Rosabeth Moss Kantor has observed that, in most American companies, nonwhites "have to do twice as much to get half as far" as their white counterparts. Even though many companies are hiring more people of color, that hasn't translated into anything like a proportionate increase in the professions and upper management.

Since most of the power in American companies and other institutions continues to be held by white males, the ongoing racial disparity comes as no great shock. People tend to be most comfortable with others like themselves, which is why a white business leader might be inclined to share power with, as Professor Kantor puts it, "someone he can relate to. Someone who reminds him of himself. Someone who looks just like him."

Without the opportunity to attain real power, which Professor Kantor defines as the ability to "participate in decisions, to gain access to resources, information and political support that ensure that their voices are heard and that they can get things done . . . even the most talented people can find themselves stuck in dead-end jobs."[8]

To achieve a high level of career success, African Americans must know how to negotiate a world in which most of the power positions are held by whites—many of whom are either biased or resistant to sharing that power with racial minorities.

Most successful African Americans know how to manipulate the system in ways that give them a competitive edge. They've learned how to take the initiative, stay focused on their long-term goals, and not to expect anything good to come without a great deal of effort.

To help children develop these attributes, parents need to teach racial intelligence, as well as racial discipline. Essentially, racial intelligence is a proven way to negotiate interracial situations or diversity encounters that increases your chances of achieving your goals. Racially intelligent people use the following workplace strategies.

1. Recognize your own emotions and how they can affect you in diversity encounters. Separate feelings from actions. Don't let anger and other potentially destructive feelings control what you say and do.

2. Take responsibility for your own racially intelligent behavior. If the opportunity presents itself, encourage the people you work with to do the same.

3. Don't expect your company or employer to implement racially equitable or fair policies.

4. Always try to cooperate with those with whom you work—regardless of their racial or ethnic background.

5. Concentrate on your own career goals. Don't get sidetracked by office politics or other people's negative agendas.

6. Avoid coworkers who are biased or racially ignorant. People with these traits often seek out allies, or audiences receptive to their prejudiced remarks. If the racially ignorant person is someone you like, remind him that people may have the right to say and do what they want in their homes. However, that right does not extend to the workplace.

7. Assume goodwill whenever possible. Instead of viewing someone from another racial group as a potential threat, use the differences between you to develop new problem-solving approaches and to generate new opportunities.

8. Embrace change. People often stick with what's familiar—even when those strategies no longer work. Your ability to use change as a positive force is a key factor in your ability to reach your long-term career goals.

9. Know your ability to tolerate bias and racial insensitivity. There are

different ways of being racially intelligent. For example, if you find yourself in a discriminatory work environment, it's up to you to decide if you're better off going elsewhere or taking some kind of action in your current workplace.

10. Take every opportunity to use race to your benefit. If you have a chance to advance, always take advantage of it. Don't sweat it if your race played a role in that opportunity. Considering how often race is used against African Americans, it makes little sense to not use it when it furthers your goals. If others feel that you were advanced at their expense, that's their problem. The best way to fight that kind of criticism is by doing an outstanding job.[9]

Reminder: Mistakes are life's most valuable learning tools.

Nobody is born with racial intelligence—or any of the other critical career skills we've discussed. The only way to acquire them is to assess what works and what doesn't work, and go from there. There are bound to be times when you make a wrong call or fall on your face. Mistakes are both unavoidable parts of life and our most valuable learning experiences.

Parents need to help children understand that mistakes are not a cause for shame; nor do they label a person a failure. On balance, people generally learn more from their mistakes than they do from their successes. There are never any surefire ways to know if what you're doing is going to work out. However, the surest road to success is to keep trying and continue learning from your mistakes.

Parents who can help children develop the strength to keep moving forward under challenging circumstances while learning from their mistakes are sharing a gift that will serve a young person well—both in and out of the workplace.

Summary

Seven Ways to Promote Financial and Career Discipline

1. Begin teaching financial responsibility early.

2. Help your son or daughter appreciate the value of a dollar.

3. Explain the relationship between what people do, and how they live.

4. Emphasize the value of hard work and self-discipline.

5. Provide positive and appropriate career role models.

6. Help young people choose a career that best suits them—even if it's not your choice.

7. Help your child develop the skills he or she needs to succeed.

8

Mind-Body Discipline: The Search for Balance

I feel I am the luckiest child in the world to have had a mother and father who taught their children that being honest was more important than being honored, and that faith was a safer and more enduring harbor than fame.

—MARIAN WRIGHT EDELMAN
founder, Children's Defense Fund[1]

In This Chapter:

◆ Understanding what goes into making a child healthy and strong

◆ Recognizing the stages of adolescent development

◆ Creating balance in the three components of good health

◆ Helping children achieve physical discipline

◆ Finding the best health care

◆ Guiding children toward mental discipline

◆ Helping children develop a strong spiritual sense

WE HAVE SEEN thousands of girls and boys during our years as practicing pediatricians, and one thing remains clear: Strong, healthy children and adolescents don't get that way by accident. Many factors, including genetics (and even luck) can influence a child's health. Nonetheless, there is no more important factor than the environment in which a child grows up—and that's largely a product of parenting.

As we see it, the job of a pediatrician or family physician is to support parents in raising strong and healthy children. Many physicians concentrate their efforts almost exclusively on physical health, in part because that's how they're trained in medical school. We believe this is far too narrow a focus—particularly when dealing with black families.

In several critical areas of health, African Americans are at greater risk and suffer worse health outcomes than many other groups—in part because of racial bias in the health-care system. Obviously, parents and physicians can't afford to neglect physical health concerns; but the only meaningful way to get an accurate read on a child's overall strength and health is to look at a combination of physical, mental, and spiritual factors. This kind of multidimensional whole-person perspective provides a window into the way your child balances these key health factors and lets you pinpoint areas that need strengthening.

A useful way to look at an individual's physical, mental, and spiritual selves with respect to the whole person is to visualize a wheel with spokes. Watch the way the wheel works. Is it wobbly, creaky? This indicates imbalance or weakness. When you watch a wheel turning effortlessly, you witness a thing of beauty—synchronized, smooth, and strong.

If something appears amiss with this wheel, start out by testing the strength of the individual spokes. The stronger the spokes, the more efficiently the wheel turns, and the more weight the wheel will bear—so long as there's balance. As you continue to help children strengthen each component—physical, mental, and spiritual—the positive carryover effect pervades every aspect of their lives.

In this chapter we explore three interrelated mind-body components. We first look at the various levels of adolescent physical development, then move to a discussion of how best to avoid physical risk factors. Next we show you how to help children achieve the mental and spiritual health that will help them attain the ideal of a strong mind and spirit within a healthy body.

THE MIND-BODY WHEEL

1. **Physical health:** *Taking proper care of a child's physical health and safety needs. Passing on positive health habits.*

2. **Mental health:** *Providing the mental tools black children need to negotiate effectively with others, and to achieve their intellectual and social goals.*

3. **Spiritual health:** *Fostering concern for others and connection to the community. Helping children develop character, values, and the ability to differentiate between right and wrong. Encouraging a relationship with a higher power or other nonmaterial forces.*

Understanding the Stages of Adolescent Psychosocial Development

Adolescence is divided into three progressive psychosocial stages: early adolescence, middle adolescence, and late adolescence. Each stage features its own particular markers in biological, mental, and spiritual spheres. Each stage also contains the platform for distinguishable zones of anticipated high-spirited growth as well areas in which caution on the part of both parents and teens is strongly advised. The following signposts characterize each of these stages.

EARLY ADOLESCENCE

The early adolescent (typical age range: 11 to 14 years) undergoes rapid body changes. Secondary sexual characteristics begin to appear, physical growth accelerates, and the young person's body becomes a major focus of everyday concerns.

At this stage, young people have difficulty projecting themselves into the future. This difficulty becomes a particular problem when parents ask children to modify their behaviors and to delay gratification—in order to avoid adverse health consequences down the road.

For example, a twelve-year-old may refuse to stop smoking cigarettes, even if his parents warn him that prolonged and habitual tobacco use is likely to lead to cardiovascular disease or lung cancer. Early adolescents are often too focused on their immediate needs to worry about these long-term risks. Boys and girls of this age may also be expected to test parental authority to see what they can get away with.

During early adolescence, teens begin to identify more strongly with their peer group. As part of their search for identity, teenage girls and boys seek out other young people whom they sense are similar to them (or who reflect the ways in which they would like to see themselves).

Teens often begin to experiment with sex during this stage, but sexual activity tends to be limited. Urban youths (especially males) who become sexually active during adolescence may have sexual intercourse during this stage, but even this group will usually not have sex on a regular basis until they reach the next developmental step.

Middle Adolescence

This middle stage of adolescence (typical age range: 15 to 17 years) is the developmental home of the majority of teenage problem behaviors. The transitions adolescents experience during this stage are so dramatic they seem to occur overnight. Secondary sexual characteristics become fully established, and the growth rate slows. Physically, these young people look more like the adults they will become and less like the children they were.

During this stage, adolescents attain a set of psychological supports that act as a kind of armor. There are three types of protective gear, to which we give the following designations:

- The helmet of omniscience—which makes teens act as if they are all-knowing
- The breastplate of omnipotence—which makes teens act as if they are all-powerful

- The shield of invincibility—which provides teens with the sense that they can defend against and defeat every foe

This armor of middle adolescence has its pros and cons. The armor provides the supportive structure, which allows young people to emancipate themselves and move outside of the family structure. At the same time, this armor can make it difficult for young people to recognize the consequences of engaging in dangerous and destructive risk-taking behaviors.

With this armor in place, teens can put themselves in harm's way, and convince themselves that they can't be adversely affected. It's not uncommon for teens at this stage to fool themselves into thinking that one or more of the following fallacies is true.

- I can pass a test without studying.

- I can drive a car even though I've never taken a driving lesson.

- I can steal a car and not get caught.

- I can put whatever I want into my body and suffer no consequences.

- I can have unprotected sexual intercourse and not get pregnant.

In some families, the struggle for emancipation is played out through major conflicts over parental control and authority. These battles often move outside the home environment—for instance, when teens begin to challenge other authority figures, such as teachers or police officers.

As adolescents participate in this process of separation from the family, they cleave more tightly to their peer group, which begins to define its own rules of behavior. Parents often cite an adolescent's peer group as the source of any and all problem behaviors, because of the pressure the group sometimes places on its members to conform to its code of behavior. However, young people don't select their peers by accident. To a great extent, these choices reflect the young person's own identity needs and parental influences. It's easy enough for a parent to say: "My son's not the problem, it's his friends," and thus get their child (and themselves) off the hook. In reality, each member of the group, including the teen in question, participates in defining its norms and behavioral code.

Sex is a major focus of the lives of middle adolescents. Both the young men and the young women suddenly seem to become sexual in all aspects of their being. From a parent's perspective (if not always the teen's), the health and social risks associated with unprotected sexual intercourse are major concerns throughout this stage.

LATE ADOLESCENCE

The late adolescent (typical age range: 18+ years) attains full physical maturity. At this stage, young people are highly evolved mentally, and are increasingly aware of their limitations and how the past will affect their future. These young women and men gradually make a major transition from the fantasies of middle adolescence to the realities of adulthood. They begin to realize that all things are not possible. More important, they become fully aware of their natural limitations, as well as the limitations that result from earlier mistakes made during middle adolescence.

The vast majority of late adolescents who come from families that instill strength and discipline negotiate this transition to adulthood successfully. However, those with unresolved emotional issues sometimes become despondent and incapacitated because they lack the strength to accept the loss of their dreams.

Late adolescents who successfully negotiate the previous stages move to a more adult-to-adult relationship with their parents; most late adolescents begin the process of establishing their independent lives. The peer group recedes as an important determinant of behavior, and sexuality becomes increasingly tied to commitment and planning for the future.

We have designed the following handy guide to help you recognize and monitor your child's physical growth and developmental progress through the stages of adolescence.

Parent Guide to Monitoring Adolescent Development

Puberty is the term commonly used to describe the physical growth and development that occurs during the teenage years. Puberty is an endocrinological process that begins in the center of the brain in an area known as the hypothalamus. This process initiates physical changes that lead to the production of testosterone (the male sexual-maturation hormone), and estrogen and progesterone (the female sexual-maturation hormones). These hormones combine with other glandular hormones to produce the growth and sexual development of the adolescent.

FEMALE PUBERTY

The first visible sign of female puberty (average age range: 9 to 13 years) is the appearance of breast buds under the nipples on the chest; the growth of pubic hair follows shortly thereafter. Pubertal growth continues typically over a three- to four-year period and includes the following developmental changes:

- Increased body height (growth spurt)
- Increased body weight
- Change in the size and shape of the breasts
- Increased amount and distribution of pubic hair
- Menarche (the first menstrual period)
- Production and release of mature ova (eggs)

Female puberty ends with menarche (the first menstrual period), which usually occurs 2½ to 3 years. after the appearance of the breast bud. Although the exact timing is variable, most girls experience menarche between ages 11 and 12½ years.

MALE PUBERTY

Puberty in the adolescent male (average age range: 11 to 18 years) begins with the enlargement of the testicles. This event is caused by the growth of sperm-producing tubules inside the testicle. Pubertal growth continues typically over a three- to five-year period and includes the following developmental changes:

- Increase in body height (growth spurt)
- Increase in body weight
- Increased amount and distribution of pubic hair
- Increase in the size (width and length) of the penis
- Deepening of the voice

- Production of facial hair
- Increased production of spermatozoa (sperm)

There is no event in male adolescent development that is exactly equivalent to the female menarche—the first menstrual period. It has been suggested, however, that the first "wet dream" indicates a time at which the male is producing sperm at a rate and amount great enough to increase significantly the chance that ejaculation during sexual intercourse will cause pregnancy. This event, called *semenarche,* usually occurs at around age 13.

PHYSICAL GROWTH AND DEVELOPMENT

Most adolescents are intensely concerned with their physical growth and development, and are likely to compare their progress with that of their peers or siblings. This is a usually a frustrating process, because the timing of growth and development differs significantly between individuals of the same age.

The following table will help you assess your child's developmental progress. The table contains a description of the developmental events at each of the five sexual maturational stages, along with an associated normal age range for the occurrence of developmental events. Keep in mind that each child develops within a standard range, according to his or her own biological time clock

Parent Guide to Monitoring Adolescent Development

DEVELOPMENTAL STAGE	MALE	FEMALE
Stage 1	**Birth–10 years** • no pubic hair • small penis • small testicles	**Birth–8 years** • no pubic hair • no breasts
Stage 2	**Begins 10–13 years; ends 11–14 years** • testicles and scrotum enlarge • pubic hair growth at base of penis • slight elongation of penis	**Begins 8–13 years; ends 9–14 years** • breast bud under nipple • sparse pubic hair growth at border of labia majora
Stage 3	**Begins 11–14 years; ends 12–15 years** • continued enlargement of testicles • penis becomes longer • public hair darker and more curled	**Begins 9–14 years; ends 9½–14½ years** • moderate breast development • darker more curled pubic hair • most rapid growth in height is experienced in this stage
Stage 4	**Begins 12–15 years; 13–16 years** • testicles larger, scrotum darker • penis becomes wider and glans penis develops	**Begins 9½–14½ years; ends 11–16 years** • continued enlargement of breast with separation of its contour • pubic hair continues to increase in amount

• sparse adult distribution of pubic hair	• first menstrual period occurs at the end of this stage
• most rapid growth in height is experienced in this stage	

Stage 5	Begins 13–16 years; ends 14–18 years	Begins 11–16 years; ends 17–18 years
	• adult testis and scrotum	• fully developed adult breast
	• adult penis	• full adult distribution and amount of pubic hair
	• adult distribution of public hair	
	• increased muscle growth	
	• deepening of the voice	

Instilling Physical Discipline in Black Youth

In general, a physically healthy child is the product of parents who foster good health habits. For better or worse, the discipline you as a parent demonstrate in maintaining your own health is likely to be mirrored by your children. If you pursue positive health habits—such as maintaining a balanced diet, exercising regularly, and avoiding tobacco and alcohol—your children are likely to follow your lead. The same principle also applies to families in which parents don't demonstrate good health habits.

When, for example, children are obese, it's likely that they've been eating a diet high in fat and sugar for a good part of their lives. Those eating patterns don't happen by accident. Young children in particular will generally eat whatever food their parents prepare or bring into the house. Whether meals are prepared in the family kitchen, in a restaurant, or at a local fast-food joint, it's a good bet that parents whose kids are gorging on greasy burgers and fries aren't themselves dining on fruits, vegetables, and whole grains.

We strongly encourage you to demonstrate discipline with respect to nutrition, exercise, and consumption of tobacco and other unhealthy substances. It's important to take these positive steps—for your family's sake as well as your own well-being.

Kids may want to eat the fast food they see advertised while they're vegging out in front of the television. They may be tempted to smoke cigarettes because they think it looks cool. Your job is to provide the example and discipline that give young people the strength to forgo their immediate wants in favor of their long-term health. We realize this is not an easy task when you're dealing with young people who are too wrapped up in the moment to worry about the future. That's why it's imperative to set a positive example and to help your son or daughter understand the long-term benefits and health risks associated with the choices they make now.

DON'T LET YOUR CHILDREN GET TOO HEAVY.

Many of our young people are simply too fat, and the problem is getting worse. There are twice as many overweight children and adolescents in the United States than there were a generation ago. When kids become obese (20 percent over their ideal weight), they greatly increase their risk of developing hypertension (high blood pressure), stroke, heart disease, diabetes, and cancer as adults.

Caution: Most overweight teenagers become overweight adults.

Very few individuals have strokes and heart attacks during adolescence. However, once patterns of unhealthy eating and physical inactivity take hold, they can be difficult to change. The sooner young people develop the habits of eating right and exercising regularly, the healthier they're likely to be throughout their lives. It's important for all parents to help children develop healthy habits in terms of diet and exercise. But it's especially vital that African Americans make sure their sons and daughters develop discipline in these areas.

Heart disease, diabetes, high blood pressure, and kidney failure are all linked to obesity—and black Americans are prone to these degenerative diseases that lead to disability and early death. When you consider that 60 percent of black women and 40 percent of black men are obese by the time they reach middle age, you're looking at the most overweight ethnic group in America.

If you want to give children the gift of lifelong health, do what you can to prevent them from becoming overweight. If a child is already too heavy, start working to reverse that trend. The following steps will help you achieve that goal.

Recognize that too much weight is a problem. Some parents are under the misconception that childhood plumpness is a sign of good health—an indication the parents are doing the right thing. This is often a misguided notion, even during the earliest stages of their child's life. As youngsters develop, they are likely to find that being heavy is not viewed as positive by peers, who may call them names like fatso or tubby. You'd think that this kind of social pressure would motivate kids to lose weight, but that's not always the case.

Studies of college students show that only 36 percent of obese black males and 40 percent of obese black females perceive themselves as heavy. Many who admit they have a weight problem don't recognize the health risks those excess pounds pose.[2]

The first step in correcting any problem is to face the fact that it exists. If your child has a tendency to overeat and is not physically active, it's important to recognize that these are important factors and to start taking corrective action.

Your pediatrician or family physician can tell you if your child is overweight—and if there is an associated medical cause. Sometimes children visibly put on weight just prior to a growth spurt, so in these instances a modest temporary increase in body fat is usually no cause for alarm. However, if there's a significant or sudden increase in your child's weight or body fat, don't necessarily dismiss it as unimportant.

Note any changes in your child's eating or exercise patterns. Is he or she eating a lot more junk food or spending more hours in front of the television? In some cases, such behavioral changes can signal depression or other emotional predicaments. From a physical standpoint, however, changes in body weight can usually be traced to a combination of poor diet and lack of exercise.

Start making positive dietary changes now. The best way to help an overweight child (and to prevent children from gaining weight) is to get the whole family hooked on healthy eating—even those family members who don't have a weight problem. Instead of telling kids that they need to go on a diet, talk in terms of eating healthier as a family—and figuring out what that entails for each family member.

Get rid of all unhealthy junk foods, and replace them with foods that are both healthful and tasty. You'd be surprised at what a difference keeping unhealthy food out of the house can make. Kids tend to eat what's available, and that is something parents can control. Purge your house of junk food. At the very least, put them out of reach of children who need to lose weight.

Try substituting fresh fruits for candy and air-popped popcorn for nachos or potato chips. Prepare meals that are rich in whole grains and fresh vegetables, and low in fat—especially animal fat.

Find a healthy way of eating that suits your family. There are long-standing debates about what kind of food regimen is best. Some believe in a strict vegetarian diet, completely free of all animal-based products. Others favor a high-protein diet that includes fish, poultry, and low-fat dairy products. Most health experts agree that diets that are high in fat and refined sugar promote obesity and increase health risks. These are the foods you want to restrict in your family's diet—particularly if there are one or more overweight children in the house.

THREE BASIC RULES OF HEALTHY EATING

1. *Watch those fats. One of the first steps to a healthier diet is cutting down on fats—which can clog arteries and eventually cause heart disease. The most harmful are saturated fats, which are found in excessive proportions in red meats—particularly the kinds featured in fast-food places—in deep-fried foods like doughnuts and French fries, and in dairy products like cheese and whole milk. Still, a certain amount of fat is essential for a healthy diet. The best kinds of fat are found in foods like fish and olives—which have been shown to enhance coronary health. There is also evidence that low-fat, high-protein milk products, like yogurt and skimmed or 1 percent milk, also contribute to a healthy diet.*

   Substituting low-fat milk for whole milk products is a relatively painless way to cut calories while preserving taste. Using olive, canola, or peanut oil in frying or baking instead of butter, margarine, or lard can reduce saturated fat and cholesterol.

2. *Replace refined carbohydrates with whole grains. The process involved in turning whole-wheat flour into white flour and brown rice into white rice effectively removes most of the fiber and vi-*

tamins (as well as a good deal of the taste) from those foods. It's important to begin replacing refined grain products with their whole grain equivalents. Studies show that the fiber in whole grains can significantly reduce one's chances of developing heart disease and some cancers.

When you buy bread or pasta, make sure the words *whole grain* are the first ingredient listed. Use brown rice instead of white rice. Try baking with whole-wheat flour instead of white flour. Make sure the cereals you serve are high in whole wheat, oats, rice, or buckwheat and low in refined sugar.

3. **Make that sweet snack a piece of fruit—or a carrot.** Refined sugar—the kind found in most candies, cakes, and cookies—is both fattening and detrimental to a child's health. These products are also likely to be high in fat, which makes them doubly dangerous. By substituting a piece of fruit for a candy bar or slice of cake, you enrich your child's diet and reduce his long-term health risk. The same goes for replacing a sugar-laden soda with a glass of fresh fruit juice, vegetable juice, or water.

Caution: School cafeteria food can be fattening and unhealthy.

Most schools include information about a so-called balanced diet as part of their curricula. So it's odd that lunch menus in many schools violate the basic rules of good nutrition. Foods like French toast sticks, pizza, hot dogs, burgers, and fried chicken nuggets were some of the featured main courses on many of the lunch menus we looked at. The token cup of canned peaches and container of milk may be in compliance with an official dietary standard. We view it as a sad statement about the effort many schools are making to address children's long-term health needs.

If at all possible, encourage children to make their own lunch and take it to school. Some choices might include a salad, or a turkey sandwich with some carrot sticks, or a container of yogurt and a piece of fresh fruit. School cafeterias may offer these and other healthier options, but they tend to appear on the bottom of the menu. By making children aware of healthy food choices, you make it more likely that that they will select these options both in and outside the home.

Be firm but flexible in setting dietary rules. You are likely to run into some resistance when you start changing the way your family eats. Kids may not automatically be receptive to munching on an apple instead of a candy bar. They may complain that the skimmed milk you've started serving is tasteless. Hold your ground, but make changes gradually.

Consider, for example, switching from whole milk to 2-percent milk, then 1-percent milk, and then skimmed milk. This kind of incremental approach will help your child adapt to these changes. At the same time, you do want to allow your child the occasional cheeseburger or piece of ice cream cake. It's important to enjoy food—and that means allowing for the occasional exception to a healthful eating regimen.

Reminder: Don't use food as a substitute for love.

Food is something all of us must live with—and need in order to live. The key to achieving and maintaining good body weight is to find a way to enjoy eating without overdoing it—and that requires a healthy attitude toward food. Well-intended parents often do things to exacerbate a child's weight problem. If you or your partner do any of the following, we strongly suggest that you stop:

♦ Insisting that children finish everything on their plate

♦ Using food as a reward or punishment for good or bad behavior

♦ Giving children fattening foods for comfort when they're upset or despondent or out-of-sorts

Limit television watching—especially at mealtime. It's important not to let youngsters get hooked on TV. In general, watching commercial television isn't particularly enlightening—nor is it a medium that necessarily portrays African Americans in a positive light. Too often, busy parents use TV as a baby-sitter for very young children. As boys and girls grow up, they develop the habit of sitting transfixed in front of the tube for hours at a time.

Imagine how much richer these children's lives would be if they spent all that wasted time reading or taking part in something that requires active involvement. Becoming a couch potato doesn't only limit children's horizons; it also expands their waistlines. The following statistics show that the percentage of children who are overweight increases in proportion to the number of hours per day they spend watching TV.[3]

Hours of TV Watched	Percentage of Kids Who Are Overweight
0–2	12
2–3	23
3–4	28
4–5	30
More than 5	33

We suggest limiting access to television or video viewing (as well as wasted time on computers or Internet) to no more than one hour per day—especially on school nights.

It's also essential that children don't get into the habit of eating their meals while watching television. Research shows that overweight kids eat 50 percent more dinners in front of the tube than normal-weight kids of the same age, and that the problem is most pronounced with black children. A recent study by researchers at Baylor College of Medicine in Houston found that black kids ate 62 percent of their meals in front of the TV—almost one-third more than Hispanic children, twice the rate of white children, and three times the rate of Asian-American children.[4]

Instead of making a strict policy of no meals in front of the television, consider eating meals as a family whenever possible. Eating together as a family fosters better parent-child communication and helps kids to avoid the high-calorie foods that in practice go along with eating in front of the TV.

One recent study found that children between the ages of nine and fourteen who eat meals with their families consume more fruits and vegetables and less fried food than those who eat meals alone in front of the television.[5] Research on teenagers conducted at Cincinnati Children's Hospital Medical Center found that "[teens] who eat with adult family members an average of at least 5 times a week are less likely to use drugs or fall victim to depression than adolescents who eat with their parent(s) only 3 times a week. They were also more motivated to do well in school and had better relationships with their peers."[6]

STAY PHYSICALLY ACTIVE AS A FAMILY.

A healthy diet goes hand in hand with a program of regular exercise. However, a better way to get this notion across to children is to talk in terms of being physically active. The idea is to use some of that wasted fat-inducing TV time to get your child's body moving and the heart pumping.

You don't need expensive sneakers or special equipment to put a family-fitness plan into place. Choose activities the child enjoys in which you and other family members can take part. Try going for brisk walks or taking bike rides after dinner. Play ball or join the "Y" together. Families who get involved in physical fitness reinforce one another's good health habits and create a positive, nonthreatening environment for the overweight child.

There are major benefits to physical activity. Aside from burning fat and calories and decreasing the risk of some major health threats, physical activity increases energy and relieves stress. Children (and adults) who exercise regularly for a period of time develop a positive habit that's hard to break. Many people who get hooked on exercise don't feel right if they miss a single day. That's because regular physical activity makes you feel better in ways that have a positive impact on everything you do—including working more efficiently and sleeping more soundly.

Encourage children to participate in organized sports. One disadvantage of excess body weight is that it slows a child's physical efforts. Any kind of exercise or sports participation will relieve this problem. However, supervised team sports have a number of advantages over informal, unsupervised game playing in streets or backyards. Team sports instill discipline by helping kids master established skills and rules. Organized sports also provide a safe setting wherein young people have an opportunity to gain recognition, develop social skills, and increase their motivation to achieve.

Similar benefits are also available to girls and boys who participate in organized music and drama groups. But organized sports give children an unparalleled opportunity to learn how to cooperate and compete—a combination of skills that will serve them well throughout their lives.

Reminder: When choosing a sport or team, make sure you're comfortable with the coaching.

Any vigorous sport will provide physical activity, and that's certain to help children stay fit. However, it's always important to look at the total environment in which you place your child. An important aspect of any sports team environment revolves around the coach's philosophy and personality. A good coach can motivate a child and instill a love of the game. A coach who is obsessed with winning (and only winning) or who plays favorites is not likely to provide an optimal sports experience. Minority parents should also assess the coach's attitudes toward different racial and ethnic groups.

In the black community, girls are more prone to obesity than boys, so their participation in organized sports is highly recommended. In general, it's best for girls over age ten to play on all-female teams. If these aren't available in your community, seek them out in neighboring areas. Keep in mind that many communities don't restrict participation to residents. That means you can choose a team where the coaching, racial balance, gender mix, and scheduling are in line with your child's needs.

DON'T LET YOUR CHILDREN SMOKE.

We originally considered discussing cigarette smoking in Chapter Four, because cigarettes contain nicotine, which is an addictive substance. Although nicotine can cause changes in behavior, these are relatively minor compared to those exhibited by people who drink or take drugs. The long-term physical dangers of cigarette smoking, however, are anything but subtle. Consequently, we treat tobacco use as more of a physical health issue than an emotional one. When you come right down to it, though, the ultimate message for parents is pretty much the same.

♦ Help children recognize the dangers of smoking so that they won't be tempted to experiment with tobacco.

♦ When young people have already started smoking, help them develop the discipline and motivation to stop.

♦ If you are a smoker, set a positive example for your child by kicking the habit.

In discussing cigarette smoking with young people, it's important to emphasize a number of well-established facts. Some of the following points are especially noteworthy for mothers and fathers who smoke.

- Tobacco smoke contains nicotine, a highly addictive drug. When people try to quit, they often experience symptoms of physical withdrawal.

- Smoking is a major cause of cardiovascular disease.

- Smoking is linked to about one-third of cancer deaths, including most deaths from lung cancer.

- Secondhand smoke (the smoke people in the same room as the smoker are forced to inhale) has been shown to make others sick.

- Pregnant women who smoke are more likely to deliver babies with low birth weights.

- During the first two years of life, children whose parents smoke are more likely to wind up in the hospital for pneumonia and bronchitis than children of parents who don't smoke.

- Children with parents who smoke have significantly more ear infections and sore throats than boys and girls whose parents don't smoke.

- Asthma, which is more common among black children than their white counterparts, is more likely to develop and persist in families where one or both parents smoke.[7]

Caution: Children whose parents smoke are more likely to become smokers themselves.

Some people smoke as a means of weight control. Tobacco can make the taste of food less appealing. Plus, a cigarette is something in the smoker's mouth that precludes eating. In general, it's counterproductive to substitute one bad habit for another—especially one as potentially deadly as cigarette smoking.

Teenagers often start smoking because they think it looks cool. But there are many social advantages to giving up tobacco that are important to teens. If your child smokes, try to point out the following negatives.

Cigarettes make the smoker's breath smell foul. The scent of stale tobacco tends to linger on hair and clothes—and that's a turnoff to nonsmokers. Ditto the hacking cough that announces your unattractive habit.

Be sure to emphasize that these unappealing symptoms usually disappear soon after a person stops smoking.

There is also a tremendous economic benefit to be gained by giving up smoking. At this writing, a pack of cigarettes costs up to five dollars. At that rate, someone smoking a pack a day would spend about $1800 on cigarettes in the course of a year. Point out to your teen all the great clothes and personal items he or she could buy with that money—things that won't ruin their health and pose a danger to others.

Find the Best Medical Care for Your Family

When a prominent African American leader referred to the need to fix inequities black people suffer at the hands of doctors and hospitals as "the new civil rights battle of the twenty-first century," he touched on a very troubling issue. Some have argued that racism in the medical system is no better or worse than it is in the society as a whole. We suspect that probably is the case—which is little consolation. Since the treatment doctors and other health care providers dispense is so critical to your child's well-being, it's important to be aware of some of the problems black Americans experience, and that you have the tools to deal with them.

We haven't encountered any physicians who would admit that their racial attitudes affect the way they practice medicine. However, there is mounting evidence that a particularly dangerous kind of racial profiling often influences the treatment of black patients.

Most doctors are not trained in racial sensitivity—nor are they required to take courses in cultural awareness. So it's not surprising that some doctors who've had little or no contact with African Americans buy into media stereotypes of what black people are like. Too often, that translates into viewing us as poor, uneducated, sexually loose, and likely to be abusing drugs.

There is another stereotype called "hardiness" that can affect the way African Americans (especially young black males) are treated. Hardiness is a stereotype that springs from the racist notion that black people are stronger and have a greater tolerance for pain than whites. In years gone by, this stereotype resulted in some white physicians doubling the strength of X rays they administered to African Americans because of the false belief that they had thicker skin than white people.

In the twenty-first century, even the most bigoted doctors wouldn't admit to using such primitive and inaccurate racial genetics as a basis for treating patients. This kind of bias is more likely to rear its head in discussions about socioeconomic status. Some doctors who harbor these beliefs have been known to extend entrenched "ghetto" stereotypes to all black people, regardless of their socioeconomic status or other truths of the situation. In practical terms, biased attitudes can result in a doctor not believing your teenage son when he complains of being in pain, and suspecting him of making up a story just to get drugs.

There are other doctors who probably mean well, but try to pass themselves off as being colorblind. People who claim that color and ethnicity make no difference are either lying to themselves or to others. Differences in racial and ethnic background can and should not be ignored by anyone—much less doctors and other health care professionals.

African Americans are more vulnerable to certain serious diseases than members of other racial groups, and less vulnerable to others. These factors should always be considered in making a diagnosis and treatment plan. At the same time, patients need to make certain that doctors aren't ignoring potentially dangerous warning signs because of cultural generalizations.

If, for example, your college-age daughter has elevated blood pressure, it would be a grave error to let a physician make light of that symptom, because African Americans tend to be hypertensive. All population groups are predisposed to certain illnesses, and that's a point doctors need to consider. It's important to make sure your child is treated as an individual, one whose racial background is factored into the doctor's diagnosis and treatment recommendations, along with other relevant factors such as medical history, family history, and age.

It's important to work with doctors you trust—and to pass that trust on to your children. We find that adolescents whose parents trust and have positive opinions about doctors are more likely to take an active role in maintaining their health. Such young people see their doctors regularly and take an active role in helping those physicians find and treat medical problems.

One reason many black Americans don't trust doctors is that only 4 percent of physicians in this country share their color. Patients who bring their children to us for the first time often remark that nobody in their family has ever been treated by a black physician.

SIX REASONS AFRICAN AMERICANS DON'T TRUST THE MEDICAL SYSTEM[8]

1. *Complaints by black patients are taken less seriously.* A study reported in The New England Journal of Medicine concluded that doctors were 40 percent less likely to order sophisticated cardiac tests for black patients that complained about chest pain than for white patients with identical symptoms.[9]

2. *Black people are less likely to receive the most sophisticated treatment. Black patients receive cardiac bypass operations and other advanced procedures about 25 percent as often as whites, even though blacks die of coronary heart disease at a higher rate than whites.*

3. *Black patients are more likely to have limbs amputated.* A survey by Newsday found that black patients with diabetes are more likely to have their feet or legs amputated, whereas whites in a comparable condition are more likely to receive surgery designed to restore blood flow and save their legs.[10]

4. *African Americans who need kidney transplants wait longer for a compatible organ, and are less likely than whites to ever receive a donor kidney.*

5. *Black patients who suffer from depression and other emotional problems are less likely than whites to be referred for psycho-therapy. When they are referred, African Americans are more likely to be treated only with drugs or sent to inexperienced therapists.*

6. *Black patients are less likely than whites to get lung cancer surgery during the disease's early stages. Consequently, a dis-proportionate percentage of African Americans die from this potentially curable condition.*

We urge you to take the following proactive steps if you want to increase your chances of getting the best available health care for all the members of your family, whatever their age.

Shop around. Ask people you trust for referrals to physicians with whom they've had good experiences. If your medical coverage is supplied by a health maintenance organization (HMO), seek out a physician who has been referred by someone whose opinion you value.

Don't be intimidated. Doctors sometimes interpret questions as challenges to what they perceive to be their absolute authority. Sometimes a doctor may not be able to answer your question. At other times, the physician may simply not want to take the time. Part of a doctor's job is to communicate effectively and courteously with patients. Unfortunately, some doctors have trouble communicating, even with people who share their background. The situation becomes that much worse when such a doctor has to communicate with someone of another race.

Even doctors with good communication skills sometimes need to be reminded that most patients don't have a sophisticated medical vocabulary. Don't let a doctor intimidate you with medical jargon or scientific terms. If the doctor says something you can't understand, politely ask him to translate that into plain English.

Today, one finds doctors from a wide variety of cultures. However, an African American physician is still somewhat of a rarity. People often feel most comfortable with those of their own cultural or racial group. Such preferences tend to be more intense when you're talking about a critical service like medical care.

Considering that your chances of getting a black doctor are only four in one hundred, it doesn't make sense to restrict your choice to a particular racial group. It's possible that the black doctor in your neighborhood may not be as competent or as easy to work with as a white or Asian physician in the same area. We would advise you to select doctors who are experienced, capable, committed to healing, and respectful to patients—whatever their race or cultural background.

Building Mental Muscles in Black Youth

Productive mental health habits are key to maintaining a balanced and disciplined lifestyle. We think of developing this aspect of a child's makeup as mental or psychological fitness—something every black child needs to possess. Mental fitness is to the mind what physical fitness is to the body. Children need to be physically fit in order to maintain high energy and good health. Similarly, girls and boys need to be mentally fit to perform at a high level, overcome obstacles, achieve scholastic and career success, and exercise greater control over their lives.

SEVEN ATTRIBUTES OF MENTAL DISCIPLINE THAT HELP KIDS WIN

- *Increased resilience for overcoming obstacles and setbacks*
- *Increased self-confidence*
- *Increased motivation*
- *Better ability to resist negative peer pressure*
- *Lower vulnerability to stress-related illness*
- *Lower vulnerability to depression*
- *Higher threshold for frustration and pain*

One way to look at the arc of a child's development is as a graduated series of challenges and problems that need to be solved. Parents must help children develop the most effective problem-solving skills, so they'll be prepared to deal with the challenges that lie ahead. For young African Americans, who will have to cope with some form of racism throughout their lives, three mental strengths are especially vital: optimism, negotiation, and balance.

OPTIMISM

Chances are you've met your share of optimists and pessimists—people who predictably see a glass filled to 50-percent capacity as either half-full or half-empty. What many people don't realize is that optimism and pessimism are largely products of parenting.

Children become optimistic when parents help them understand that their successes and achievements are due to ability, and not blind luck. This is an empowering message because it makes girls and boys feel that their actions have an impact. Optimistic children are highly motivated and less prone to depression. When adversity strikes, an optimistic child doesn't ask "why me?" Nor does he look to assign blame.

Optimistic children have been taught to externalize bad events—even when they bear some of the responsibility personally. Rather than allowing themselves to be paralyzed by gloom and doom and a sense that the bad times will never end, optimistic children maintain a positive outlook. They view adversity and setbacks as temporary conditions, and feel confident they'll be able to weather the storm.

By contrast, pessimistic children have been taught to blame themselves when bad things happen. They see positive events as the product of good luck, an accident, or something propelled by outside forces. Somewhere along the line, parents of pessimistic children have taught their children to feel helpless. Consequently, these children interpret every failure as being their fault—or due to forces outside of their control. Even when pessimistic children do succeed, they are likely to conclude that their triumphs were due to an accident of good luck or some other external factor.

Because pessimistic children don't believe their efforts will be rewarded, they are not highly motivated. This pervasive feeling gives them an easy excuse for failure. If, for example, you ask an optimistic child why she didn't do well on a test, she is likely to point to a flaw in the test or something external that impeded her performance. It's highly unlikely, however, that she'll tell you that she didn't give it her best shot.

On the other hand, a pessimistic child is likely to claim he didn't do well on the test because he didn't try. The underlying reason pessimists don't try is that they have a poor self-image, which is partly a product of a history of poor performance. This feeling of not being able to do anything right eventually becomes self-fulfilling and pervasive. Fortunately, parents have the power to make their children more optimistic.

In his book *Learned Optimism*, psychologist Martin Seligman counsels parents to "teach [children] how to tolerate frustration, not avoid it, and to view adversity as a challenge, not a forerunner of failure."[11]

The following guidelines, which draw from Seligman's work, can help you help your child develop a more optimistic approach to life.

Be watchful of how your child interprets problems and setbacks. Does your child blame himself for difficulties that aren't his fault? If your child demonstrates this pattern, discuss alternate ways of looking at problems. Then focus on a few small behavioral changes that might help him turn things around. If, for example, your son blames himself for a poor test score, suggest a change in the way he studies, or relaxation techniques that might help him to improve concentration while taking tests.

Help children focus on changing behaviors—not traits. Behaviors are discrete actions that are much easier to change than personality traits, which tend to be relatively fixed. If, for example, a child explains failing a test by saying she's stupid, she's effectively saying that she has little or no control over the outcome. By demonstrating that a student can improve her performance by studying harder or more efficiently, you put the control largely in the young person's hands.

Teach children to tolerate frustration and value mistakes. Children who aren't equipped to deal with frustration tend to become passive or immobilized when confronted by challenging situations. When they do make an effort, such children give up at the first hint of a false start or mistake.

UNDERSTANDING THE VALUE OF OPTIMISM

P sychologist Martin Seligman finds that optimists have "self-serving illusions enabling them to maintain good cheer and health in a universe that is essentially indifferent to their welfare." His research demonstrates that optimists have important advantages in the following areas:

Physical health: optimists are more resistant to infectious disease and are better at fending off chronic midlife illnesses like cancer and heart disease.

School performance: A study comparing optimistic and pessimistic high school students with the same SAT scores and grade-point averages revealed that optimists do better in college than pessimists.

Sports: *Optimists use defeat as motivation to try harder the next time, while pessimists get discouraged. In a study of Olympic swimmers who had been defeated in their previous race, the optimists swam the next race faster, while the pessimists swam more slowly.[12]*

Reminder: Never belittle children when their efforts fall short.

Always encourage children to put forth their best effort in whatever they do. Explain that mistakes and false starts are not just roadblocks that need to be tolerated. They are important opportunities for improvement and essential learning experiences that underlie success in any meaningful venture. For example, the young baseball player who strikes out can interpret the event in one of two ways.

The pessimist says: "I can't hit a baseball to save my life."

The optimist says: "Next time I'll adjust my swing."

There are few worthwhile goals in life that are accomplished without a learning curve—and that requires errors and false starts. When parents adapt an optimistic approach to their own lives and instill this mental discipline in their children, they provide an invaluable tool for meeting the challenges that lie ahead.

Negotiation

The main objective of any negotiation is to win; still, it's not always clear what that means. Even in war, where the primary objective is defeating the enemy, farsighted victors will often go to great lengths to rebuild their vanquished adversaries. The United States took this approach after World War II. As a result, we now count Germany and Japan among our staunchest allies. Some have suggested that our ongoing problems with terrorism are partly the result of not taking a similar tack in our encounters with Arab nations.

A similar principle applies in the realm of personal dealings. Black children in particular often have to fight in order to achieve their objectives. However, it's important for parents to help children understand that they are not at war with any single person or group of people, and that there are frequently ways to win without creating losers.

Popular expressions such as "winning isn't everything, it's the only thing," and "looking out for number one" reflect the highly competitive nature of our society. There's no question that children must learn how to act in their own self-interest. At the same time, parents need to convey the message that winning entails achieving a positive result, both for yourself and the people you're dealing with.

In their book *Getting to Yes,* Roger Fisher and William Ury lay out the principles of a "win-win" negotiation—a process in which each participant's interests are addressed. We have adapted some of the authors' principles to help parents show children of color the most effective way to resolve differences and achieve their objectives.[13]

Separate personal issues from the problems you're trying to solve. Encourage children to concentrate on the issues at hand. Never resort to personal attacks, simply because someone won't give you what you want. If you must attack, channel that energy toward confronting the issues. Encourage children to establish and respect boundaries—that is, what they and others are and are not willing to do. Parents can strengthen a child's skill in this area by doing the following:

- Help children develop the confidence to ask for what they want.
- Make children feel comfortable about expressing their feelings and opinions.
- Teach children to set personal boundaries—and to say no when necessary.
- Teach children to recognize and honor other people's boundaries.
- Role-model empathy and mutual respect in your own dealings with others.

Focus on what you're trying to accomplish. Teach young people to keep their eye on the ball—and not get sidetracked by unproductive emotions. When dealing with people of other racial groups, it's especially important not to allow stereotypes to interfere with efforts to achieve win-win solutions.

Help children recognize stereotypes that fuel racial anger so they don't allow those attitudes to undermine what they're trying to achieve. When dealing with people of other racial groups who can either further or impede your goal, it's generally unwise to accuse them of racism directly—even if you believe them guilty of it.

People who judge others on the basis of racial stereotypes don't necessarily harbor ill will against particular groups—they may merely have a simplistic way of seeing individuals. Even when you perceive someone to be a racist, you may still want or need to deal with that individual.

The key to being effective at this aspect of negotiation is developing the discipline to stand back and simply observe differences in the way people think and act, without allowing your emotions to guide your behavior. Young people who develop this observational skill and control inspire trust and confidence in others. When people trust you, they are more likely to express themselves openly—and this openness is likely to help you get what you want.

Try to not make your win a total loss for the other party. As we point out in the opening of this section, even warring nations aren't well served when their foe feels crushed. The most successful negotiations are those in which neither party feels defeated—even when the ultimate result clearly favors one player over the other. A win-win result is especially important when you're negotiating with someone of another race, because bad feelings tend to invoke racial tensions and harden entrenched stereotypes.

THE PROCESS IN ACTION: HOW TO NEGOTIATE ACROSS RACIAL LINES

Ken is a full professor at a large university in the Midwest—and the only African American department head at the institution. As part of a recent cost-cutting policy, the white university president announces that Ken's department is going to be downsized and combined with another department. Ken will continue to retain his full professorship with no loss of salary. However, his loss of the department chairmanship will greatly reduce his power and influence at the institution.

Ken knows exactly what he wants: to retain his department chairmanship. The only question is the best way to achieve that goal. It's clear that, so far as the university president is concerned, his cost-cutting announcement is a statement of economic and administrative policy, not an invitation to negotiate.

Ken spends some time considering his options. He thinks about quitting and looking for another job, but quickly dismisses the idea. At the same time, he's not prepared to accept this directive as the final word.

Ken wonders whether the president's decision is racially motivated, and finds no clear evidence either way. The president has never said or done anything to make Ken think he's a racist. Then again, Ken knows too well that a good deal of racism is covert—sometimes even to the person harboring it.

It doesn't take Ken long to figure out the most effective course of action. He sets up an appointment with the university president. After exchanging pleasantries, the president expresses his regret about relieving Ken of his chairmanship. The president then shakes his head and says that hard times require hard decisions.

Ken assures the president he understands the economic realities and that tough choices are in order. He then proceeds to remind the president that he is the only African American department head at the university. "Under the circumstances," Ken adds, "eliminating the only black department chair might reflect poorly on the institution's commitment to diversity."

The president doesn't respond to Ken's comment. However, a few days later, the president revises his reorganization plans: all department heads will retain their positions; cuts will be made in other areas.

The negotiating strategy Ken used was designed to help him keep his position. But in the process, he may actually have saved the university a good deal of embarrassment. Some might argue that Ken played the race card to get what he wanted; perhaps there's a grain of truth in that. Still, Ken played his hand in a way that yielded a positive result for himself and his institution—which is the essence of a disciplined, win-win negotiation.

In explaining scenarios like the one described above to young people, be sure to emphasize the three key negotiating principles we've discussed, and how they contributed to a successful outcome:

♦ *Separate personal issues from the problems you're trying to solve.* Ken had a deeply personal response when he was informed that his chairmanship was being taken away. However, he quickly began to formulate a solution that would help him realize his goal.

♦ *Focus on what you're trying to accomplish.* Ken considered the possibility that there might have been a racial basis for his position being eliminated. Instead of wasting his energies on feeling angry or labeling the president of the university a racist, Ken found a constructive way to use race to help him accomplish his objective.

◆ *Try to not make your win a total loss for the other party.* In the final analysis, Ken got everything he wanted. However, he accomplished his goal without denigrating the person who was attempting to take away a position he valued. Instead of confronting the university president as an adversary, Ken framed his case in a way that created a victory for both parties—and for the institution.

Achieving Balance

Part of growing up involves an ongoing struggle to figure out who we are and what we want out of life. Some people never answer those questions, and go through life in a permanent state of psychological imbalance. The search for balance is an attempt to create harmony among all facets of our lives.

In the course of a given day, children may have to deal with any number of people and systems—their family, their peers, their schoolteachers, their minister and fellow parishioners, their sports coach and teammates. When children's dealings in any one of these areas get out of sync, their sense of balance gets disrupted, and they feel splintered or out of control. Balance is the mechanism that gives young people the strength and fluidity to address the demands of these different situations and personalities, while maintaining a singular sense of who they are.

Psychologists use the term *identity* to describe the way people define themselves in relation to personal, social, and historical time. Adolescence is a crucial period for sorting out these issues.

By late adolescence, most young people have a sense of who they are sexually (sex-role identity) and what they might like to do for a living (occupational identity).

Racial and ethnic identities also factor in to who a person is. However, research on adolescents from different racial and ethnic backgrounds shows that this aspect of identity is a relative nonissue to whites, but very important to African Americans. This should come as no surprise. After all, race has a lot less of an impact on the lives of white people than it does on racial minorities.

People are taught to make judgments on the basis of skin color—judgments that often don't work in favor of racial minorities. That's why black people are so much more concerned about race than white people; and this has a major impact on a young person's quest to answer the question: Who am I?

Parents need to instill a kind of dual consciousness in order to help girls and boys become successful and attain mental balance. It's essential that young African Americans learn to find their place in a white-dominated mainstream system that has a long history of devaluing and oppressing their people. At the same time, it's equally important that these young men and women embrace their African American heritage and develop a healthy racial identity. When these two forces are at odds with one another, there's bound to be a state of imbalance:

Seventeen-year-old Jared, the son of two professional parents, lives in a mostly white upper-middle-class neighborhood. Jared is one of the few black kids in the local public high school. He is a good student who is well liked by his teachers and popular with his classmates.

Jared's parents attend a local church that has few black parishioners. They have little connection to the African American community, and don't find it necessary to encourage their only son to pursue black friends and other relationships within the African American community. After years of hearing his parents disparage poorer black people by referring to them as "ghetto types," Jared acquired a similar attitude.

"I can't feel sorry for these women who keep having babies and collecting welfare," he would sometimes remark. A number of Jared's more politically liberal white friends would kid him about being politically conservative—a good candidate for the Young Republicans.

One evening Jared took an unfamiliar route on his walk home from baseball practice. Suddenly, a gang of tough white teenagers converged on him. They called Jared nigger, beat him with his own baseball bat, and sent him to the emergency room.

This incident brought about a striking change in the young man. He'd never really thought of himself as being black; this violent event threw him for a loop. For a while, Jared was depressed and confused. By the time the dust settled, Jared had done a lot of thinking about where he fit in. He started seeking out black friends in a nearby working-class neighborhood, and grew distant from his white friends.

Jared's grades began to drop and his teachers and classmates noticed that he'd developed what they took to be a militant black attitude.

"What's up with Jared?" one of his white friends wondered. "It's like he suddenly discovered that he was black and decided to hit everyone over the head with it."

That wasn't a totally inaccurate assessment of the changes Jared was going through. The young man's parents were very concerned when they brought him in to see us.

We assured Jared's folks that their son's sudden change was part of a normal search for identity. The process had been supercharged by a violent racist encounter that had a number of post-traumatic consequences. We were eventually able to help Jared work through these feelings—including his anger at white people. The young man came to understand that he didn't need to hate the whole white race to feel connected to his own people.

Reminder: Parents can't shield their sons and daughters from racism.

This is a reality some mothers and fathers have difficulty accepting. Nevertheless, this realization is an important first step in helping children develop the balance they need to succeed in a society that is increasingly diverse—but where being white remains the gold standard. It takes strength for young people to fend off affronts to their racial identity and to control their emotions while keeping long-range goals in sight. Parents can foster this strength by following these five steps.

1. **Help children understand where their interests lie.** Discuss with your child the benefits of cooperating and working well with people of different races in all areas of life. Explain that people who possess these skills are at a great advantage in today's increasingly diverse environment.

2. **Teach children not to judge others solely on the basis of race.** Explain that the differences that exist between people of different racial groups are based on their experience and culture—not on one group's being better than another. Stress that there are people of good will in all racial groups, as well as those who would do harm to others.

3. **Encourage children to find common ground with others.** Race is

only one part of a person's being, and it often serves to divide one group from another. Still, there are many other things that people share—for instance, ethics and religious values. We find that most black Americans have more similarities and share more values with white Americans than they do with black Africans. It sometimes takes a war or other crisis to bring that common ground to the fore. But it is something all people would do well to keep in mind during both good and bad times.

4. Teach children to learn from experience. The attitudes and advice you share are part of a child's experience. The young person's observations of how you deal with others is another. As children develop, they increase their own repertoire of experience. Parents can do much to help children process and learn from their own negotiations with the world.

Encourage children to talk to you about their dealings with others—including interactions with people of other races and cultures. Help children reflect on the course of those interactions. Try to identify what they've learned about their own mindset, as well as that of others. Help children pinpoint mistakes as well as opportunities to use these insights in future encounters.

5. Encourage children to walk a mile in the other guy's shoes. It's easy to get so caught up in your own viewpoint that you're completely blind to the other person's perspective. This is a common trap in interracial dealings, because people too often allow stereotypes to mask what's really taking place.

Young people can have an especially tough time stepping outside themselves because the immediacy of their emotions is so intense. When children have a problem with someone of another race, it's important for parents to encourage them to talk it out. Then, once things calm down, invite the child to role-play the incident.

Offer to portray your child in the interaction, and encourage him to portray the other person. Then reverse roles. Next, try changing the dialogue and discussing how this can affect the result. Helping a child to see things from the other person's vantage point provides a vital learning experience that can serve to change the course of future encounters.

Helping African American Children Develop a Strong Personal Identity

In developing their identities—both as human beings and black Americans—young people are bombarded by conflicting influences and messages. One test of mental discipline is the ability to respond to the voices and cues around you while staying true to your own internal compass. In *The Lonely Crowd*, David Reisman describes these clashing voices in terms of two distinct personality types:[14]

Inner-directed people are self-reliant and purposeful. These individuals use the rules and principles instilled by their parents as a compass that guides them through life.

Other-directed people rely on the external cues, such as those displayed by peers, coworkers, and the media, to navigate the world.

The contrast between these two personality types was depicted on a cover of *Time* magazine following the release of *The Lonely Crowd*. The inner-directed person was portrayed by a hardworking businessman who is guided by a gyroscope—a navigational device directed entirely by its own internal compass—without considering any outside influences. The other-directed person was portrayed as a glad-handing salesman who uses a radar dish to figure out what those around him think he should do next.

Reisman believed that, in order to raise inner-directed children, parents have to foster a "rigid though highly individualized character," and a permanent moral "set" that would enable them to weather the storms and stresses of an unpredictable, often unfriendly, world. While this portrayal draws on some of the values we endorse, it is far too simplistic to address the realities black youth face in the twenty-first century.

The need for effective interracial negotiation and other so-called people skills is critical in today's world. Consequently, no successful person can afford to be completely disinterested in the external information on the radar screen—even those independent souls who manage to follow their own muse.

There is clearly a great deal wrong with our society, especially when it comes to its treatment of racial minorities. Ultimately, however, an individual's ability to achieve balance and find true inner freedom goes beyond the limits of any kind of social order. That, as one commentator has noted, is the core message of *The Lonely Crowd*:

"There is no conceivable set of social arrangements that can make us free. The freedom to which we can reasonably aspire is to be found neither in acts of mindless conformity nor in acts of mindless rebellion." Ultimately, the key to achieving this freedom is to find a way to operate within the social limits without being psychologically bound by them.[15]

Helping African American Children Develop a Spiritual Center

Spiritual health is a more abstract concept than physical or mental health. As a result, it has been the subject of less research and scientific discussion than the other components of mind-body discipline. Nevertheless, spirituality is an essential aspect of total health—one that lends strength to every part of a person's being.

A major article on spiritual health in the journal *Wellness Perspectives* identified the internal and external benefits of spirituality as follows:

> Internally, spiritual health seems to provide the individual with life purpose and ultimate meaning; oneness with nature and beauty and a sense of connectedness with others; deep concern for and commitment to something greater than self; a sense of wholeness in life; strong spiritual beliefs, principles, ethics, and values; and love, joy, peace, hope, and fulfillment.
>
> In terms of their external interactions, spiritually well individuals express themselves through trust, honesty, integrity, altruism, compassion, and service. In addition, they . . . have some sort of personal relationship and experience with a higher power or larger reality that transcends an observable physical reality.[16]

People with a spiritual center feel a connection to nonmaterial forces. In traditionally religious cultures, this is expressed by belief in a higher power, God—or some guiding or organizing principle. Spirituality provides the glue that keeps our youth connected to their people, and the moral compass that helps them know the difference between right and wrong.

In Chapter Three we talked about how important it is for African American families to participate in a black church or mosque—even for families who are not particularly religious. Black churches have historically provided a variety of useful outlets and constructive activities for young people, including those who don't attend weekly services.

Spirituality can be found within the walls of churches and mosques. However, even families who choose not to participate in organized religion can impart a spiritual sense to children. Families can nurture this aspect of self through a variety of spiritual activities or ethical values. Some people connect to their spiritual selves through nature, or music, or other art forms.

Spirituality has played an important role in the lives of many African Americans, including those who don't participate in organized religion. The roots of spirituality in the black community can be found in the tradition of African religions. Those who partake feel a sense of power and purpose beyond the tangible, and a sense of comfort in the face of adversity.

When the road gets hard, uncertainty and fear can derail people. Those who possess a strong spiritual center are better able to ride out these difficulties, because they believe that there's an underlying purpose to the ebb and flow of life—even if its meaning isn't always apparent.

Black Americans have certainly known their share of hard times, which partly explains why spirituality is woven into the very fabric of who we are. But a strong spiritual center is equally important when times are good—when folks are in a position to do for others.

Children who grow up without a spiritual dimension may not readily understand the purpose of values and principles that don't have an immediate, concrete result. This type of individual tends to be shortsighted, and unable to envision or shape a better future for himself and those he touches.

We have talked before about how important it is for black youth to develop a sense of connectedness with their community. This entails a certain amount of selflessness or altruism. Yet there is a growing body of research suggesting that people who give freely of themselves derive benefits that are quite tangible.

In his book *The Healing Power of Doing Good,* Allan Luks presents evidence that those who help others derive a multitude of benefits. Luks found that over 90 percent of people who participate in volunteer work at least once a week rate their health as being better than people of the same age and general health. Participants also reported reversals of lower-back pain and chronic headache, as well as dramatic improvements in heart conditions. Luks concludes that "helpers" can expect to reap the following benefits:

- A fortified immune system that is better able to fend off disease.

- Activation of positive emotions that underlie good health

- Reduction of negative, stress-related emotions[17]

The health-based rewards of doing for others may not have much resonance for young people—most of whom feel invulnerable to the ravages of chronic disease. Still, giving of yourself is an act that feels good at any age, and it's something parents would do well to encourage and reward.

We are not in the business of advising people about their spiritual lives and the way they choose to convey those values to their children. But in our experience, spiritually grounded black children are often better able to resist negative temptations and postpone gratification. These young people are more likely to develop into adults who go through life with a strong sense of purpose, and who will always treasure the gift of strength and love their parents have given them. These young women and men recognize that giving is often better than receiving. They are the ones whose commitment is to the betterment of the black community—and the human race.

Summary

A Seven-Step Program for Raising a Well-Balanced Child

1. Know what to expect during the various stages of your child's development.

2. Help your child maintain healthy eating habits and an appropriate weight.

3. Explain the dangers of tobacco to discourage smoking before it starts.

4. Understand the special health and health-care issues African Americans face.

5. Help your child become an effective problem solver.

6. Teach your child the value of staying true to one's own internal compass.

7. Provide your child with a strong spiritual grounding.

9

Questions and Answers
Across the Five Disciplines

The story of the African American—our story—is one of survival. We survived slavery. We survived segregation. I am certain we will survive [today's] problems, too. The key is personal discipline.

—CAROL MOSELEY BRAUN[1]
former U.S. Senator

IN THIS CHAPTER, we answer questions that cut across the various disciplines and which may have not been fully addressed in previous chapters. These are some of the questions parents most often ask at our lectures and seminars—as well as in our professional practice. When feasible, we key our answers to the various disciplines and refer you to sections in the book where additional prescriptive guidelines are available.

My son, who is a college freshman, called to say he was bringing his new girlfriend home to spend Thanksgiving weekend with the family. He then added that the girl happened to be white. Our son knows that

226

we don't approve of interracial dating. How should we handle the situation?

Interracial dating seems to be a pressing concern for many black parents. It's also common knowledge that white parents aren't too enamored with it either. Interestingly, today's teens are increasingly open to dating someone outside their race. By the time they get to college, many have already done so.

In general, there's nothing to be done if kids choose to date someone of another race. In regard to your specific question, our advice is to welcome the young lady into your home. You are certainly entitled to express your surprise to your son—but it's important to do so privately, without creating a scene.

Decisions about dating people of particular racial and religious groups are highly personal matters. It's important that parents state their feelings about these issues—without implying that their love is contingent on the child's compliance. Children will ultimately have to make their own choices, and some of these may not be in line with your values and preferences.

Most young people won't wind up marrying their current girlfriends or boyfriends. It's more than likely that this (or any) youthful relationship will be history in six months or a year. In the end, you might be surprised to find that the values you've stressed are more deeply ingrained than they may appear to be at this point in your son's development. If the young man eventually does choose to marry someone of whom you don't approve, there's not very much you can do to prevent it.

For the present, it's important not to overreact. Such behavior on your part can only make the situation worse. By taking an inflexible position, you may push the young person into doing things he might not otherwise do. If you have very strong feelings on the matter, find a private time to discuss your views. Remember, you can't change behavior by trying to dictate a young person's choices.

My husband and I often have wine or mixed drinks with dinner. We're trying to keep our sixteen-year-old daughter substance-free, but she says, "If you drink, why can't I drink?" How should we handle this?

Parents have to negotiate a tightrope in this regard. It's legal for adults to consume alcohol—but not for kids. It's also true that many children do learn to drink by observing their parents. Therefore, mothers and fathers need to model what constitutes acceptable drinking behavior around their kids, but that's not the same as giving a teenager permission to drink.

It may not be the world's strongest argument, but there are things that adults can do that kids can't do. The family is not a total democracy—which means that parents have rights and responsibilities that children simply don't have. Those rights may be based on a family member's age, experience, and contribution to the household. That said, it might be prudent to take your daughter's protests as an opportunity to assess your own drinking behavior.

There are many "social drinkers" who are in fact alcoholics, and whose behavior may be inviting serious physical or emotional consequences down the road. A *yes* answer to one or more of the following questions may indicate that you are a problem drinker:

+ Do you drink alone on a regular basis?

+ Do you drink to gain courage or increase self-confidence?

+ Do you regularly miss work because you're hung over?

+ Have you been cited for driving under the influence of alcohol?

+ Do you hide bottles or sneak drinks so others won't know?

(Please see Chapter Four for a complete discussion of alcohol and drug abuse.)

My husband and I are in the process of divorcing. There's a lot of anger on both sides. How can I best protect my two children?

There are few things kids hate worse than the separation of their parents. In one study, middle-school students rated divorce as being the most stressful life event, next to the death of a parent or sibling. These kids rated divorce as more stressful than the death of a friend, being seriously injured, feeling that nobody liked them—even being hit by a parent.

Divorce is a major threat to children's health, because the separation of parents shatters their sense of stability and order. Many kids have told us that the worst day of their lives came when their father or mother moved out of the family home. Divorce often has a negative impact on a child's school performance. It can also precipitate depression and substance abuse. Even when kids manage to ride out the storm, we often see long-term negative effect on their sense of optimism and their perception of male-female relationships.

This is not to say that parents should stay in troubled marriages solely for the sake of their children. In the long run, some children do benefit from their parents' divorce, but it takes time and a great deal of care. Above all, parents need to make a conscious effort not to drag children into their battles. They should do everything possible to avoid undermining the child's relationship with the other parent. Whatever their problems with each other, parents need to remain partners in ensuring the welfare of their children.

The following is a list of guidelines for mothers and fathers who are considering or going through divorce. If it turns out that you or your ex-spouse can't live with these commonsense principles, consider seeking appropriate professional help as soon as possible.

◆ Make sure to keep telling (and showing) children that the breakup of the marriage is not their fault—and that they will continue to retain the love of both parents.

◆ Don't fight or call each other names in front of the children.

◆ Don't ask children to choose whom they love more.

◆ Don't use children to deliver messages to each other.

◆ Don't make children feel as if they're being shuttled between parents.

◆ Don't use children as sources of emotional support, or as confidants.

◆ Make it easy for children to have a continued relationship with the other parent.

◆ Do your best to create and maintain a calm atmosphere and a stable environment.

◆ Don't say negative things about your ex-spouse—even if you feel that they are true.

◆ Make teachers and school administrators aware of your divorce and about any accompanying changes in living arrangements.

◆ Don't prevent an ex-spouse's parents and other relatives from having access to children.

- Try to include your ex in important decisions and events in the child's life.

- Continue to reassure children that even though you and your spouse will no longer be living together, both of you will always love and care for them.

My eighteen-year-old son just dropped out of college and moved back home. He refuses to get a job and sits around the house all day, watching TV. What should I do?

The right path in this all-too-common scenario is clear. While you may be willing to support the young man while he's obtaining a higher education, it would be a mistake to allow him to sit around the house and do nothing. Be sympathetic to his need for a transition period and encourage him to talk about his plans for the future. But while he's in the process of getting all this together, make it plain that you expect him to be involved in something productive. If he's not ready to attend school, he must find some sort of job, and pay for his room and board.

This kind of hard stand on your part serves a dual purpose. It demonstrates that you now consider your son to be an adult, and expect him to behave like one. By demanding that the young man get a job, you highlight the limited options he's likely to have without an education, thereby increasing the possibility that he will eventually decide to resume his schooling.

My husband and I are white. We are in the process of adopting an African American girl. Is there anything special we need to do in raising this child?

The principles and disciplines we cover in the chapters apply to all parents of African American children. However, there are a number of issues families face in terms of transracial adoptions.

All adopted children have to deal with an additional identity issue—assuming their adoptive parents have been honest about their background. There is a process adopted children go through in trying to understand what it means to have two sets of parents. Along the way, they are bound to ask questions such as "Why did my birth parents give me up for adoption?" and "Why did you want to adopt me?"

The rule of thumb for answering such complicated questions is to tell the child the truth, without going beyond the specifics of what the child is asking. As adopted children develop, their level of understanding increases, and so does the depth of their questions. It's a parent's job to provide a steady hand in helping kids navigate this road. That's why honesty is so important.

There are instances of people who go through their entire childhood without knowing they were adopted. When the truth finally does come out, these men and women understandably become confused about their identity and often suffer great emotional pain.

One reason adoptive parents hide the truth is because they want to avoid having to answer complicated questions. Also, any adoption involves loss. First, the child has lost his or her birth parents. Many parents who adopt have had difficulty conceiving a biological child, so there's loss on that end as well. Adoption also comes with its own set of negative connotations—particularly that of somehow being second best.

In a transracial adoption, there is generally no way to hide the truth. The contrast between your skin color and the child's announces that this is not the standard family arrangement. This difference does not have to be a negative in a child's life, but it does require special handling. No matter how successfully a child of a different race is absorbed into your family, this difference must be honored and taken into consideration. That means giving careful thought to the neighborhood in which you choose to live and the social and cultural opportunities you make available to the child.

When white parents adopt black children, they incur an implicit obligation to learn about the child's cultural heritage, and to help the child understand that this is an important part of who he or she is. It helps when adoptive parents take a genuine interest in the culture and share that learning experience with the child. In the best scenario, the black child and white parents find a way to appreciate the differences in each other's background and to use those differences to strengthen their bonds.

I'm concerned about my seventeen-year-old son. He has never had a girlfriend, but all his best friends are females. He's also not interested in sports or any of the other "normal" boy things. Should I worry that he's gay? And if that turns out to be the case, what can I do about it?

There's a lot of confusion and many misconceptions about sexual identity—and we like to clear them up when questions like this are raised. Let's first look at the wide range of concerns parents express about these issues.

On one end of the spectrum, there are nine- and ten-year-old girls whose mothers worry because they are tomboys. These are girls who would rather play ball than with dolls, and who prefer wearing jeans to dresses. Such behavior at this age has nothing at all to do with sexual identity, and is usually more a matter of style or comfort. At the other extreme are teenage boys who tell their folks that they are attracted to or sexually active with other males.

It's important to understand that homosexuality is not an abnormality. It is simply a sexual identity in which the individual is attracted to someone of the same sex. That expression of same-sex attraction or love doesn't necessarily mean that the young person is having sexual activity.

Some young people feel this attraction, but go through life never having any same-sex contact. There are large numbers of bisexual people—those who are attracted to both males and females. There are also men and women who are confused and not really sure about how they feel. We call that *questioning*. *Transgender* is when someone feels he has a different personal sexual identity. For example, a boy who feels that he's a female, despite his male physiology.

The fact that a seventeen-year-old isn't sexually active and prefers female friends tells you little or nothing about his ultimate sexual identity. In any case, there is absolutely nothing parents can do to change their children's sexual feelings and preferences. Keep in mind that whatever a young person says or does about his sexuality is merely an expression of how he or she feels right now. The best thing parents can do is to accept the teen's statements and feelings without passing judgment. Children who feel comfortable enough to discuss sexual feelings with their parents are demonstrating a great deal of trust. It's important to continue building on that.

The key is to love your child, no matter what his sexual identity. If you're curious, encourage your son to talk about his feelings. Should it turn out that your son is homosexual, don't overreact or try to discipline it out of him. Again, the most important issue is not that he's gay—but that you love him.

Children who are unsure of their sexual identity or who have feelings they don't deem as normal often feel upset and confused. In that case, you need to help him seek counseling. Young people who are gay are subject to ridicule and loss of friends. They also have an exceptionally high rate of suicide. Homosexual teens often have nobody to turn to. Parents may be shocked or concerned or disappointed, but it's essential that mothers and fathers subjugate their own emotions and expectations. Remember, your main job as a parent is to protect your child and love him for who he is.

(Please see Chapter Four for more information on talking about sex with your child.)

I have reason to believe that my son has been sexually active with another boy of the same age. Does that mean he's gay?

The short answer to that question is no. Having one or more sexual experiences with someone of the same gender does not necessarily identify that person as a homosexual or bisexual. However, there's a larger issue to consider. It's not uncommon for kids to experiment and have one or two same-sex experiences, and parents should be careful not to jump to any conclusions. At the same time, there are serious health concerns that relate to same-sex behavior that need to be addressed.

Boys who've had homosexual experiences sometimes mistakenly think they are gay. For example, boys who've been sexually abused by older men may conclude that they're homosexual—as might boys who've had a few same-sex experiences with peers. There are also boys who've had same-sex experiences who will answer no when asked if they are homosexual or bisexual. These boys are not necessarily being dishonest; the fault lies more with the question.

In our work with HIV and AIDS, we've come across a growing number of girls who contracted these diseases by having intercourse with young men who engaged in homosexual behavior.

"But I asked him if he was a homosexual," girls in this position will complain, "and he said no."

One of the questions girls need to ask boys of any age to assess their risk is: "Have you had sex with another boy or man?" Another is: "Have you had sex without using a condom?" Of course, truthful answers may not be forthcoming, but at least the right questions have been posed.

Boys who've engaged in same-sex activity may or may not consider themselves to be gay. That's not the most important concern for them—or for you as a parent. The main thing is that the young person gets the appropriate health screening, which may include probing for a variety of diseases in the mouth and rectum. At the end of the day, the issue is not one of labeling your child. It is one of overcoming your feelings of embarrassment and making your child's health your top priority.

(Please see Chapter Four for more information about sexually transmitted diseases.)

My seven-year-old daughter came home from school crying because a white classmate said: "I don't want to play with you because you're black." What is the most effective way to handle the situation?

Kids say hurtful things to one another for all sorts of reasons. Any visible difference can be used as a weapon of attack. For example, kids can be verbally attacked for wearing glasses, for being short or fat—or because of racial differences.

In some cases, these kinds of exchanges between young kids are not signs of racism. If you know the parent of the child who hurled the insult, call her and calmly discuss the incident. A sensitive parent will almost always apologize, promise to talk to her child and ask you to inform her of any recurrence. If, on the other hand, the parent denies or brushes off the incident, you can reasonably conclude that you're dealing with someone who is not racially sensitive—or possibly an outright racist.

In discussing the incident with your daughter, it's important to explain that some people are brought up to fear those who are different from themselves—and that race is a difference that's easy to see. If your child's classmate winds up apologizing, encourage your child to accept that gesture. As your daughter gathers more experience in dealing with people, she will become better able to fend off such insults, and choose friends who don't resort to racial slurs.

(Please see Chapter Three for a detailed discussion on racial discipline.)

My seventeen-year-old daughter's boyfriend recently broke up with her. She has made a few offhand comments about committing suicide. How seriously should I take those remarks?

When kids bring up suicide, they are usually crying out for help.

Parents who ignore such cries can be making a grave error. Any reference to suicide needs to be treated with the utmost seriousness. Young people who use irony or humor in making such references are just as likely to follow thorough as those who are visibly depressed. If a child raises the possibility of committing suicide, immediately seek the assistance of a mental health professional who has experience with both adolescents and in suicide prevention.

If you don't know where to turn for help, call your pediatrician or family physician and ask for a referral. If the situation appears to be acute, immediately take the child to the hospital emergency room to get a psychiatric evaluation.

Our eighteen-year-old son recently announced that he wants to join the Nation of Islam. We are a church-going Christian family, and this violates our beliefs and traditions. Should we order him not to go, try to discourage him, or let him do as he wishes?

This is a complex question. You can make a case that a child who is still living at home ought to abide by the longstanding traditions of the family. On the other hand, it's not at all unusual or undesirable for a young person to seek out an independent spiritual path. Rather than focussing on your own disappointment, try to assess what's going on with your son at this time.

Does the young man seem upset or troubled? Are things going reasonably well in school and in other areas of his life? If everything else seems in order, it's likely that your son's desire to switch religious affiliation is an attempt to find his own independent spiritual identity. Some young people may decide that they are atheists or agnostics, or that they prefer the Baptist Church to Catholicism. In general, it's not helpful to make too much of these pronouncements. In any case, it's a mistake to try to force an eighteen-year-old to do something he doesn't want to do—particularly when it relates to as highly personal an issue as religion.

Keep in mind that young people who are interested in joining the Nation of Islam are often searching for their racial, as well as their religious, identity. While there is some controversy surrounding the Nation of Islam, they have done a lot of good in the African American community, and have rebuilt many lives. Rather than going through the futile effort of trying to dictate what your son should or shouldn't believe, try to maintain a positive attitude toward his need for spiritual searching.

Consider learning a bit more about what your son finds attractive about the Nation of Islam. Encourage him to discuss his progress with you, and make it clear that the door to your church will always be open, should he choose to return.

(Please see Chapter Eight for a discussion of spirituality and issues of identity.)

My fifteen-year-old son has started hanging out with a rough crowd of boys who cut school and don't get good grades. What can I do?

Before you jump to any conclusions, it's a good idea to see your son's new friends close up. Consider inviting the whole group over for a meal, or taking them all out for pizza. This way, you can get an idea of what these boys are really like—underneath the superficial impression one might get from their clothes or style of speech. Create a friendly atmosphere as you encourage the boys to talk about their families, their attitudes toward school, and their future goals. It may well be that your son's association with this crowd is not a matter of concern.

If, on the other hand, you do conclude that these boys are likely to pull your kid in the wrong direction, it's essential that you intervene in the right way. Parents often don't realize the power they have in changing a child's behavior. The key is using that power in a nonconfrontational way. Instead of ordering your son not to associate with a particular crowd, simply state that you're not happy with these new associations and that you would prefer that he didn't hang out with these people.

There's a better than even chance that your son will say that he's not going to give up these friends. If so, don't get bent out of shape. Just reiterate your position—and leave no doubt that by refusing, your son is going against your wishes. When parents have laid the disciplinary groundwork, children will often come around and honor their wishes.

There are two approaches that almost never work. The first is yelling and ordering the child to obey, which only serves to invite rebellion. The second is not stating a clear position, which leads children to believe it's okay to do as they wish. Most teens are well aware that parents are limited in their power to enforce rules. Your best chance of getting your son to comply is to build on his respect for your opinions and his desire to meet the high standards you set. (Please see Chapter Two for a discussion of setting down disciplinary guidelines. See Chapter Three for a discussion on peer group concerns.)

My sixteen-year-old daughter is pregnant. Should I advise her to get an abortion?

This needs to be a family decision, though, ultimately, the young person should have the final say. Either way, you should do everything in your power to support the young woman. As a practical matter, parents often try to push the expectant mother in one direction or another—according to their own needs and wishes.

We know mothers of pregnant teens who want a new baby in the family, and who will discourage the young girl from having an abortion. There are other situations in which teens want to keep their babies, but the parents take a strong stance against it.

It's important to help a pregnant teen understand the long-term responsibility having a child entails—even if the family is willing to absorb a good deal of that responsibility while the young mother completes her schooling. Some families are against abortion on religious grounds. In such cases, a teenager who doesn't want to keep her baby can seek placement through adoption.

In counseling a pregnant teen to come to an informed decision, it's important to help her understand all the ways having a baby can change her life. You might explain, for example, that babies get sick and mothers sometimes have to stay up all night caring for them. Also, a baby can greatly restrict a young person's social life, and make it harder for her to complete her education.

There are, of course, many examples of young mothers who have gone on to have successful careers and satisfying lives. If your daughter does decide to have the baby, it's important to provide enough support so that she's not forced to drop out of school. Explain that it takes a good deal of money to support a child until he's eighteen or twenty-one. Consequently, obtaining a good education and career skills is, if anything, even more important than it would have been had she not become pregnant. (Please see Chapter Ten for a listing of programs and resources for young single mothers.)

My fourteen-year-old daughter came home from school complaining that boys are feeling her breasts and touching her inappropriately. How should I handle this?

First, believe your daughter, and make it clear that you are ready to protect and comfort her. Kids rarely bring these things to parents unless they are quite serious. The child has obviously decided that this is a significant event, one that goes beyond normal teasing or fooling around. The worst thing a parent can do is minimize what happened or treat it as an everyday occurrence. Your daughter has told you she was harmed and that she's upset about it. That's all you need to know to start taking action.

Keep in mind that sexual harassment is a crime. While you may not want to involve the legal system at this point, you should immediately pull your child out of school. Next, report the incident to the school principal as a crime. State your complaint both verbally and in writing. At that point, you may want to request a forum with the principal, the boy or boys involved, and their parents. Depending on how the school administrators handle the situation, you may choose to bring in the police.

In many instances, the offending boys may not be arrested. Depending on their history and the exact nature of the incident, the principal may be able to remedy the matter with appropriate punishment. The bottom line is, however, that a crime has been perpetrated against your child—and you want to know what measures school administrators plan to take in order to avoid a repetition.

Again, the three key steps are: assume your child is telling the truth; provide all the support and comfort she needs; and make certain that she is no longer at risk.

(Please see Chapter Five for a discussion on dealing with school administrators. See Chapter Four for a discussion on bullying.)

My seven-year-old daughter is very upset over the death of her fifty-eight-year-old grandmother. Should we have her attend the funeral?

Parents often have a tough time talking about death with their children. That's not surprising, since many adults haven't come to terms with their own mortality. All living things die, and concealing that reality from a child is not helpful.

Children are likely to become upset at funerals of loved ones. At the same time, the experience can help them achieve a sense of closure.

Death from old age is the most natural conclusion to life. Sometimes, people die before their time—whether from an accident or an illness. This too is part of life, though death is always harder to accept when it occurs outside the natural course of events.

Mothers and fathers with a strong religious faith may have an easier time helping kids cope with death and answering questions like, "Why do people die?" and "What happens after we die?" But, in general, the most important thing is to help children understand the arc of life and the importance of grieving for every loss. We all need to mourn our losses and deal with our feelings in order to heal and move on with our lives. The earlier children develop these strengths, the better off they will be.

Parents need to talk frankly to children about death—whether it's the death of a relative, a friend, or a pet. Shielding children from loss and mourning can wind up causing much greater pain. In time, children learn to celebrate the loved one's life through memories and stories, to come to terms with the circumstances of her death—and to allow their own emotions to run a natural course.

My ten-year-old son and twelve-year-old daughter are very fearful of being killed by terrorists. I try to shield them from the horrors we see and hear on the news, but it's impossible. How can I soothe their fears without being dishonest?

Wars and terrorist acts can provoke fear and shake a child's sense of security. In the wake of the attacks on the World Trade Center on September 11, 2001, we received many calls from parents who had questions on this matter. The subsequent war and terrorist threats have provoked ongoing fear and undermined some children's sense of security. We live and work only a few miles from lower Manhattan, so we've dealt with a number of families who lost loved ones in the attacks and who required counseling. However, in most families, parents should be able to calm children's fears by using the following guidelines:

♦ In general, it's best to answer questions honestly, but without dwelling on frightening details. Don't underestimate children's intelligence. They will be more worried if they think you are too scared to tell them what is happening. Children of all ages should be encouraged to express their thoughts and feelings. You can help children accomplish that by being a good listener.

♦ Don't embellish or speculate about what has happened and what might happen. Don't raise issues the child doesn't bring up. Always take a child's age and level of understanding into consideration.

Early elementary school children need brief and simple information, balanced with reassurances that the daily structure of their lives will not change.

Upper elementary and early middle school children will be more vocal in asking questions about whether they truly are safe and what protective steps are being taken. They may need your assistance separating reality from fantasy.

Upper middle school and high school students are likely to have strong and varying opinions about the causes of violence and wars. They may share concrete suggestions about how to prevent wars and tragedies in society.

♦ Model calm and control. Children take their emotional cues from the significant adults in their lives. Do your best not to appear anxious or frightened.

♦ Let children know that it is okay to feel upset. Explain that fear is a natural response in the face of war and similar tragedies. Encourage children to talk about their feelings, and help put them into perspective. Children will express their emotions differently, and will look to you for assurance that there's nothing wrong with what they're feeling.

♦ Observe children's emotional state. Depending on their age, children may not express their concerns verbally. Changes in behavior, appetite, and sleep patterns can also indicate an elevated level of grief, anxiety, or discomfort. Make extra time to be with your children, and go out of your way to express warmth and reassurance—especially at bedtime. If a behavioral change is ongoing or seems unusually intense, seek appropriate counseling.

♦ Limit the amount of your child's television viewing of troubling events. Many adults feel compelled to sit mesmerized watching news programs. In general, kids are better off without much exposure to the never-ending parade of opinion and speculation about what terrible thing might or might not happen next.

◆ Seek spiritual comfort. In times of tragedy and uncertainty, many people find it helpful to pray or attend religious services. If you believe this will help you and members of your family, by all means do so.

◆ Safeguard your children's health. Stress and fear can take a physical toll on children as well as adults. Make sure your children get appropriate sleep, exercise, and nutrition.

(Please see Chapter Eight for more information on mind-body health. See Chapter Ten, Selected Resources, for places to turn to for help.)

Lately, I've been taking my frustrations out on my kids. I always feel bad afterwards, but sometimes it all gets to be too much to handle. Does this mean that there's something wrong with me? Do I need counseling?

Nobody ever said that being a parent was easy. It's important not to let yourself get too stressed out. We recognize that this is easier said than done, but there are things you can do when your stress level goes into the red zone. Sometimes, having a friend to talk to or a shoulder to cry on is enough to put people in a better state. There are also community- and church-based parenting groups where mothers and fathers can network and share their concerns.

Parents Anonymous is a national volunteer group whose mission is to help parents who feel that they are at the end of their rope. When parents feel frustrated and overwhelmed, they can act against their better judgment by doing and saying things that can hurt their children. Before that happens, it's important to seek some kind of competent outside help. The appropriate type of help depends largely on the nature of the problem.

Parents often become frustrated when children have serious physical or emotional disabilities. Such problems can disrupt a family's emotional balance and keep parents on a short fuse. Fortunately, there is plenty of help available. There are, for example, groups for parents of children with diseases ranging from cancer to cerebral palsy. There are also parent groups of children with emotional disabilities ranging from autism and behavioral disorders to learning problems like dyslexia and ADHD. These groups can generally direct you to counselors and other specialists who deal with families on an individual basis.

Some problems that require outside help stem more from the parent than the child. These include alcoholism, drug abuse, gambling, and violent or abusive behavior. Physically abusive parents sometimes portray themselves as strict disciplinarians who are doing right by their kids. Parents who are verbally abusive can have an even harder time facing up to their problem, because their hurtful behavior leaves no physical marks. However, the emotional damage they inflict can hurt a child just as much. The following are some signs that you might need help in controlling your temper.

- You leave marks on your child's body when you administer discipline.
- Your main forms of discipline are spanking or berating the child.
- Your child fears you and seems afraid when you come near.
- You sometimes have thoughts of hitting or otherwise harming your child.
- You berate your child or embarrass her by criticizing her—rather than her actions.
- You sometimes fantasize leaving your child, or feel sorry that he or she was born.
- You notice the child mirroring your aggressive behavior in his or her treatment of siblings and peers.

Recognizing that you need help is often the most difficult step in making positive changes. Once you've gotten past that hurdle, you want to make sure you get the right kind of help. The following is a listing of some of the generally available kinds of counseling and therapy. Please note that some sources of help are free, some charge a modest fee or work on a sliding scale, while others can run upwards of $100 per hour. Medical insurers and HMOs sometimes provide full or partial coverage for certain kinds of counseling or therapy. Please consult your health-care provider for specific information.

SOURCES OF OUTSIDE HELP

- Friends and relatives can be of help when sharing everyday complaints and frustration. Their time and advice is cost-free, and can be tremendously helpful. However, people close to you may have trouble offering the kind of well-considered advice you need to navigate certain situations.

◆ Clergy members in the African American community often provide counseling services. Pastoral counselors who've been trained to work with families can be especially effective in this work. In most cases, their services are free to congregation members.

◆ Twelve-step programs can help women and men cope with a wide variety of personal and family difficulties. These include the afore-mentioned Parents Anonymous, as well as more well-known groups like Alcoholics Anonymous, Narcotics Anonymous, and Gamblers Anonymous. These groups are free and run by the members, who form a network of mutual support. Twelve-step groups now exist for a variety of addictive behaviors. These include Overeaters Anonymous, Emotions Anonymous, Sex Addicts Anonymous, and many others. Most twelve-step groups have counterparts for children and spouses of partic-ipants.

◆ Targeted support groups, such as the kind mentioned above, help families deal with a wide variety of issues, including infertility, teenage pregnancy, adoption, the death of a parent, and a wide variety of chil-dren's problems. Most of these groups are run by not-for-profit organiza-tions that require little or no payment. Such groups are good sources of information and also put people in contact with others who are experi-encing similar difficulties.

◆ Psychiatrists, pediatricians, and physicians who are trained and ex-perienced in dealing with family issues can offer help and guidance to children, parents, and entire families. These are the only helping profes-sionals who can prescribe medication.

◆ Psychologists, clinical social workers, and nurse practitioners com-plete a prescribed course of training and are licensed by the state. Be ad-vised that in many states, you don't need a license to call yourself a counselor or therapist. Consequently, consumers have to shop carefully for these services.

To make certain the person you're considering is properly trained and certified, consult a professional organization such as the American Psychiatric Association, the American Psychological Association, or the National Association of Social Workers. These organizations can verify the credentials of the therapist and also refer you to qualified individuals in your community.

(Please see Chapter Ten, Selected Resources, which lists organizations offering help with specific problems and parenting issues.)

My son and daughter are both in their teens. Neither one has any serious problems. Still, as I read this book, I notice a number of things I've done wrong in raising my kids. For example, my son doesn't work up to his potential at school, and my daughter has a weight problem. I feel that I've been too lenient in the past. Is there anything I can do at this point?

Parenting is a lifelong learning process, and there is no such thing as a perfect or mistake-free parent. Every day provides some kind of new challenge and learning opportunity for parents. The best you can do is to try to take advantage of them, and not be too hard on yourself when something goes wrong. Just because your child overeats or gets a failing grade doesn't mean that you're a bad parent.

Loving, well-meaning parents make all sorts of decisions in raising their children, not always anticipating the likely result. Some mothers and fathers are overbearing and overcritical; others aren't demanding enough. We also know parents who try hard to duplicate their own childhood, and others who would move heaven and earth to do the opposite of what their own parents did. Mothers and fathers sometimes favor one sibling over another, and this too is bound to have an impact.

Many of these parenting choices are made pretty much on the fly, without a lot of advance thought. Our purpose in writing this book is to help mothers and fathers become more thoughtful in their parenting choices. Still, there is no such thing as a perfect parent—or a perfect child. Quite often, it is the desire for perfection that creates problems. Rather than worry about not being a perfect parent, try to profit from your mistakes and make positive changes as you go forward. It's always easier to instill discipline early. However, it's never too late for parents to start making adjustments and improvements.

The key is to live in the present, learn from the past, and try to do better in the future—and to teach your children to do the same.

10

❦

Selected Resources

Raising children is like hanging wallpaper—just when you figure out what you're doing, you're done.

—ANONYMOUS

W E HAVE DESIGNED our Five-Discipline Program to address many of your key concerns as African-American parents. However, no single book can answer every question or help parents anticipate every problem that might come up. We hope this book will inspire you to seek out more information on issues or problems that interest or concern you. To that end, we devote this final chapter to providing a listing of selected resources that can help you in your quest to be the best possible parent to your child or teen.

In this chapter, we supply a selected list of books, videos, and Web sites that provide further information about areas or topics of interest to parents. We also list addresses, phone numbers, and Web site addresses that offer help with various kinds of problems. Of course, we want you to think of us as an ongoing resource, and we invite you to contact us at either of our Web site addresses—www.strengthfortheirjourney.com or www.blackparents.org—with your questions, comments, and concerns.

Parenting

TELEPHONE ADVICE

Childhelp USA National Hotline
800–4–A–CHILD (422–4453)
Offers 24-hour advice and referrals nationwide, for children and adults with questions or in crisis.

National Parent Information Network
800–583–4135
Features a large database of parenting information.

WEB SITES

ParenTalk
www.tnpc.com/parentalk/index.html
Informative Web site featuring articles by physicians and psychologists.

ParenthoodWeb
parenthoodweb.com
Pediatricians and psychiatrists answer e-mailed questions.

Parenting Q&A
www.parenting-qa.com
This site is "solely devoted to providing parents with answers to their most pressing questions." Also offers essays on spirituality and other subjects.

ParentSoup
www.parentsoup.com
Discussion forums address a wide range of topics including disciplining, stepfamilies, and learning problems.

BOOKS

Brooks, Robert, and Goldstein, Sam, *Raising Resilient Children.* Chicago: Contemporary Books, 2000.

Comer, James P., and Poussaint, Alvin F., *Raising Black Children: Two Leading Psychiatrists Confront the Educational, Social, and Emotional Problems Facing Black Children.* New York: Penguin, 1992.

Hopson, Darlene Powell, and Hopson, Derek S., *Different and Wonderful: Raising Black Children in a Race-Conscious Society.* New York: Prentice-Hall, 1990.

Sachs, Brad E., *The Good Enough Child: How to Have an Imperfect Family and Be Perfectly Satisfied.* New York: Quill, 2001.

Seligman, Martin E. P.; Reivich, Karen; Jaycox, Lisa; and Gillham, Jane, *The Optimistic Child.* New York: HarperPerennial, 1996.

Thompson, Michael; Grace, Catherine O'Neill; and Cohen, Lawrence J., *Best Friends, Worst Enemies: Understanding the Social Lives of Children.* New York: Ballantine, 2001.

Wright, Marguerite A., *I'm Chocolate, You're Vanilla: Raising Healthy Black and Biracial Children in a Race-Conscious World.* San Francisco: Jossey-Bass, 1998.

Therapy and Counseling

PROFESSIONAL ORGANIZATIONS

American Association for Marriage and Family Therapy
1100 17th Street, N.W.
Washington, DC 20036
Telephone 202–452–0109
www.aamft.org
American Association for Marriage and Family Therapy publishes its own helpful *Consumer's Guide for Marriage and Family Therapy.* The organization also provides online referral and other information through its Web site.

American Association of Pastoral Counselors
9504A Lee Highway
Fairfax, VA 22031–2303
Telephone 703–385–6967

American Association of Sex Educators, Counselors, and Therapists (AASECT)
435 N. Michigan Avenue, Suite 1717
Chicago, IL 60611
Telephone 312–644–0828

American Mental Health Counselors Association
Telephone 800–326–2640
Provides referrals to professionals in your area.

American Psychiatric Association
1400 K Street, N.W.
Washington, DC 20005
Telephone 202–682–6000

American Psychological Association
750 First Street, N.E.
Washington, DC 20002
Telephone 202–336–5500

Association of Black Psychologists
P.O. Box 55999
Washington, DC 20040–5999
Telephone 202–722–0808
Admin@ABPsi.org

Mental Health Directory
Superintendent of Documents
Washington, DC 20402
Telephone 202–783–3238
Comprehensive listing of outpatient mental health clinics, psychiatric hospitals, mental health centers, and general hospitals with separate psychiatric services.

National Institute of Mental Health (NIMH)
5600 Fishers Lane, Room 15CO5
Rockville, MD 20857
Telephone 301–443–4515
NIMH conducts research and provides information on depression and other mental disorders.

Takes Two
Telephone 301–439–0024.
Organization designed specifically for
African-American couples.

American Academy of Pediatrics
www.aap.org
Organization provides information
and education on health issues for
parents of infants, young children,
and adolescents.

Single Parents

ORGANIZATIONS

Single Parents Association
Telephone 800–704–2102
Helps single parents find support
groups and resources in their communities, and fields a wide range of parenting questions.

**African American Self-Help
  Foundation**
182 Farmers Lane, Suite 200
Santa Rosa, CA 95405
Telephone 707–528–3499;
707–525–1310 fax
www.aashf.org

Mentoring

ORGANIZATIONS

100 Black Men, Inc.
141 Auburn Avenue
Atlanta, GA 30303
Telephone 800–598–3411
fax 404–688–1024
100blackmen.org

Big Brothers/Big Sisters of America
230 North 13th Street
Philadelphia, PA 19107

**Clearinghouse on Urban Education
  (EIRC)**
Teachers College,
Columbia University
Main Hall, Room 300, Box 40
525 West 120th Street
New York, NY 10027–9998
Telephone 212–678–3433

Project RAISE
Fund for Educational Excellence
616-D North Eutaw Street
Baltimore, MD 21201

One Plus One
4802 Fifth Avenue
Pittsburgh, PA 15213

Public/Private Ventures
399 Market Street
Philadelphia, PA 19106

Save the Children
54 Wilton Road
Westport, CT 06880
Telephone 1-800-729-1446
Web site
savethechildren.org

African American Service Organizations

The Links, Inc.
1200 Massachusetts Avenue, N.W.
Washington, DC 20005
Telephone 202–842–8686
www.linksinc.org

Jack and Jill International
Carla D. Williams,
National President
P.O. Box 70635
Pasadena, CA 91117
Telephone 626–584–6410
jack-and-jill.org

Adoption

Resolve, Inc.
Telephone 617–643–2424
Based in Belmont, Massachusetts,
Resolve, Inc., provides information
on infertility, adoption, high-tech
pregnancies, and insemination. This
national organization runs support
groups and seminars, and provides
references to support groups and
physicians who specialize in treating
infertility.

**Child Saving Institute Adoption
Center**
115 South 46th Street
Omaha, NE 68132
Telephone 888–588–6003
Organization specializing in minority
and interracial adoption.

Stepfamilies

Stepfamily Association of America
650 J Street, Suite 205
Lincoln, NE 68508–2916

Divorce

WEB SITES

Divorce Helpline
www.divorcehelp.com

Divorce Info
www.divorceinfo.com

DivorceNet
www.divorcenet.com

Divorce Online
www.divorceonline.com

Divorce Support
www.divorcesupport.com

Attention and Learning Problems

The Learning Disabilities Association of America
www.ldanatl.org
A national nonprofit organization with a purpose "to advance the education and general welfare of children and adults of normal or potentially normal intelligence who manifest disabilities of a perceptual, conceptual, or coordinative nature." Contains links to resources for specific learning, perceptual, and/or attention deficits.

Gifted Children

ORGANIZATIONS

For information regarding the care and nurturing of gifted children, contact one of the following organizations:

National Association for Gifted Children
1155 15th Street, N.W.
Washington, DC 20005

Educational Information and Resource Center (EIRC)
606 Delsea Drive
Sewell, NJ 08080

Mensa Gifted Children Pen Pals International
Dr. Debby van de Vender
166 E. 61st Street, Box 11G
New York, NY 10021

Gifted Child Society
190 Rock Road
Glen Rock, NJ 07452
Telephone 201–444–6530

College and College Scholarships

WEB SITES

The following Web sites allow students to access college and university online applications. They also provide useful tips and advice on topics, such as financial aid.

CollegeQuest
www.collegequest.com/cgibin/ndCGI/
CollegeQuest/pgGateway
This free service lets students apply to over a thousand schools.

CollegeEdge
apply.embark.com
This free service offers over 400 electronic applications to undergraduate, business, and graduate schools.

CollegeLink
www.collegelink.com/html/index.htm
Students can apply to more than 1000 schools through this Web site, which is affiliated with the College Board. It is free to fill out questionnaire and first application. Additional applications cost $5.

E-Apps
www.eapp.com/firstfl.htm
This Web site provides links to online applications and university homepages for undergraduate, graduate, and community colleges.

XAP
www.xap.com
Students get the latest computerized university and college admissions applications and interactive campus tours at this Web site.

Educational Information and Resource Center
www.ericweb.tc.columbia.edu/hbcu/
financial_aid/finaid.html
Features a listing of minority-aid resources for African-American students.

BOOKS

There are a number of useful books with information and listings about potential scholarships, including these:

Beckham, Barry, ed. *The Black Student's Guide to Scholarships: 700+ Private Money Sources for Black and Minority Students.* 5th ed. Madison, WI: Madison Books, 1999.

Black, Issac. *Black Excel African American Student's College Guide: Your One-Stop Resource for Choosing the Right College, Getting In, and Paying the Bill.* New York: John Wiley and Sons, 2000.

Laveist, Thomas. *The DayStar Guide to Colleges for African-American Students.* New York: Kaplan, 2000.

Parham, Marisa. *The African American Student's Guide to College.* Princeton, NJ: Princeton Review Series, 1999.

Wilson, Erlene B. *The 100 Best Colleges for African-American Students.* 2nd ed. New York: Plume, 1998.

Money and Careers

WEB SITES

MainXchange
www.mainXchange.com
Interactive game in which teens invest 100,000 virtual dollars in publicly traded companies. Top portfolios win prizes from featured companies.

Investing for Kids
hyperion.advanced.org/3096
Produced by kids for kids. Introduction to basics of investing that adults will appreciate as well.

KidsBank.Com
www.kidsbank.com
Geared for elementary school children.

Taxi Interactive
www.irs.gov/taxi
The IRS set up this site that shows teens how much they'd earn from various summer jobs and much more.

The Mad Money Room
www.nbc.com/atthemax/money
Site features "Reality Check" and "Should I Buy It?" Teens take a quiz to see how much they'd have to earn to support their lifestyle, and whether it makes sense to make a particular purchase.

Moneyopolis
www.moneyopolis.org
Kids in grades six through eight use math skills to solve real-life problems of earning, spending, and saving.

Lemonade Stand
www.littlejason.com/lemonade/index.html
A summertime livelihood becomes a life lesson, in the form of a game that reveals the realities of running a small business.

Kids' Money
pages.prodigy.com/K/I/Y/kidsmoney
Children (and parents) can discover how other families dole out allowances and save for college. Kids learn the basics of ATMs, credit cards, and checking accounts.

Kiplinger.com
www.kiplinger.com
Financial publisher's Web site features additional money Web sites for parents, children, and teens.

BOOKS

Useful books on money and careers include:

Boston, Kelvin. *Smart Money Moves for African Americans*. New York: Perigee, 2000.

Harris, Fran. *In the Black: The African-American Guide to Raising Financially Responsible Children*. New York: Fireside Books, 1998.

Schoenbrun, Muriel Karlin. *Make Your Child a Success: Career Guidance from Kindergarten to College*. New York: Perigee, 1983.

Scheele, Adele. *Skills for Success*. New York: Ballantine, 1979.

Stress and Stress Management

ORGANIZATION

The American Institute of Stress
Telephone 212–410–9043
Located in Yonkers, New York, the American Institute of Stress provides information on stress and stress management as well as referrals to experts in your area.

PUBLICATIONS

Superintendent of Documents
US Government Printing Office
Washington, DC 20402

Diet and Nutrition

ORGANIZATIONS

American Dietetic Association
216 W. Jackson Boulevard
Chicago, IL 60606
Telephone: 800–366–1655
www.eatright.org

American Society for Nutritional Sciences
9650 Rockville Pike, Suite 4500
Bethesda, MD 20814

Telephone 301–530–7050
www.faseb.org/asns

Council for Responsible Nutrition
1875 Eye Street, N.W., Suite 400
Washington, DC 20006–5194
Telephone 202–872–1488
www.crnusa.org

Center for Science in the Public Interest
1875 Connecticut Avenue, N.W., Suite 300
Washington, DC 20009
Telephone 202–332–9110
www.cspinet.org

International Food Information Council Foundation
110 Connecticut Avenue, N.W., Suite 430
Washington, DC 20036
Telephone 202–296–6540
ificinfo.health.org

Nutrition Information Service
University of Alabama, UAB Station
Webb Building, Room 206
Birmingham, AL 35294
Telephone 800–231–DIET (3438)

Office of Dietary Supplements
National Institutes of Health
31 Center Drive
Building 31, Room 1B29, MSC 2086
Bethesda, MD 20892–2086
Telephone 301–435–2920
dietary-supplements.info.nih.gov

Weight-Control Information Network (WIN)
1 WIN Way
Bethesda, MD 20892–3665
Telephone 301–984–7378
www.niddk.nih.gov/health/nutrit/win.htm

VIDEOS

Beyond Nutrition: Eating for Health (Learning Seed, 1999; VHS, 22 min. #232).

Diet and Weight Management: What Really Works? (Cambridge Educational, 2000; VHS, 30 min.).

Food for Thought: The Critical Elements of Good Nutrition (Aquarius Health Care, 2001; VHS, 28 min.).

Weighing In: The Problems of Obesity (Aquarius Health Care, 2001; VHS, 28 min.).

WEB SITES

American Dietetic Association
www.eatright.org

Arbor Nutrition Guide
www.arborcom.com

Center for Food Safety and Applied Nutrition
vm.cfsan.fda.gov/list.html

Cyberdiet
www.cyberdiet.com

Dietsite.com
www.dietsite.com

Food & Nutrition Information Center
www.nal.usda.gov/fnic

Healthy Weight Network
www.healthyweight.net

Nutrition.gov
www.nutrition.gov/home/index.php3

Mayo Clinic Food and Nutrition Center
www.mayoclinic.com

BOOKS

American Academy of Pediatrics, *Guide to Your Child's Nutrition.* New York: Villard, 1999.

Bijlefeld, Marjolijn K., and Zoumbaris, Sharon. *Food and You: A Guide to Healthy Habits for Teens.* Westport, CT: Greenwood Press, May 2001.

Goldberg, Albert C., M.D. *Feed Your Child Right: From Birth Through Teens.* New York: M. Evans, 2000.

Litt, Ann Selkowitz. *The College Student's Guide to Eating Well on Campus.* Bethesda, MD: Tulip Hill Press, 2000.

Tamborlane, William V., M.D. *The Yale Guide to Children's Nutrition.* New Haven, CT: Yale University Press, 1999.

Sex Education

WEB SITES

iwannaknow.org
www.iwannaknow.org
Sexual health and STD prevention information for teens, including games, chat, education, and resources.

Scarleteen
www.scarleteen.com
With Pink Slip and Boyfriend, a sex education and sexuality information site for teens.

Teen Health
www.chebucto.ns.ca/Health/Teen Health
Provides information and links on sexuality, STDs, pregnancy, sexual orientation, and more.

Sex, Etc.
www.sxetc.org
Newsletter written by teens for teens on important health and sexuality issues.

All About Sex
www.allaboutsex.org
Offers open discussion about sexuality for adults, teens, and preteens.

Teen Sexuality in a Culture of Confusion
www.intac.com
Seven teens talk about their lives, sex, being gay, being straight, and being HIV+.

Choosing the Best
www.choosingthebest.org
Abstinence-based sex education curriculum aimed at preventing teen pregnancy and sexually related problems.

It's Your (Sex) Life
www.itsyoursexlife.com
Provides objective sexual health information for both young adults and parents who want to address these issues with their teens.

Teenwire
www.teenwire.org
Sexuality and relationship information from the Planned Parenthood Federation of America.

Youth Embassy
www.youthembassy.com
Dedicated to providing youth, parents, and teachers with science-based responses to questions about sex.

Sexuality Information & Education Council (SIECUS)
www.siecus.org
Develops, collects, and disseminates sexuality education information.

Cigarette Smoking

WEB SITE

Tobacco-Free Kids
www.tobaccofreekids.org

Alcoholism and Substance Abuse

ORGANIZATIONS

Many twelve-step programs are listed in your local phone book and newspaper. For additional help and information, contact the following:

The Alcohol Abuse Emergency 24-Hour Hotline
Telephone 800–252–6465
Hotline provides twenty-four-hour information on treatments available for alcoholics, alcohol detox programs, and referrals to local treatment facilities and support groups.

The Alcohol and Drug Helpline
Telephone 800–821–4357
Sponsored by the American International Hospital Services; offers referrals to alcohol and drug dependency units.

Children of Alcoholic Families National Clearinghouse on Alcohol Information
P.O. Box 2345
Rockville, MD 20852

Elderly Alcohol Abuse Information Center
National Institute on Aging
2209 Distribution Circle
Silver Spring, MD 20910
Telephone 301–495–3455

The Cocaine Hotline
Telephone 800–COCAINE
(262–2463)
Sponsored by the American
Psychiatric Institute and Fair Oaks
Hospital in New Jersey; provides information on the health risks of using
cocaine and offers referrals to local
counseling services.

The National Clearinghouse for Drug Abuse Information Helpline
Telephone 301–468–2600
At the National Institute of Mental
Health in Rockville, Maryland; offers
programs, information, and referrals
on drug abuse.

The National Drug Information and Referral Line
Telephone 800–662–4357
Sponsored by the National Institute
of Drug Abuse; provides phone counseling and referrals to support groups
and treatment programs.

American Mensa, Ltd.
2626 E. 14th Street, Dept. GC
Brooklyn, NY 11235–3992
Telephone 718–934–3700

Violence and Abuse

ORGANIZATIONS

Parents Anonymous
Telephone 909–621–6184
www.parentsanonymous-natl.org
Parents Anonymous has more than
two thousand branches nationwide
that provide a nonjudgmental place
for parents to share their frustrations
and learn better childrearing skills.
The program (including childcare
during meetings) is free.

Childhelp USA
Telephone 800–4–A–CHILD
(422–4453)
National twenty-four-hour hotline is
staffed by trained counselors who can
help with a range of problems, from
"How do I stop his crying?" to "I
think I'm going to harm my baby."

Children's Defense Fund
25 E. Street, N.W.
Washington, DC 20001
Telephone 202–628–8787

Health Resource Center on
    Domestic Violence
Family Violence Prevention Fund
383 Rhode Island Street, Suite 304
San Francisco, CA 94103–5133
Telephone 800–313–1310
fax 415–252–8991

National Hotline for Battered
    Women
Telephone 800–799–SAFE (7233)
www.famvi.com/htlines.htm

Wife Beating and Elder Abuse Help
    Center
Clearinghouse on Family Violence
P.O. Box 1182
Washington, DC 20013
Telephone 703–385–7565

Center for the Prevention of Sexual
    and Domestic Violence
936 N. 34th Street, Suite 200
Seattle, WA 98103
Telephone 206–634–1903
fax 206–634–0115

United Nations Development Fund
    for Women (UNEFEM)
304 E. 45th Street
New York, NY 10017
Telephone 212–906–6400

WEB SITES

National Clearinghouse on Child
    Abuse and Neglect Information
www.calib.com/nccanch

National Committee to Prevent
    Child Abuse
www.childabuse.org

Shaken Baby Syndrome Prevention
    Plus
www.sbsplus.com

National Council on Child Abuse
    and Family Violence
www.nccafv.org

Gangs and Bullying

WEB SITES

Bully B'ware Productions
www.bullybeware.com

Children First (National PTA)
www.pta.org/programs

National Crime Prevention Council
www.weprevent.org

National School Safety Center
www.nsscl.org

Kidscape
www.kidscape.org.uk/kidscape

Safe Child
www.safechild.org

Southern Poverty Law Center and
    the Teaching Tolerance Program
www.splcenter.org

BOOKS

Decker, Scott H., et al. *Life in the Gang: Family, Friends and Violence*. New York: Cambridge University Press, 1996.

Webster-Doyle, Terrence. *Why Is Everybody Always Picking on Me?: A Guide to Understanding Bullies for Young People*. (Tokyo: Weatherhill, 1999.

Fried, Suellen, and Fried, Paula. *Bullies & Victims: Helping Your Child Survive the Schoolyard Battlefield*. New York: M. Evans, 1998.

Notes

1.
Teaching Black Children to Love Themselves

1. Opening quotation by Dr. Marilyn Benoit is from Ylonda Gault-Caviness, "Wise Words (Raising African-American Children)," *Essence*, May 2000.

2. Alex Haley, *Roots* (New York: Dell, 1997).

3. The attitudes of African American parents toward their children's education is detailed in John Immerwahr, *Great Expectations: How the Public and Parents—White, African American and Hispanic—View Higher Education.* Report by *Public Agenda,* issued by National Center for Public Policy and Higher Education, May 2000.

4. Jodi Wilogren, "College Education Seen As Essential." *The New York Times,* May 4, 2000.

5. A coauthor interview with Muriel Karlin Trachman is quoted in Muriel Karlin Trachman and Gene Busnar, "*Raising a Successful, Happy Child,*" an unpublished paper. The discussions on "Giving Children Responsibilities" and "Helping Children Become Effective Decision Makers" also draw on these sources.

2.
Traditional Discipline:
Setting Behavioral Limits

1. Statistics on how African American parents discipline children are based on Carla R. Bradley, "Child Rearing in African American Families: A Study of the Disciplinary Practices of African American Parents," *Journal of Multicultural Counseling & Development,* October 1998.

2. David M. Kleist, "Single-Parent Families: A Difference That Makes a Difference?" *Family Journal,* October 1999.

3. The description of multiple mothering and gender flexibility in African American families is from Beverly Greene, "African American Families," *National Forum,* Summer 1995.

4. Tips in the sidebar Helping Kids Relieve Stress draw on information in Barbara M. Dixon, "Stress Busters for Kids," *Heart & Soul,* December 1996, January 1997.

5. The section on stepfamilies draws from material in Steven Simring and Sue Klavans Simring, *Making Marriage Work for Dummies* (Chicago: IDG, 1999).

3.
RACIAL DISCIPLINE: DON'T LEAVE HOME WITHOUT IT

1. Quotation is from Don Terry, "Getting Under My Skin," *The New York Times,* July 16, 2000.

2. The discussion on racial discipline draws from material in Robert L. Johnson and Steven Simring, *The Race Trap: Smart Strategies for Effective Racial Communication in Business and in Life* (New York: HarperCollins, 2000).

4.
EMOTIONAL DISCIPLINE:
SAYING NO AND OTHER STRENGTH-BUILDING STRATEGIES

1. Quotation is from Robert Brooks and Sam Goldstein, *Raising Resilient Children* (Chicago: Contemporary Books, 2000).

2. "When Parents Are a Part of the Drug Problem," *Christian Science Monitor,* August 28, 2000.

3. Catherine Gourley, "Get Smart About Drugs in the Media," *Current Health,* April/May 2000.

4. Tips for saying no to drugs draw on material cited in "Winning the Fight Against Drugs," *Current Health,* February 1, 1999.

5. Joseph P. Shapiro, "Teenage Sex: Just Say 'Wait.' " *U.S. News & World Report,* July 26, 1993.

6. Statistics on sexual activity of black, white, and Hispanic teens are from *Youth Risk Behavior Surveillance,* Department of Health and Human Services (Atlanta: Centers for Disease Control and Prevention [CDC], September 2000).

7. Statistics on adolescent pregnancy and childbearing: "National Vital Statistics Report," September 25, 2001. Statistics on sexually transmitted diseases in adolescents: *Sexually Transmitted Disease Surveillance, 1999.* Department of Health and Human Services (Atlanta: Centers for Disease Control and Prevention [CDC], September 2000).

8. Statistics on sexually transmitted diseases: *Sexually Transmitted Disease Surveillance, 1999.*

9. Statistics on AIDS: *Sexually Transmitted Disease Surveillance, 1999.*

10. Jim Impoco and Robin M. Bennefield, "TV's Frisky Family Values," *U.S. News & World Report,* April 15, 1996.

11. Timothy R. Jordan, James H. Price, and Shawn Fitzgerald, "Rural Parents'

Communication with Their Teen-agers About Sexual Issues," *Journal of School Health,* October 2000.

12. Allen L. Hixon, "Gangs: Preventing Street Gang Violence," *American Family Physician,* April 15, 1999.

13. Allen L. Hixon, "Gangs."

14. Association for Children of New Jersey.

15. Allen L. Hixon, "Gangs."

16. Sue Smith-Heavenrich, "Kids Hurting Other Kids: Bullies in the Schoolyard," *Mothering,* May/June 2001.

17. Terrence Webster-Doyle, "Saved by the Bell: Self-Defense as Conflict Education," *Mothering,* May/June 2001.

18. S. S. Gregory and D. E. Thigpen, "The Hidden Hurdle," *Time,* March 16, 1992.

5.
PRACTICAL DISCIPLINE: SCHOOL DAYS

1. Reva Klein, *Defying Disaffection: How Schools Are Winning the Hearts and Minds of Reluctant Students* (London: Trentham Books, 2000).

2. Sources of information on the achievement gap include Michael Markowitz, "The Achievement Gap—Teaneck Is Pressed to Narrow Disparities in Performance Between Whites, Minorities," *The Bergen Record,* April 9, 1995.

3. Brad E. Sachs, *The Good Enough Child: How to Have an Imperfect Family and Be Perfectly Satisfied* (New York: Quill Press, 2000).

4. *The Autobiography of Malcolm X* (New York: Grove, 1966).

5. Sylvester Monroe, "Brothers," *Newsweek,* March 23, 1987.

6. Robert Sam Anson, *Best Intentions: The Education and Killing of Edmund Perry* (New York: Random House, 1987).

7. An additional source of material for this section is Signithia Fordham, "Racelessness in Private Schools," *Teachers College Record,* Spring 1991.

8. Research from the National Dropout Prevention Center is cited in Wendy Struchen and Mary Porta, "From Role-Modeling to Mentoring for African American Youth," *Preventing School Failure,* Spring 1997.

9. Dortch is cited in *Ebony Man,* July 1997.

10. Wendy Struchen and Mary Porta, "From Role-Modeling to Mentoring."

11. Staples's story about the teacher who inspired him can be found in his book *Parallel Time* (New York: Pantheon Books, 1994).

12. Barbara Jordan is quoted in a September 1986 interview with Bill Moyers, [Sound recording], CBS-TV.

13. Muriel Karlin Trachman's insights on picking teachers, monitoring children's school performance, and special education draw on coauthor interviews and material from Muriel Karlin Trachman and Gene Busnar, "Raising a Successful, Happy Child," an unpublished paper.

14. "Report: Blacks More Likely to Be Placed in Special Education," *Black Issues in Higher Education,* March 29, 2001.

15. *Diagnostic and Statistical Manual of Mental Disorders,* 4th Ed. (Washington, DC: American Psychiatric Association, 2000).

16. *Diagnostic and Statistical Manual of Mental Disorders.*

17. "ADD: Acronym for Any Dysfunction or Difficulty," *Journal of Special Education,* Spring 1992.

18. *Diagnostic and Statistical Manual of Mental Disorders.*

6.
PRACTICAL DISCIPLINE: TO COLLEGE AND BEYOND

1. Cathy J. Cohen and Claire E. Nee, "Educational Attainment and Sex Differentials in African American Communities," *American Behavioral Scientist,* April 2000.

2. "Blacks Make Higher IQ Gains in College Than Whites," *Jet,* October 20, 1997.

3. James P. Comer, "The Black Collegian and the American Future," *Black Collegian,* April 1991.

4. Coretta Scott King, "Celebrities Offer Words of Inspiration for College Graduates," *Jet,* June 26, 2000.

5. Abraham H. Maslow, *Toward a Psychology of Being* (New York: Wiley, 1999).

6. Na'im Akbar and Benjamin S. Carson, "The Mission of African-American Collegians," *Black Collegian,* October 1995 (1st Semester).

7. The discussion of Maslow's relevance to parenting draws on Joan M. Kiel, "Reshaping Maslow's Hierarchy of Needs to Reflect Today's Educational and Managerial Philosophies," *Journal of Instructional Psychology,* September 1999.

8. Carol Moseley-Braun is quoted in Akbar and Carson.

9. Joan Ryan, "Blacks and Sports—Lifeline or Noose?" *San Francisco Chronicle,* September 20, 1998.

10. Jim Eickhoff, "Acquiring Financial Aid That Is Right for You," *Black Collegian,* February 2000.

11. "Student Loan Survey Shows Black Students Feel Weight of Debt," *New York Amsterdam News,* June 4, 1998.

12. Lawrence Otis Graham, *Member of the Club: Reflections on Life in a Racially Polarized World* (New York: HarperPerennial Library, 1996).

13. Graham.

7.
PRACTICAL DISCIPLINE: MONEY AND CAREERS

1. James P. Comer, "The Black Collegian and the American Future." *Black Collegian,* April 1991.

2. Kelvin Boston is quoted in "Teaching Your Children About Money." *Ebony,* October 2000.

3. Ellis Cose, Ana Figueroa, John McCormick, Vern Smith, and Pat Wingert, "The Good News About Black America." *Newsweek,* June 7, 1999.

4. The discussion on introducing children to careers and the workplace draws on ma-

terial in Muriel Karlin Trachman and Gene Busnar, *Raising a Successful, Happy Child*, an unpublished paper. For more information on this topic, see Muriel Karlin Schoenbrun, *Make Your Child a Success: Career Guidance from Kindergarten to College* (New York: Perigee, 1983).

5. Adele Scheele's theories and comments about self-presentation, positioning, and connecting are from coauthor interviews. These three career skills are the focus of Scheele's book *Skills for Success* (New York: Ballantine, 1979).

6. Adele Scheele, cited previously.

7. Reasons for companies to promote racial and gender diversity are cited in Robert L. Johnson and Steven Simring, *The Race Trap: Smart Strategies for Effective Racial Communication in Business and in Life* (New York: HarperCollins, 2000).

8. Rosabeth Moss Kantor, Foreword, Lawrence Otis Graham, *The Best Companies for Minorities* (New York: Plume, 1993).

9. *The Race Trap.*

8.
MIND-BODY DISCIPLINE: THE SEARCH FOR BALANCE

1. Marian Wright-Edelman quotation from Walter Scott, "Personality Parade," *Newsday,* May 8, 1994.

2. Nancy P. Brener and Vanu R. Gowda, "U.S. College Students' Reports of Receiving Health Information on College Campuses," *Journal of American College Health,* March 2001.

3. "Tune In, Fill Out," *Health,* September 1996.

4. "Black Children Eat Most of Their Meals While Watching TV," *Jet,* March 12, 2001.

5. Rosemary Black, "Let's Eat Together," *Parenting,* September 2000.

6. Research on teenagers conducted at Cincinnati Children's Hospital Medical Center is quoted from *Tufts University Health & Nutrition Letter,* October 1997.

7. Adapted from *Smoking: Facts & Quitting Tips for Black Americans,* 1995.

8. An important source of information on the racial disparity in medical care is the series "The Health Divide: A Difference of Life & Death," *Newsday,* November 29–December 5, 1998.

9. *The New England Journal of Medicine*'s revelation that doctors were 40% less likely to order sophisticated cardiac tests for blacks is cited in Kirk A. Johnson, "The Color of Health Care," *Heart & Soul,* March 31, 1994.

10. The difference in the way black and white diabetes and kidney patients are treated is detailed in Ford Fessenden, "The Health Divide: A Difference of Life & Death/For Blacks, Medical Care and State of Health Trail Whites," *Newsday,* November 29, 1998.

11. Martin Seligman, *Learned Optimism* (New York: Alfred A. Knopf, 1991).

12. "How to Make Friends and Win Presidential Elections: Try a Little Optimisim," *Omni,* September 1992.

13. Roger Fisher and William Ury, *Getting to Yes: Negotiating Agreement Without Giving In* (New York: Penguin Books, 1983).

14. David Riesman, Nathan Glazer, and Reuel Denney, *The Lonely Crowd: A Study of the Changing American Character* (New York: Doubleday Anchor Books, 1955).

15. Reisman's message is quoted in Wilfred M. McClay, "Fifty Years of the Lonely Crowd," *Wilson Quarterly*, Summer 1998.

16. Steven Hawke, "Spiritual Health: Definition and Theory," *Wellness Perspectives*, Summer 1994.

17. Allan Luks, *The Healing Power of Doing Good: The Health and Spiritual Benefits of Helping Others* (New York: Fawcett, 1991).

9.
QUESTIONS AND ANSWERS ACROSS THE FIVE DISCIPLINES

1. Opening Carol Moseley-Braun quotation from Na'im Akbar and Benjamin S. Carson, "The Mission of African-American Collegians," *Black Collegian*, October 1995 (1st Semester).

Index

Discussion Points for Parents

ALL CHILDREN NEED PARENTS who provide love and discipline. However, it's important never to underestimate the extraordinary challenges black youngsters face. There are certain realities that come with being a racial minority, and there's no way to avoid them completely, no matter how wealthy or accomplished one becomes. You can help your child develop the strength and resilience he or she needs to succeed by reflecting on the following questions.

◆ What would you list as the most critical skills and attributes a young African American needs to succeed, both in society and as a person?

◆ What steps should African American parents take to help children feel good about themselves and their heritage?

◆ Do you believe it's necessary to set a positive example in your actions, or do you think it's enough just to talk to your child about doing what's right?

◆ What do you think is the most effective approach to disciplining children: strict, lenient, or balanced?

◆ Do you think it's important for African American parents to talk to children about racial prejudice and offer guidance about how to deal with it?

◆ Given the choice, would you prefer to raise your family in a mostly white, primarily black, or racially mixed neighborhood?

◆ If your teen started to date someone of a different race, would you allow things to run their course or take steps to put an end to the relationship?

◆ Are you aware of the added pressures black students often face in achieving academic success—and what parents can do about them?

◆ Do you feel that a higher education is more or less important for African Americans?

◆ Do you feel that a historically black college is a better choice for most African Americans than an institution in which most of the students are white?

◆ Do you believe parents should shoulder the primary responsibility for educating young people about the dangers of substance abuse and unsafe sex?

◆ If you thought your child was either being bullied or bullying others, what steps would you take to correct the problem?

◆ Do you think parents should make an effort to connect children with mentors and other positive role models, especially in areas where they themselves are weak or limited?

◆ If your child was having a problem you couldn't handle on your own, where would you turn for help?

◆ Do you agree that it's most important for young African Americans to develop a strong spiritual center and sense of place?

About the Authors

DR. ROBERT L. JOHNSON is chairman of the Department of Adolescent and Young Adult Medicine and professor of pediatrics and psychiatry at the University of Medicine and Dentistry of New Jersey (UMDNJ). The author is the former president of the New Jersey State Board of Medical Examiners and a distinguished social activist who has mentored hundreds of black professionals and inner-city youth. He currently serves on the U.S. Department of Health and Human Services Council and the Board of Healthcare Services of the National Academy of Sciences. Dr. Johnson is an accomplished public speaker who has appeared on such television programs as *Now With Bill Moyers,* *20/20,* and *The O'Reilly Factor.* He is coauthor of *The Race Trap,* a book on interracial communication.

DR. PAULETTE STANFORD is professor of pediatrics and codirector of adolescent and young adult medicine at the University of Medicine and Dentistry of New Jersey. The author has over twenty years of experience in child and adolescent care, preventive guidance, and counseling. Dr. Stanford is medical director of Screening, Treatment, and Risk Reduction for Teens (START), an adolescent HIV treatment program, and the principal investigator of a National Institutes of Health research study of high-risk adolescent behavior. She is the mother of a grown daughter who is an attorney.

Drs. Johnson and Stanford are African American pediatricians who specialize in giving both anticipatory and corrective guidance to parents and young people. The authors are often the first ones consulted when a child is having emotional, scholastic, or social problems. They are also experts in counseling parents on dealing with teens who are engaging in high-risk sexual behavior, are abusing drugs, or who have been the target of racial profiling.

Drs. Johnson and Stanford have worked together for nearly a quarter of a century, during which time they developed and refined the Five-Disciplines Program that is at the heart of this book. In addition to using the program in their professional practice, the authors share these techniques with groups of parents through frequent appearances at parent-teacher conferences and black civic organizations.

The authors invite readers to share their own comments, experiences, and questions. Those who would like to join the dialogue or want updated information about upcoming seminars, workshops, and appearances can contact Drs. Johnson and Stanford at www.strengthfortheirjourney.com or www.blackparents.com